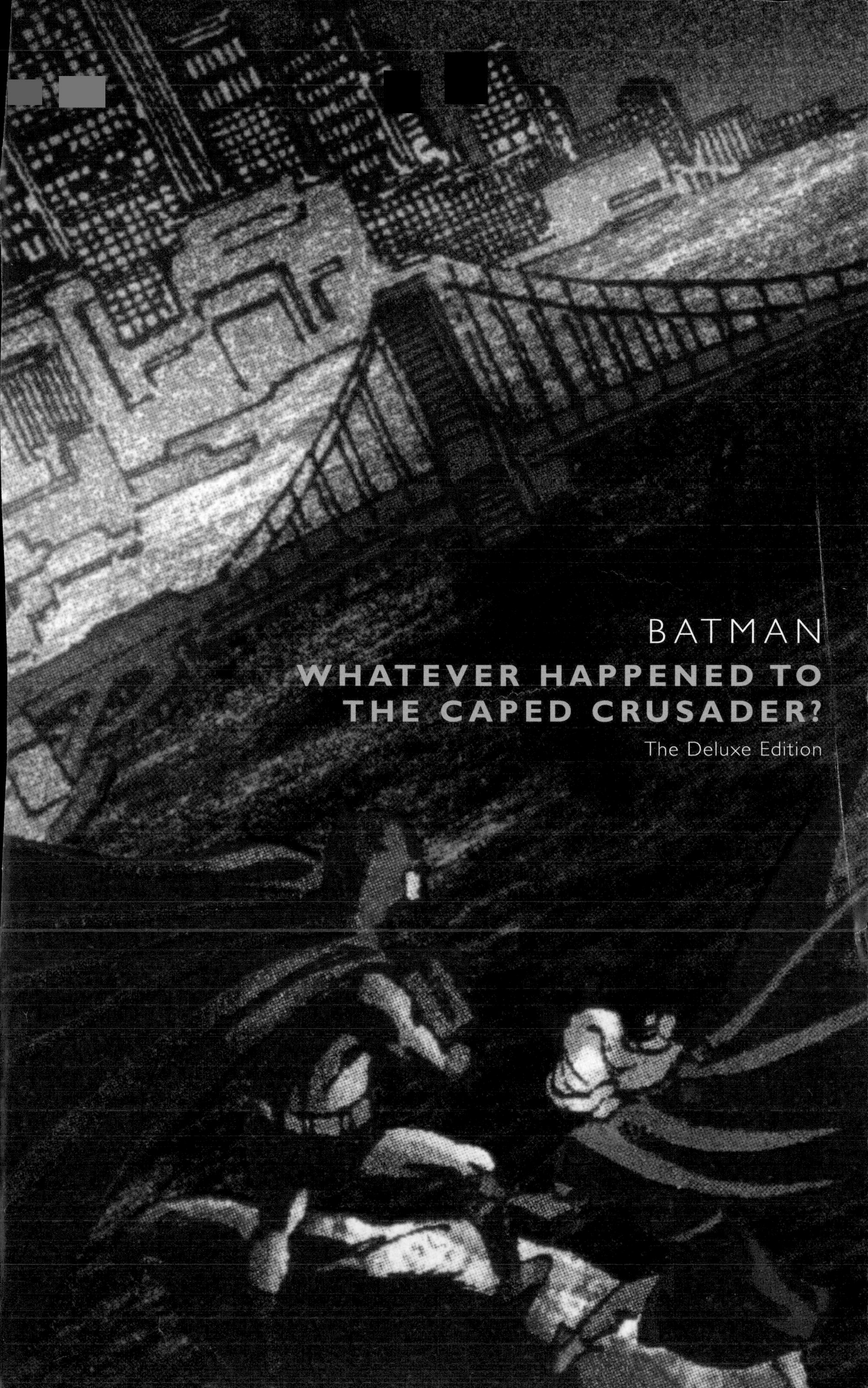

BATMAN
WHATEVER HAPPENED TO THE CAPED CRUSADER?
The Deluxe Edition

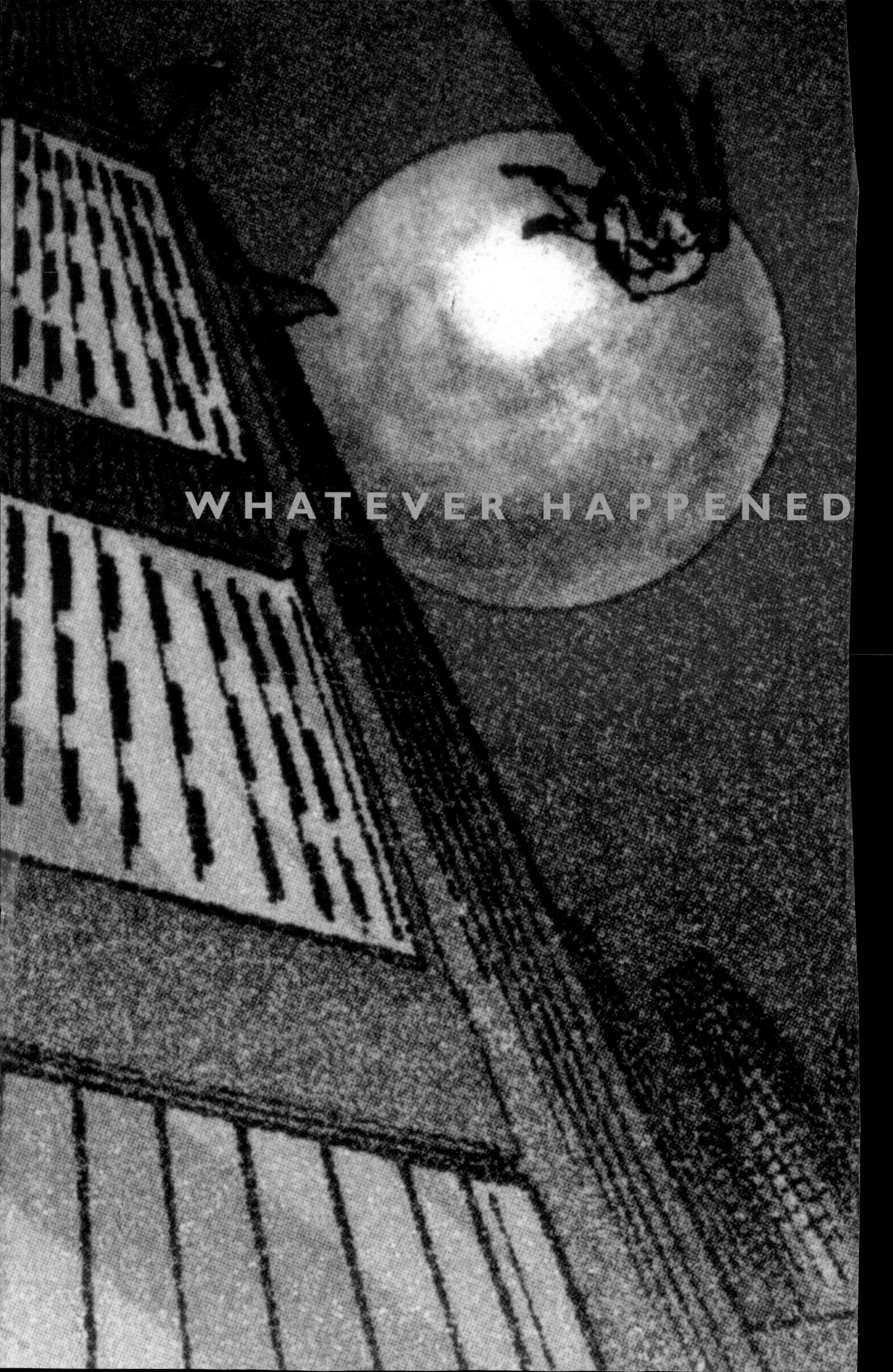
WHATEVER HAPPENED

writer
Neil GAIMAN

pencils
Andy KUBERT

inks
Scott WILLIAMS
colors
Alex SINCLAIR
letters
Jared K. FLETCHER

BATMAN
TO THE CAPED CRUSADER?
The Deluxe Edition

With other tales of the
Dark Knight written by
NEIL GAIMAN

A BLACK AND WHITE WORLD
artist Simon BISLEY
letterer John COSTANZA

PAVANE
artist Mark BUCKINGHAM
colorist Nansi HOOLAHAN
letterer Agustin MAS

ORIGINAL SINS
penciller Mike HOFFMAN
inker Kevin NOWLAN
colorist Tom McCRAW
letterer Todd KLEIN

WHEN IS A DOOR
penciller Bernie MIREAULT
inker Matt WAGNER
colorist Joe MATT

Batman created by Bob KANE

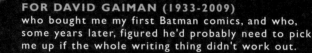

FOR DAVID GAIMAN (1933-2009)
who bought me my first Batman comics, and who,
some years later, figured he'd probably need to pick
me up if the whole writing thing didn't work out.
Thank you, Dad.
Neil

MURIEL KUBERT (1931-2008)
With unrelenting encouragement, she loved the fact
that I followed in my father's footsteps and somehow
got footprints of my own. This is for my mom,
Muriel Kubert. We miss you so much.
Andy

DAN DIDIO Senior VP-Executive Editor
MIKE MARTS MARK WAID
SCOTT PETERSON Editors-original series
JANELLE SIEGEL Assistant Editor-original series
BOB JOY Editor-collected edition
ROBBIN BROSTERMAN Senior Art Director
PAUL LEVITZ President & Publisher
GEORG BREWER VP-Design & DC Direct Creative
RICHARD BRUNING Senior VP-Creative Director
PATRICK CALDON Executive VP-Finance & Operations
CHRIS CARAMALIS VP-Finance
JOHN CUNNINGHAM VP-Marketing
TERRI CUNNINGHAM VP-Managing Editor
AMY GENKINS Senior VP-Business & Legal Affairs
ALISON GILL VP-Manufacturing
DAVID HYDE VP-Publicity
HANK KANALZ VP-General Manager, WildStorm
JIM LEE Editorial Director-WildStorm
GREGORY NOVECK Senior VP-Creative Affairs
SUE POHJA VP-Book Trade Sales
STEVE ROTTERDAM Senior VP-Sales & Marketing
CHERYL RUBIN Senior VP-Brand Management
ALYSSE SOLL VP-Advertising & Custom Publishing
JEFF TROJAN VP-Business Development, DC Direct
BOB WAYNE VP-Sales

Cover art by Andy Kubert. Cover color by Alex Sinclair.

WHATEVER HAPPENED TO THE CAPED CRUSADER?
AN INTRODUCTION, OR A LOVE LETTER.

I love Batman. There are other characters I like. There may be other characters I like better. And there are characters I invented, and I love all of them like children. But I loved, and still love Batman, unshakably, unquestioningly, as one loves a parent. He was the first. He's always been there.

Listen, I've loved him since the first time I heard his name. My father told me there was a television show in America about a man who dressed as a bat and fought crime. I was five years old, the only bats I had ever encountered were used to hit cricket balls, and I was still ridiculously interested. The TV show came to the UK next, and, honest, I used to worry about him. End of every first bat-episode, he would be in the death trap and I would worry for a week. If I missed the second part I would have to get friends who saw it to fill me in on how he escaped ("He had a bat bird-whistle in his utility belt, and got the birds to peck holes in the balloon, and got down safely...").

Batman hooked me on comics. I made my father buy me *Smash!* comics, which reprinted the US newspaper strips and were the gateway drug to the American comics I found soon enough — first in a box of American comics, soon enough in local newsagents. They were the real things: four-color dreams made real.

I loved the comics more than the TV show. I read other comics too, and I liked other comics' characters, but Batman was best. He just was. He was *Batman.*

And the glorious thing about Batman was the way he kept pace with me as I grew up. There were the Neal Adams comics when I was twelve, which transmuted the reassuring Batman I'd grown up with into a lonelier, more shadowy creature, who kept pace with me through my early teens. There was Frank Miller's DARK KNIGHT RETURNS when I was twenty-five, the subject of my first big academic essay. All of it was Batman — all of it was glorious.

So, over Dave McKean's sighs, I put Batman into the first DC comic I ever wrote, BLACK ORCHID, as a shadowy figure, speaking in white on black lettering (something I liked so much I stole it for SANDMAN, causing untold heartache in the years to come for Todd Klein and DC Comics' production department). I wrote a SECRET ORIGINS of Poison Ivy. I wrote a SECRET ORIGINS SPECIAL — a framing story about Gotham, and a Riddler story inside, which said everything I thought about the loss of one kind of story. I even wrote a BATMAN BLACK & WHITE story, with Batman and the Joker sitting around like off-duty Warner's Cartoon characters, behind the scenes at a comic, waiting to go on and perform. I put a tiny Batman cameo into THE WAKE, the last *Sandman* story, just to remind people that yes, *this* was still part of *that.*

Those were stories about Batman, though: he was there, but only seen from the outside, his effects on the world more important than his story.

There was one other Batman story, one that didn't happen: I proposed a story in about 1989 called (if memory serves) *Nights at the Circus*. I was even paid a $900 advance for it. But for one reason or another (mostly because the artist who was meant to draw it at the time signed an exclusive contract with another publisher) it never happened. It would have been a good Batman story, I think, about three nocturnal visits, over the course of Bruce Wayne's life, to a very strange circus indeed. But it never got written.

And then life happened, and one day I mostly wasn't writing comics anymore. I didn't have time, and, mostly, didn't have the smallest inclination. It would, I told people who asked, take something very special to get me to make the time to write something for comics. Or even, truthfully, to write something that I didn't own...

Then the phone rang and Dan DiDio asked if I would like to write a Batman story.

I asked Dan if this meant they were calling in their $900 and wanted me to write my *Nights at the Circus* story. He said, no, what he wanted was a two-part story — whatever I wanted to write, he said — that would be the final episode of BATMAN and the last episode of DETECTIVE. I could really write the last one of all.

"It would be," he said, "kind of like 'Whatever Happened to the Man of Tomorrow?'" That was Alan Moore's two-part story that was the last issue of the original numbering of SUPERMAN and of ACTION COMICS, the story to mark the end of Superman's Silver Age, the Mort Weisinger-Julie Schwartz years. The end of an era. It was the best last Superman comic there could ever have been, a wonderful paean to a Superman who would soon be reimagined and reinvented, and whose comics would soon be renumbered, each starting at #1.

I don't remember thinking about it: I just said yes.

Honestly, what would you have said? I think I told Dan that I didn't have time, and didn't think I could pull it off, but sure. Until the day he died, Julie Schwartz told the story of how Alan Moore physically grabbed him, and would not let him go until Julie had agreed that Alan could write "Whatever Happened to the Man of

Tomorrow?" and Alan said that it didn't matter that it wasn't actually true, and he had simply said Yes when Julie asked, it was Julie's story and it was a good one. Probably in Dan's version of the story, he and editor Michael Marts were kidnapped, and blindfolded, and were tied to chairs in a basement, and then I walked in with henchmen and said, "Now listen up, youse guys. The Last Batman Story. Anyone else so much as tries to write it, and I'll have Lefty and Knuckles teach everyone a lesson, see?" which is actually really nice of me to suggest because it means that Dan DiDio doesn't have to attempt an English accent. It could have happened like that. You never know.

I got off the phone.

I thought about Alan Moore's "Whatever Happened to the Man of Tomorrow?" This was not that, and it would not even try to be what Alan did: a celebration of the end of an era, the swan song of the greatest of Superman artists, something that ended with a smile and a wink.

Batman stories don't end with smiles and winks. And Batman had survived many eras, and would, undoubtedly, survive many more. If I were going to tell the last Batman story, it would have to be something that would survive Batman's current death or disappearance, something that would still be the last Batman story in twenty years, or a hundred.

Because if there's one thing that Batman is, it's a survivor. He'll be around long after all of us are gone. So what could be more appropriate than the story of his death?

I was delighted and thrilled when editor Michael Marts told me that I would have Andy Kubert as my artist. I don't think there's anything Andy cannot do if you ask him to, and I asked him to do some very strange things in this issue. Where other artists might have traced or swiped or copied, Andy did something much odder and more interesting — as he explained to me, "I didn't try to draw like them. I tried to draw as if the artists you were talking about were trying to draw like me." And so we see Bob Kane and Dick Sprang and Carmine Infantino and Neal Adams and Dick Giordano and Brian Bolland and all the rest of them — so many amazing artists who had left their mark on Batman, so many wonderful artistic styles — through an Andy Kubert-shaped filter. (I even tried to write like other people, to sound like Bill Finger and Gardner Fox and Denny O'Neil and Steve Englehart and Bob Haney and Frank Miller and Alan Grant and many of the other fine writers who have stared at a blank sheet of paper and tried to think of something for the Darknight Detective to do, but I'm afraid mostly it just sounded like me.)

I was lucky to have Andy, and Andy was lucky to have Scott Williams, an excellent artist in his own right, and an inker's inker, taking what Andy had created in shaded pencils and turning it into beautiful inked comic book art. I wrote things just to see how they drew them, asked the impossible because I knew they could give it to me.

Alex Sinclair colored it with rapidity and aplomb, Jared K. Fletcher lettered the hell out of it, and I got my first ever Alex Ross cover.

In my head, the story was simply called *Batman: The End*, but the first time DC Comics people talked about it, they described it as "Whatever Happened to the Caped Crusader?" and the title sort of stuck.

Due to the strangeness of printing schedules, I'm writing this before the last issue has reached the stands. I have no idea if people will like it or hate it. And truly — and oddly — I don't mind.

It's *my* last Batman story, after all; if Batman had to end, I guess that, for me anyway, it would end like this.

And it's a small thank-you: to Batman, and to all the writers and artists and inkers and colorists and letterers and editors who gave him to us over the years.

NEIL GAIMAN

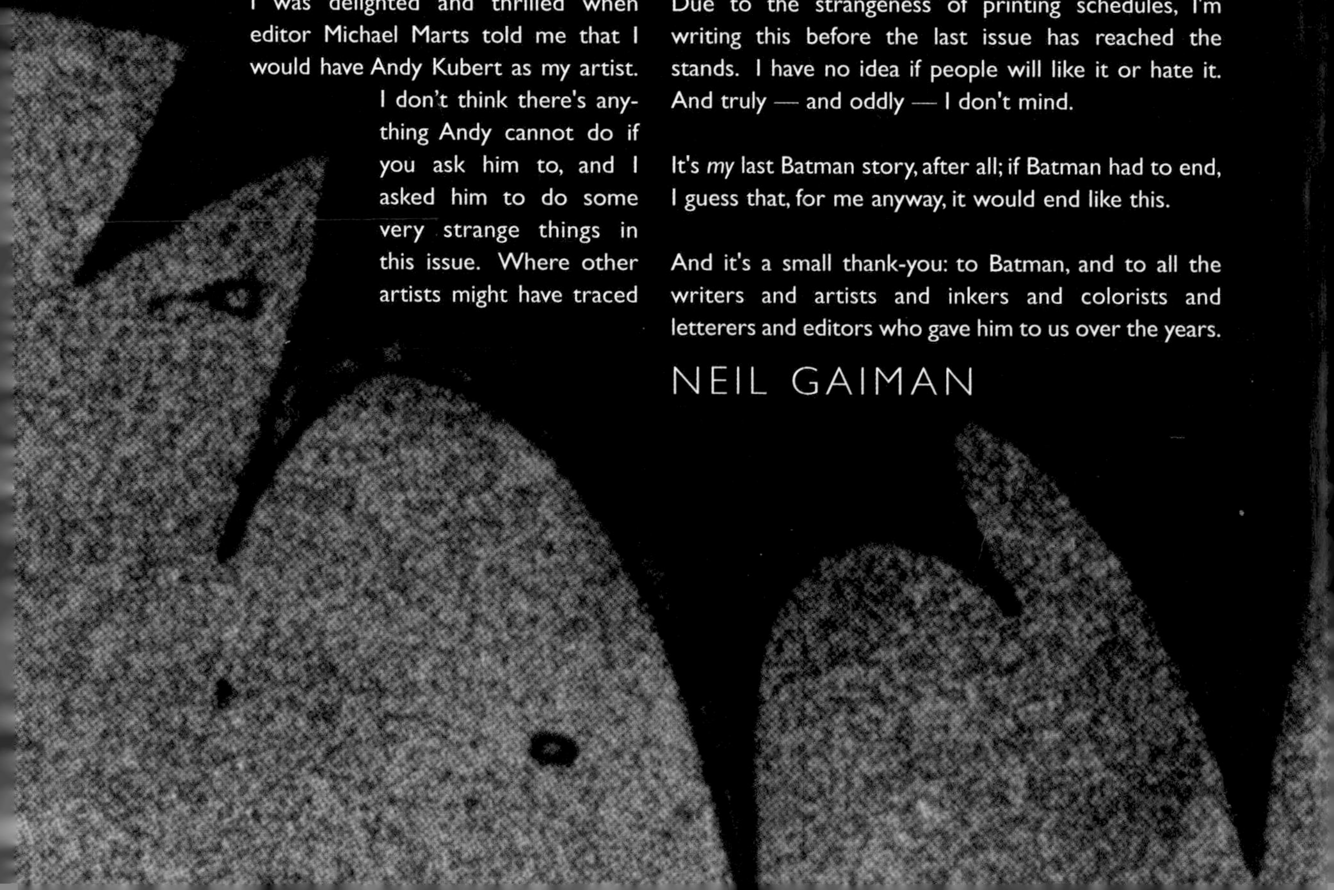

BATMAN 686
Andy KUBERT with Alex SINCLAIR

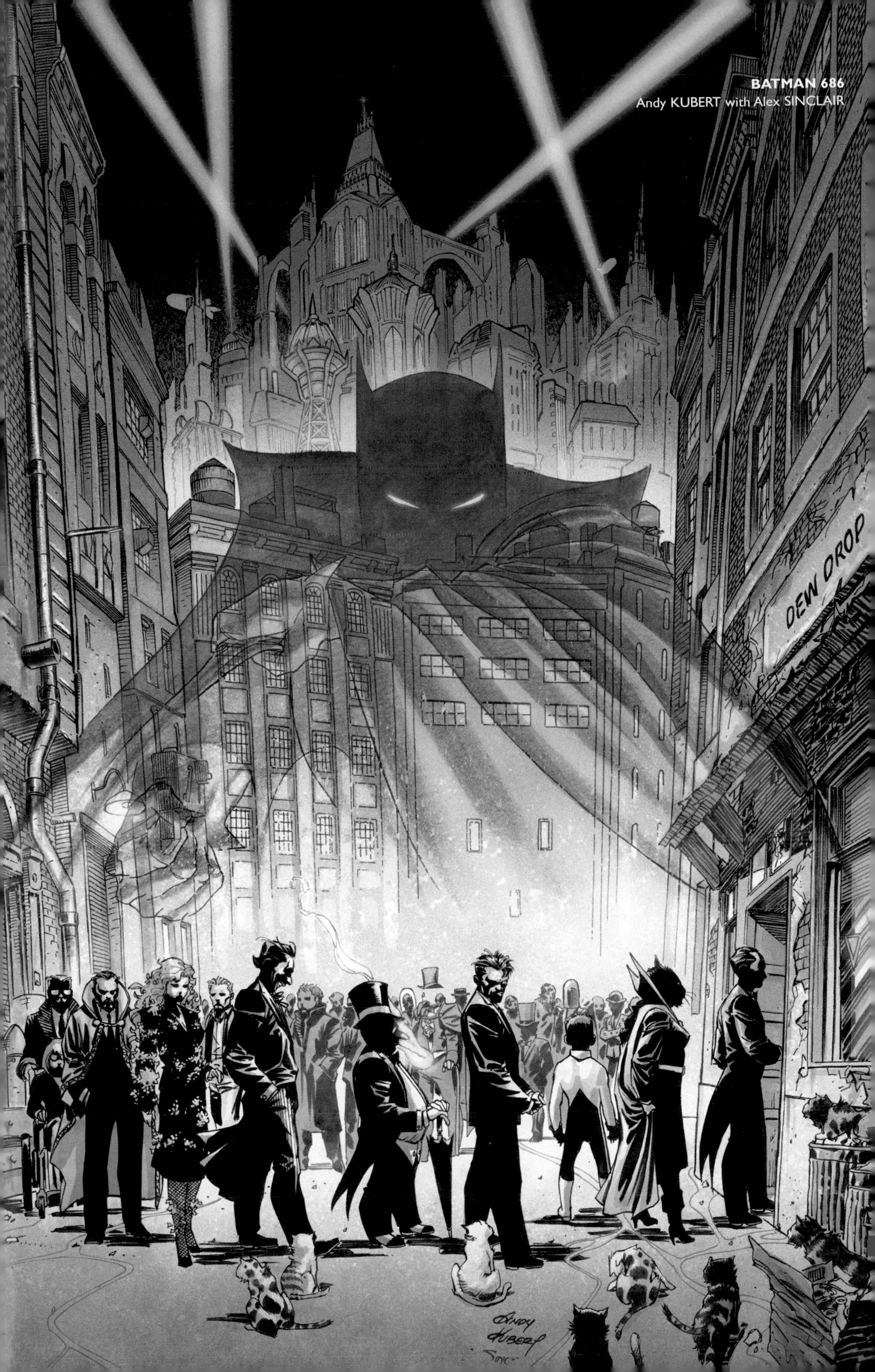
DEW DROP

WHATEVER HAPPENED TO THE CAPED CRUSADER?

Part 1 of 2

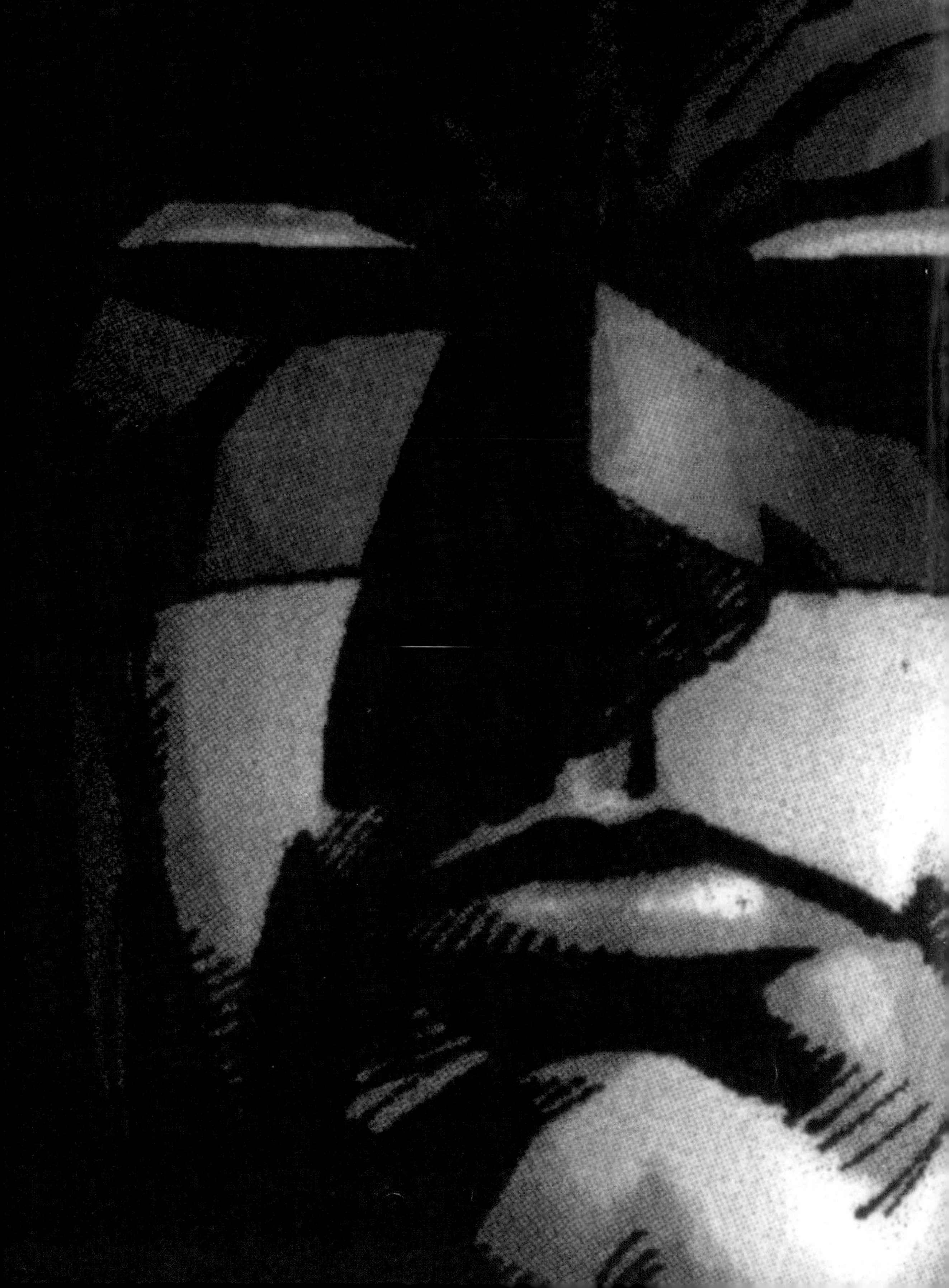

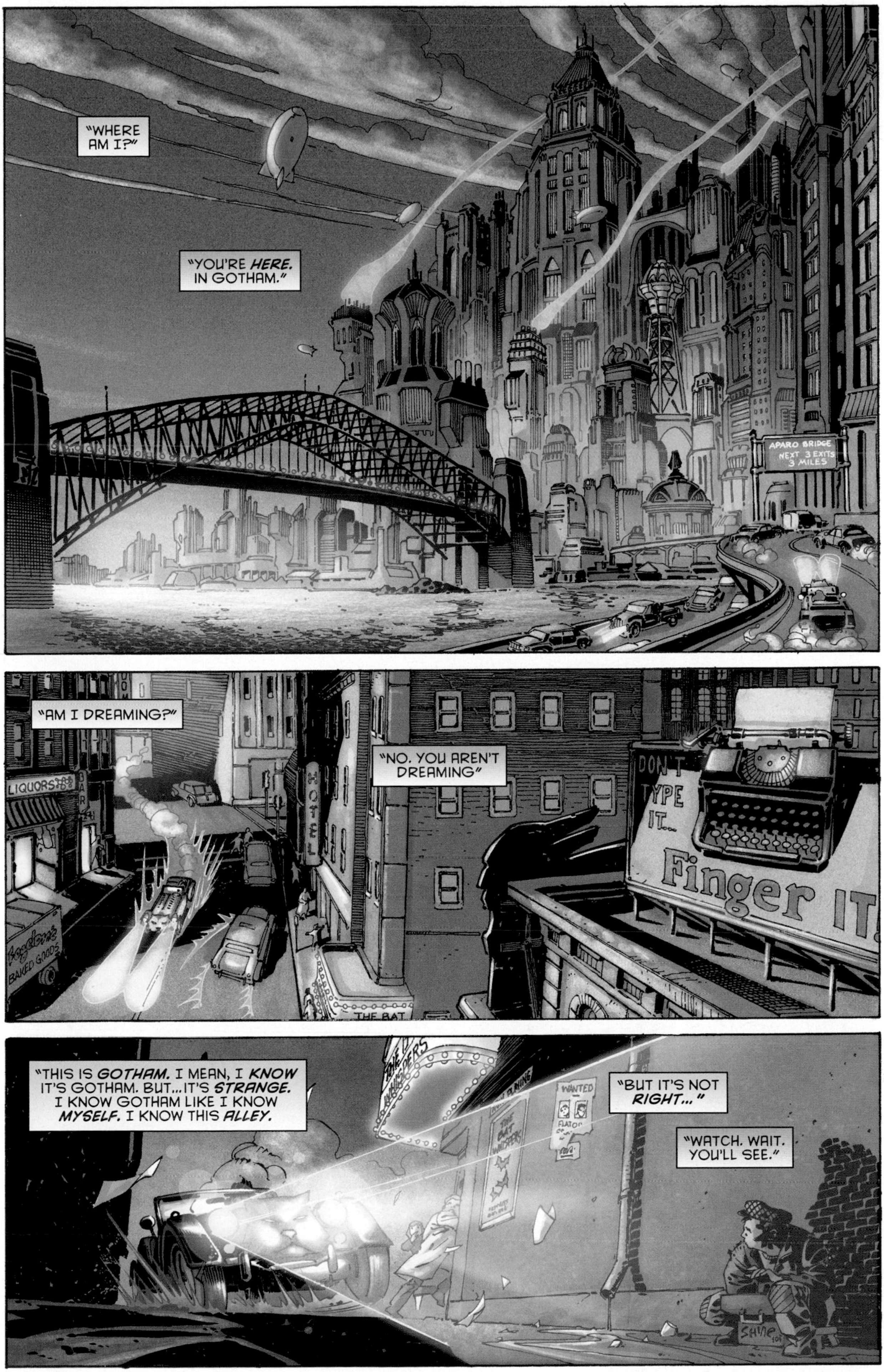
"WHERE AM I?"
"YOU'RE *HERE.* IN GOTHAM."
APARO BRIDGE
NEXT 3 EXITS
3 MILES
"AM I DREAMING?"
LIQUORS
BAR
HOTEL
"NO. YOU AREN'T DREAMING"
DON'T TYPE IT...
Finger IT!
BAKED GOODS
THE BAT
"THIS IS *GOTHAM.* I MEAN, I *KNOW* IT'S GOTHAM. BUT...IT'S *STRANGE.* I KNOW GOTHAM LIKE I KNOW *MYSELF.* I KNOW THIS *ALLEY.*
WANTED
THE BAT WHISPERS
"BUT IT'S NOT *RIGHT...*"
"WATCH. WAIT. YOU'LL SEE."

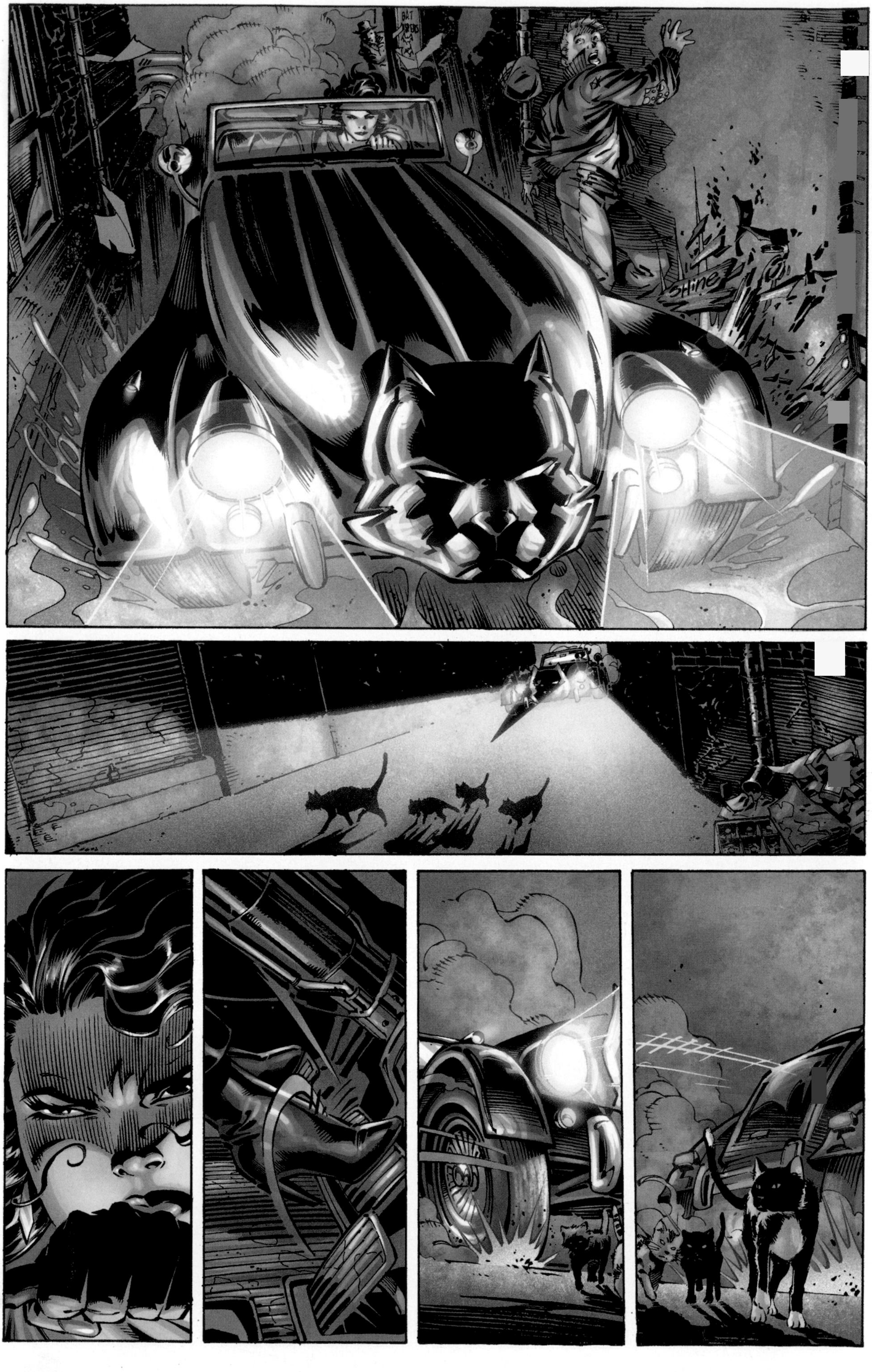
SHINE

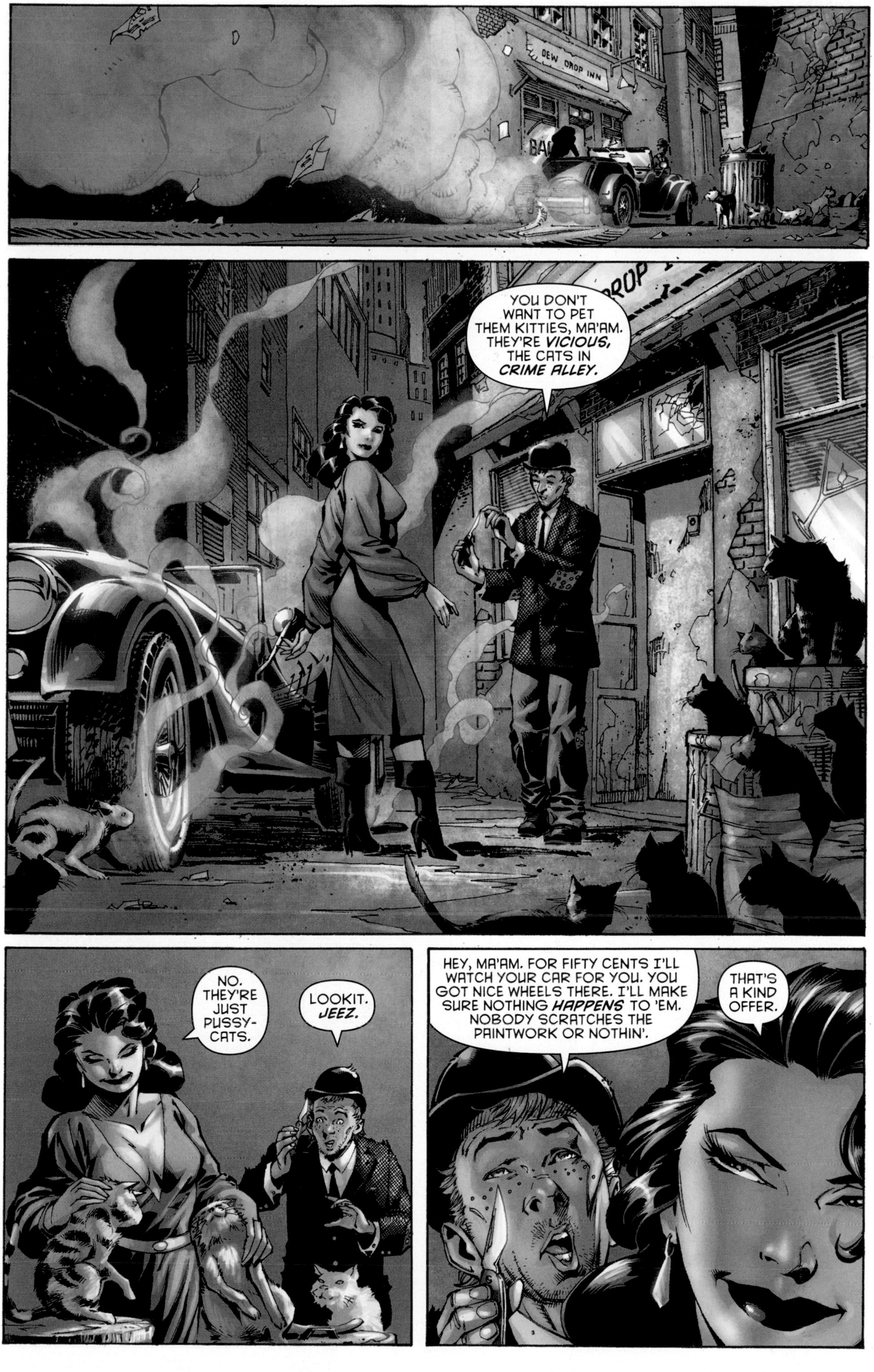
DEW DROP INN
YOU DON'T WANT TO PET THEM KITTIES, MA'AM. THEY'RE *VICIOUS,* THE CATS IN ***CRIME ALLEY.***
NO. THEY'RE JUST PUSSY-CATS.
LOOKIT. ***JEEZ.***
HEY, MA'AM. FOR FIFTY CENTS I'LL WATCH YOUR CAR FOR YOU. YOU GOT NICE WHEELS THERE. I'LL MAKE SURE NOTHING ***HAPPENS*** TO 'EM. NOBODY SCRATCHES THE PAINTWORK OR NOTHIN'.
THAT'S A KIND OFFER.

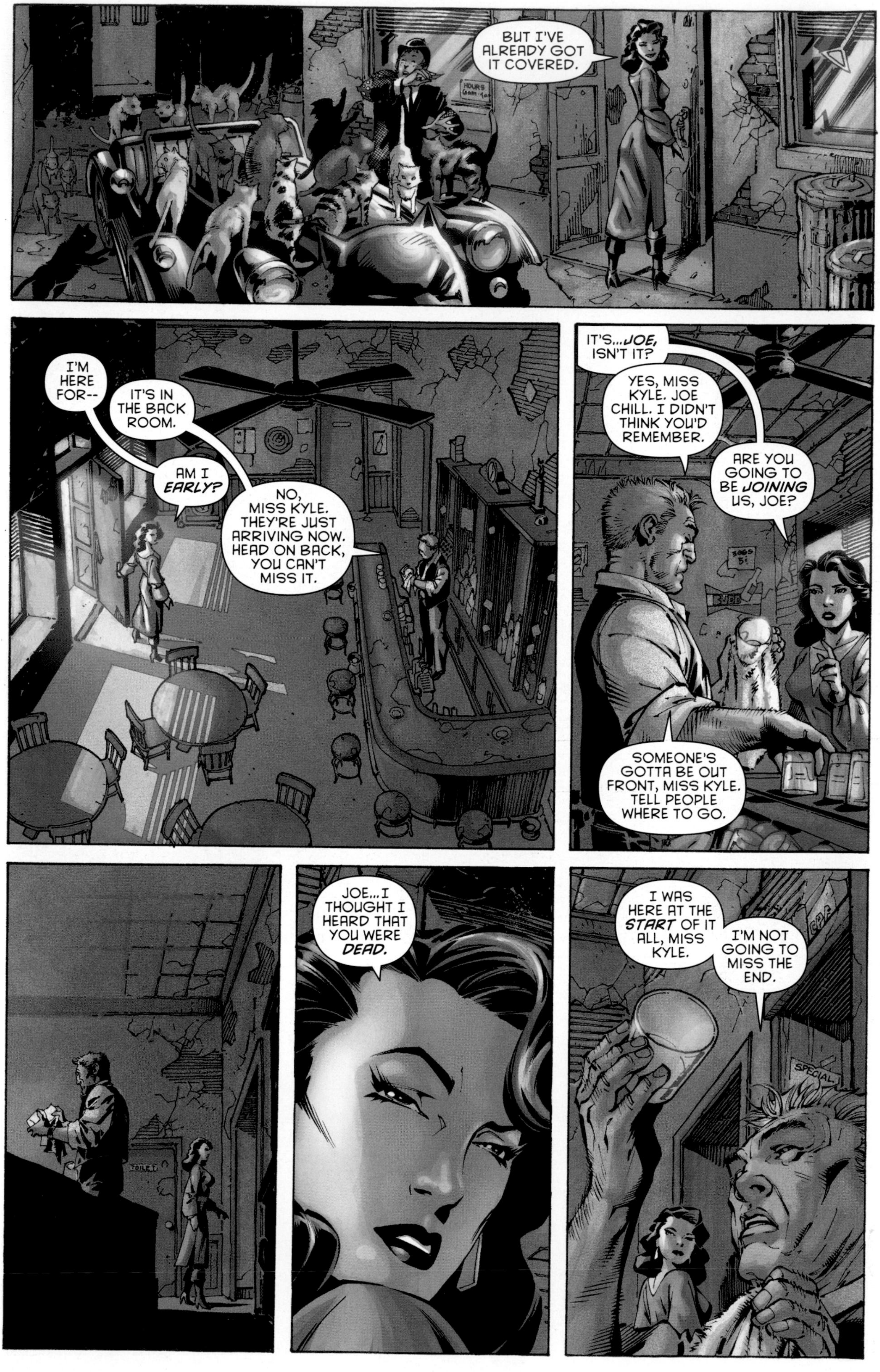
BUT I'VE ALREADY GOT IT COVERED.
HOURS 6am-1am
I'M HERE FOR--
IT'S IN THE BACK ROOM.
AM I *EARLY?*
NO, MISS KYLE. THEY'RE JUST ARRIVING NOW. HEAD ON BACK, YOU CAN'T MISS IT.
IT'S...*JOE,* ISN'T IT?
YES, MISS KYLE. JOE CHILL. I DIDN'T THINK YOU'D REMEMBER.
ARE YOU GOING TO BE *JOINING* US, JOE?
SOMEONE'S GOTTA BE OUT FRONT, MISS KYLE. TELL PEOPLE WHERE TO GO.
TOILET
JOE...I THOUGHT I HEARD THAT YOU WERE *DEAD.*
I WAS HERE AT THE *START* OF IT ALL, MISS KYLE.
I'M NOT GOING TO MISS THE END.
SPECIAL

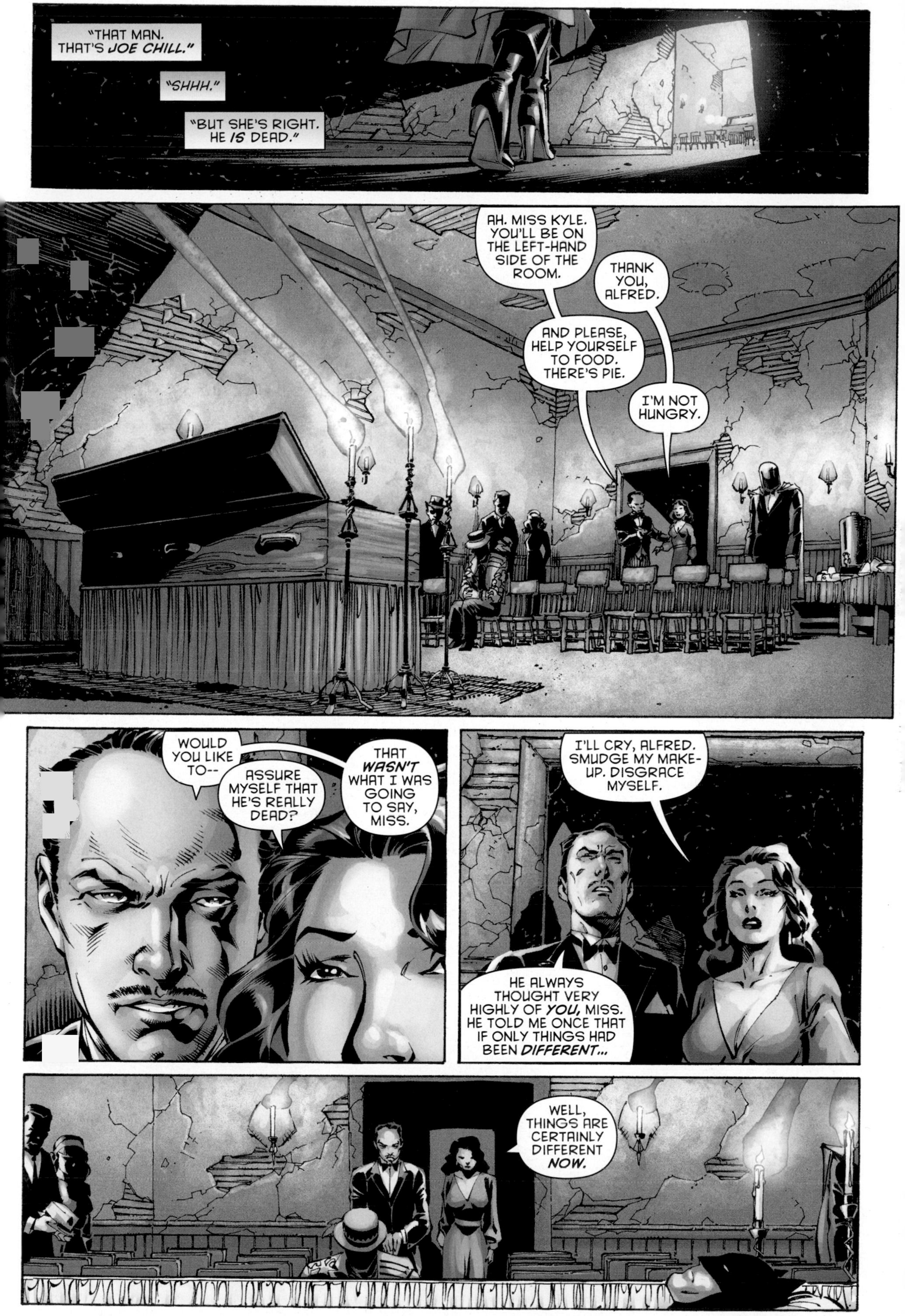
"THAT MAN. THAT'S JOE CHILL."
"SHHH."
"BUT SHE'S RIGHT. HE IS DEAD."
AH. MISS KYLE. YOU'LL BE ON THE LEFT-HAND SIDE OF THE ROOM.
THANK YOU, ALFRED.
AND PLEASE, HELP YOURSELF TO FOOD. THERE'S PIE.
I'M NOT HUNGRY.
WOULD YOU LIKE TO--
ASSURE MYSELF THAT HE'S REALLY DEAD?
THAT WASN'T WHAT I WAS GOING TO SAY, MISS.
I'LL CRY, ALFRED. SMUDGE MY MAKE-UP. DISGRACE MYSELF.
HE ALWAYS THOUGHT VERY HIGHLY OF YOU, MISS. HE TOLD ME ONCE THAT IF ONLY THINGS HAD BEEN DIFFERENT...
WELL, THINGS ARE CERTAINLY DIFFERENT NOW.

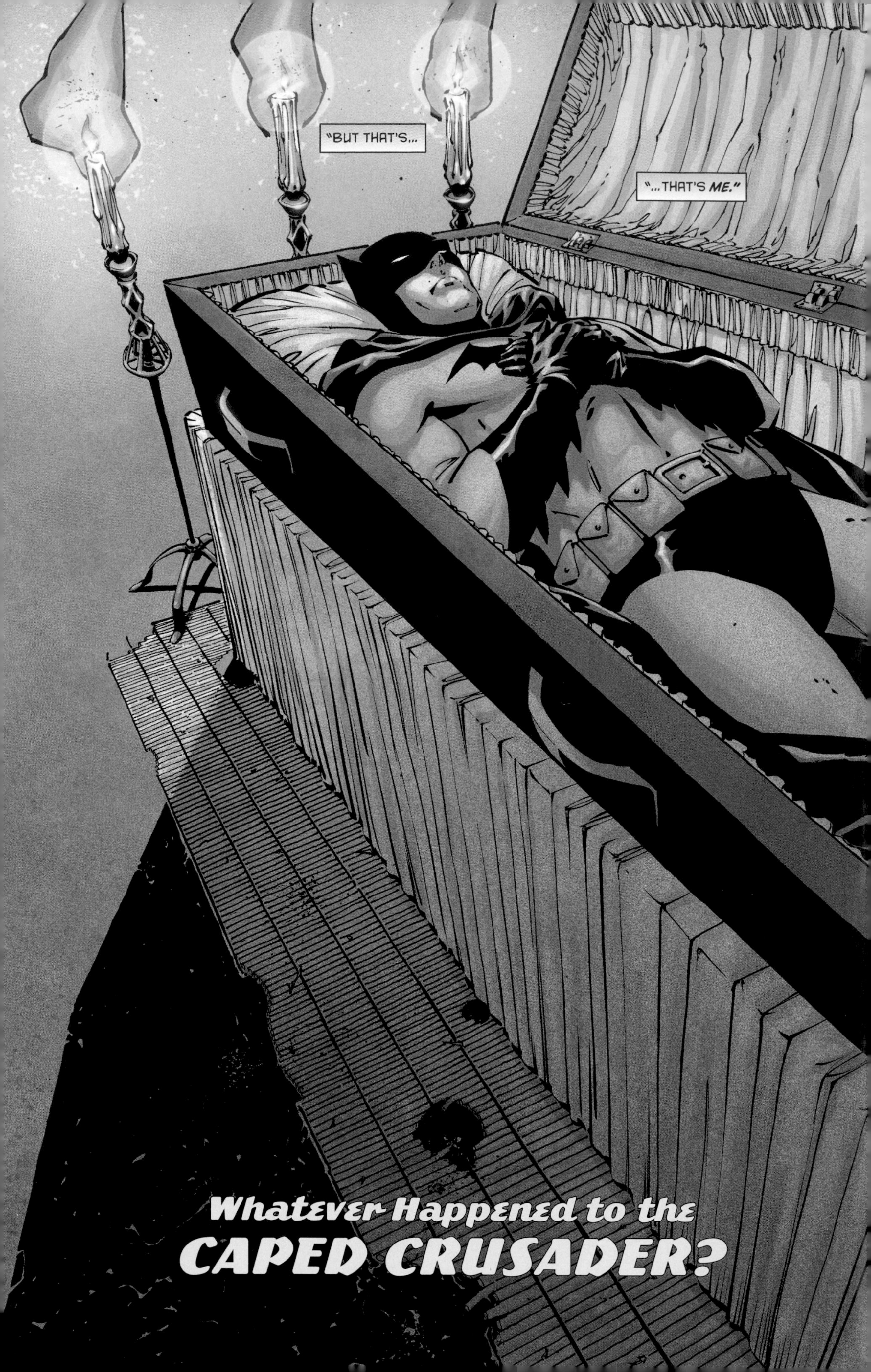
"BUT THAT'S...
"...THAT'S *ME.*"
Whatever Happened to the
CAPED CRUSADER?

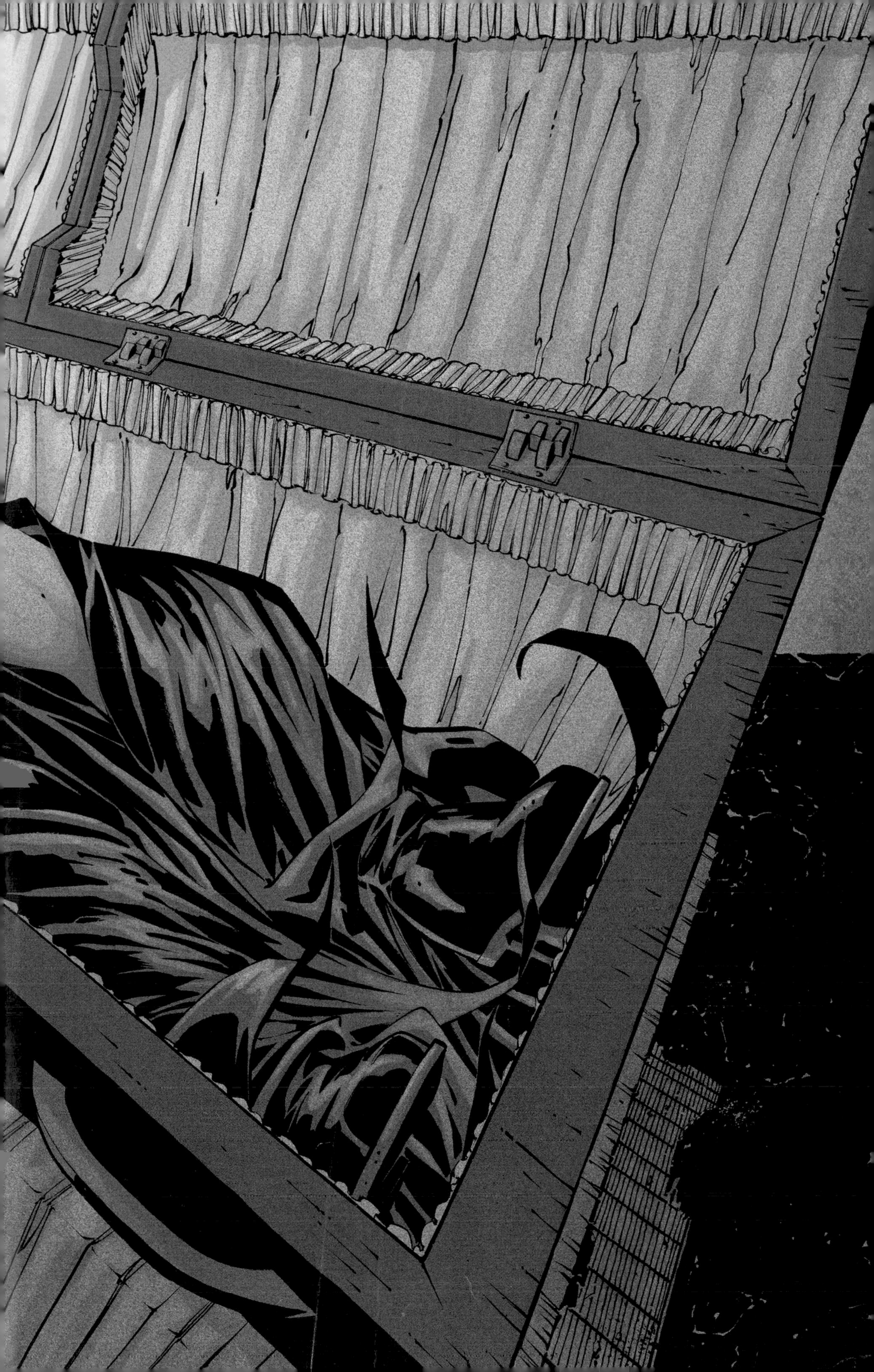

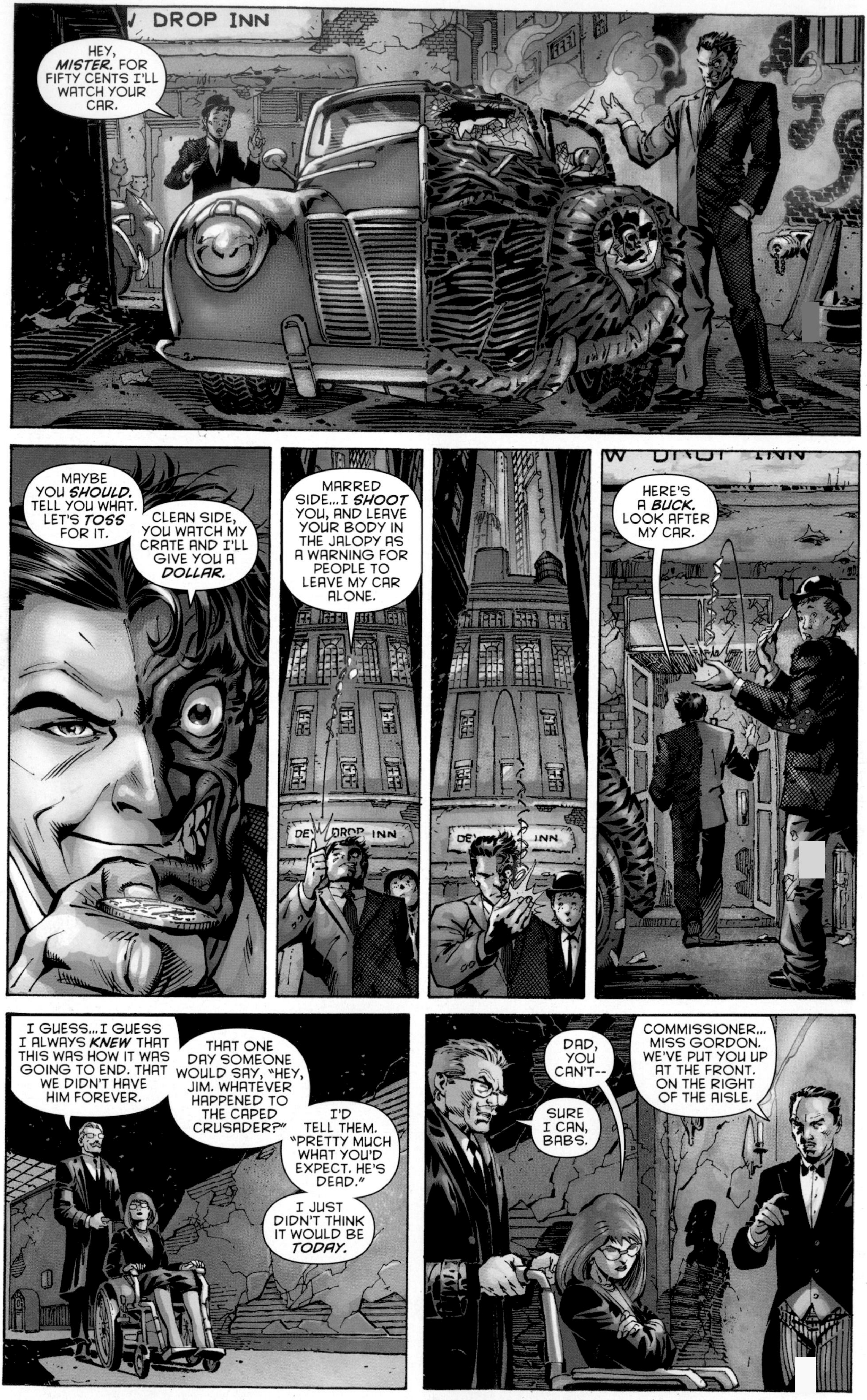
W DROP INN
HEY, MISTER. FOR FIFTY CENTS I'LL WATCH YOUR CAR.
MAYBE YOU SHOULD. TELL YOU WHAT. LET'S TOSS FOR IT.
CLEAN SIDE, YOU WATCH MY CRATE AND I'LL GIVE YOU A DOLLAR.
MARRED SIDE...I SHOOT YOU, AND LEAVE YOUR BODY IN THE JALOPY AS A WARNING FOR PEOPLE TO LEAVE MY CAR ALONE.
DEW DROP INN
HERE'S A BUCK. LOOK AFTER MY CAR.
I GUESS...I GUESS I ALWAYS KNEW THAT THIS WAS HOW IT WAS GOING TO END. THAT WE DIDN'T HAVE HIM FOREVER.
THAT ONE DAY SOMEONE WOULD SAY, "HEY, JIM. WHATEVER HAPPENED TO THE CAPED CRUSADER?"
I'D TELL THEM. "PRETTY MUCH WHAT YOU'D EXPECT. HE'S DEAD."
I JUST DIDN'T THINK IT WOULD BE TODAY.
DAD, YOU CAN'T--
SURE I CAN, BABS.
COMMISSIONER... MISS GORDON. WE'VE PUT YOU UP AT THE FRONT. ON THE RIGHT OF THE AISLE.

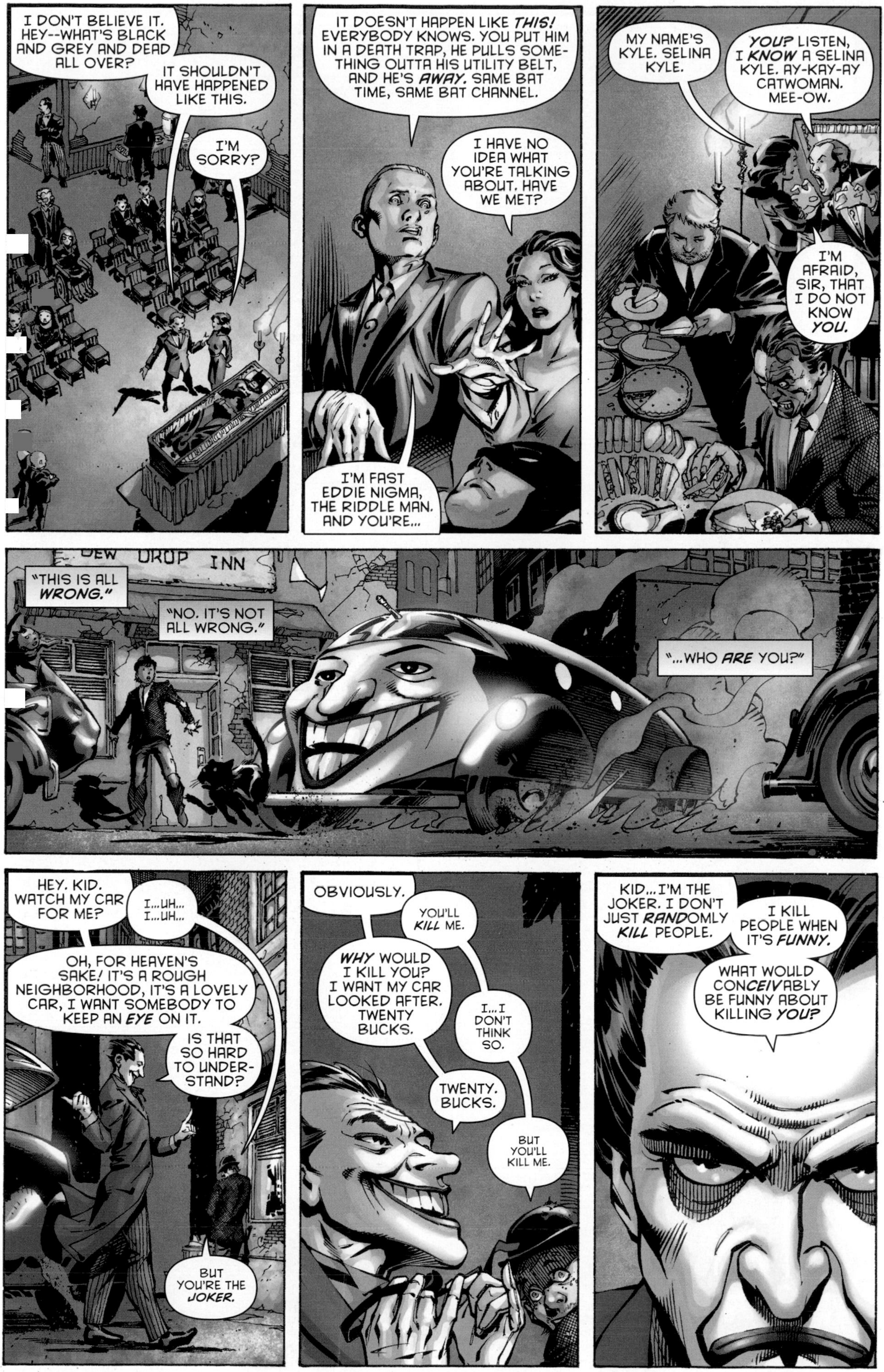
I DON'T BELIEVE IT. HEY--WHAT'S BLACK AND GREY AND DEAD ALL OVER?
IT SHOULDN'T HAVE HAPPENED LIKE THIS.
I'M SORRY?
IT DOESN'T HAPPEN LIKE THIS! EVERYBODY KNOWS. YOU PUT HIM IN A DEATH TRAP, HE PULLS SOMETHING OUTTA HIS UTILITY BELT, AND HE'S AWAY. SAME BAT TIME, SAME BAT CHANNEL.
I HAVE NO IDEA WHAT YOU'RE TALKING ABOUT. HAVE WE MET?
I'M FAST EDDIE NIGMA, THE RIDDLE MAN. AND YOU'RE...
MY NAME'S KYLE. SELINA KYLE.
YOU? LISTEN, I KNOW A SELINA KYLE. AY-KAY-AY CATWOMAN. MEE-OW.
I'M AFRAID, SIR, THAT I DO NOT KNOW YOU.
DEW DROP INN
"THIS IS ALL WRONG."
"NO. IT'S NOT ALL WRONG."
"...WHO ARE YOU?"
HEY. KID. WATCH MY CAR FOR ME?
I...UH... I...UH...
OH, FOR HEAVEN'S SAKE! IT'S A ROUGH NEIGHBORHOOD, IT'S A LOVELY CAR, I WANT SOMEBODY TO KEEP AN EYE ON IT.
IS THAT SO HARD TO UNDERSTAND?
BUT YOU'RE THE JOKER.
OBVIOUSLY.
YOU'LL KILL ME.
WHY WOULD I KILL YOU? I WANT MY CAR LOOKED AFTER. TWENTY BUCKS.
I...I DON'T THINK SO.
TWENTY. BUCKS.
BUT YOU'LL KILL ME.
KID...I'M THE JOKER. I DON'T JUST RANDOMLY KILL PEOPLE.
I KILL PEOPLE WHEN IT'S FUNNY.
WHAT WOULD CONCEIVABLY BE FUNNY ABOUT KILLING YOU?

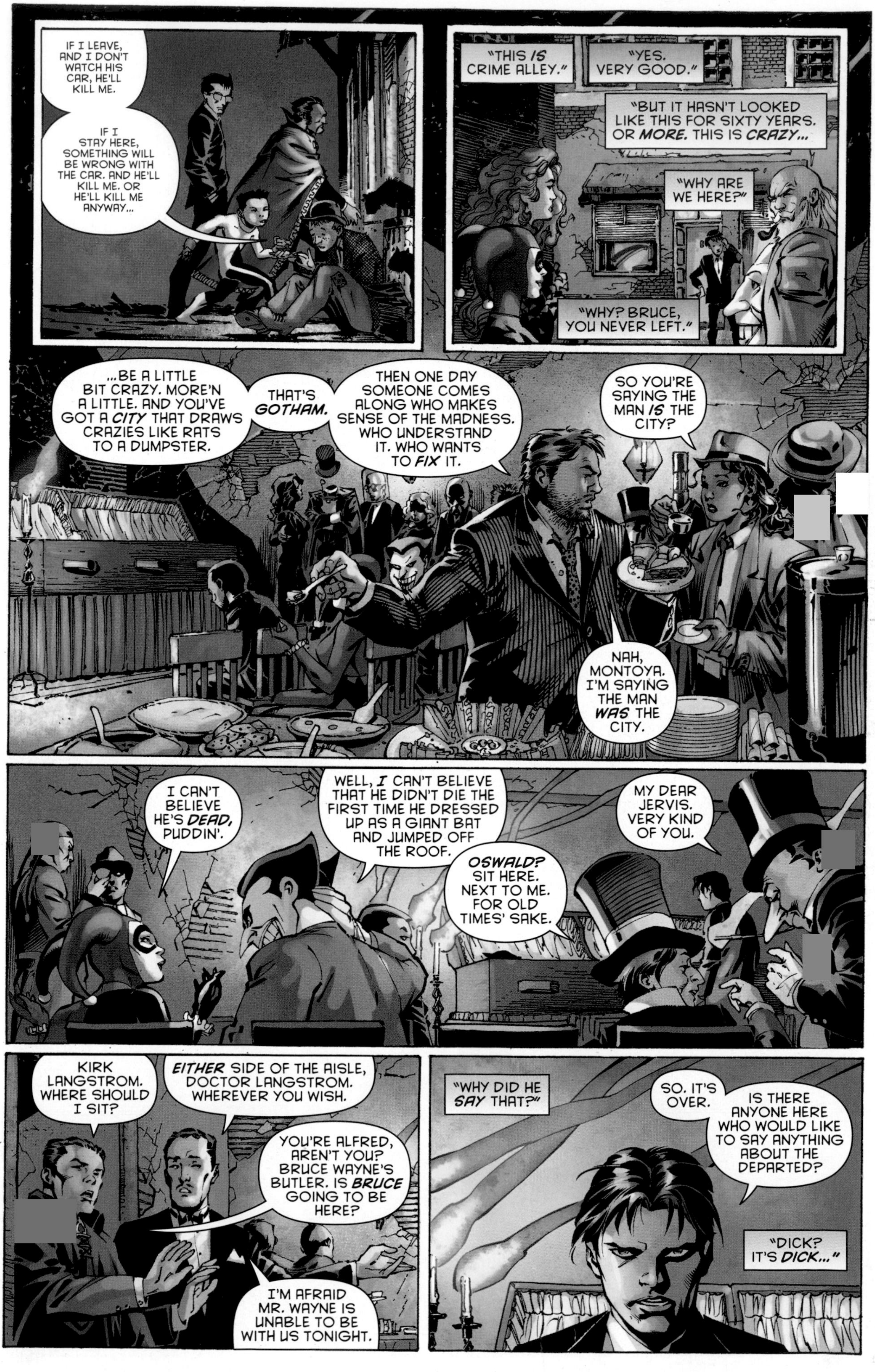
IF I LEAVE, AND I DON'T WATCH HIS CAR, HE'LL KILL ME.
IF I STAY HERE, SOMETHING WILL BE WRONG WITH THE CAR. AND HE'LL KILL ME. OR HE'LL KILL ME ANYWAY...
"THIS *IS* CRIME ALLEY."
"YES. VERY GOOD."
"BUT IT HASN'T LOOKED LIKE THIS FOR SIXTY YEARS. OR *MORE.* THIS IS *CRAZY...*
"WHY ARE WE HERE?"
"WHY? BRUCE, YOU NEVER LEFT."
...BE A LITTLE BIT CRAZY. MORE'N A LITTLE. AND YOU'VE GOT A *CITY* THAT DRAWS CRAZIES LIKE RATS TO A DUMPSTER.
THAT'S *GOTHAM.*
THEN ONE DAY SOMEONE COMES ALONG WHO MAKES SENSE OF THE MADNESS. WHO UNDERSTAND IT. WHO WANTS TO *FIX* IT.
SO YOU'RE SAYING THE MAN *IS* THE CITY?
NAH, MONTOYA. I'M SAYING THE MAN *WAS* THE CITY.
I CAN'T BELIEVE HE'S *DEAD,* PUDDIN'.
WELL, *I* CAN'T BELIEVE THAT HE DIDN'T DIE THE FIRST TIME HE DRESSED UP AS A GIANT BAT AND JUMPED OFF THE ROOF.
OSWALD? SIT HERE. NEXT TO ME. FOR OLD TIMES' SAKE.
MY DEAR JERVIS. VERY KIND OF YOU.
KIRK LANGSTROM. WHERE SHOULD I SIT?
EITHER SIDE OF THE AISLE, DOCTOR LANGSTROM. WHEREVER YOU WISH.
YOU'RE ALFRED, AREN'T YOU? BRUCE WAYNE'S BUTLER. IS *BRUCE* GOING TO BE HERE?
I'M AFRAID MR. WAYNE IS UNABLE TO BE WITH US TONIGHT.
"WHY DID HE *SAY* THAT?"
SO. IT'S OVER.
IS THERE ANYONE HERE WHO WOULD LIKE TO SAY ANYTHING ABOUT THE DEPARTED?
"DICK? IT'S *DICK...*"

I WOULD.

HELLO. MY NAME IS *SELINA KYLE.* I WAS *SADIE KELOWSKI* WHEN I WAS A KID, BUT THAT WAS TOO LONG AGO. I'VE KNOWN THE DEPARTED SINCE...WELL, IT WAS A COUPLE OF YEARS BEFORE PEARL HARBOR.

I GUESS THAT *DATES* ME.

I WANT TO TELL YOU WHAT KIND OF A *MAN* HE WAS.

AND *HOW* HE DIED. I SHOULD TELL YOU *THAT.*

THE CAT-WOMAN'S TALE

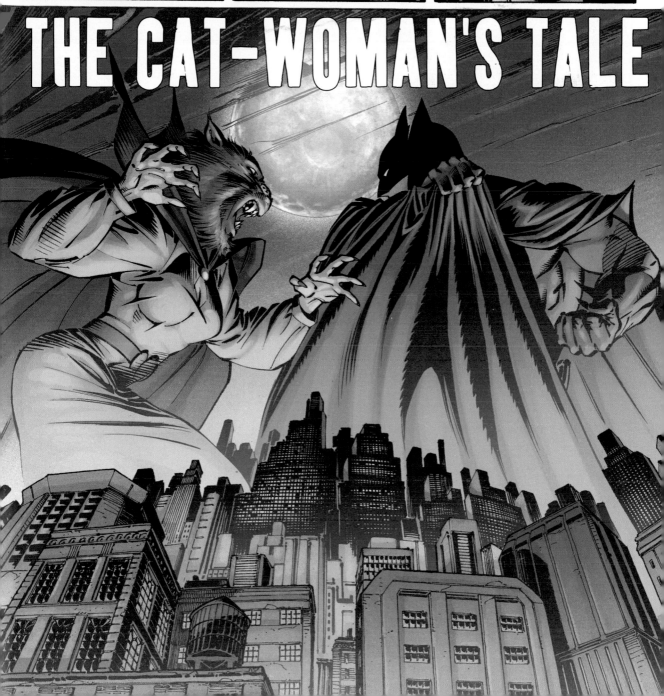

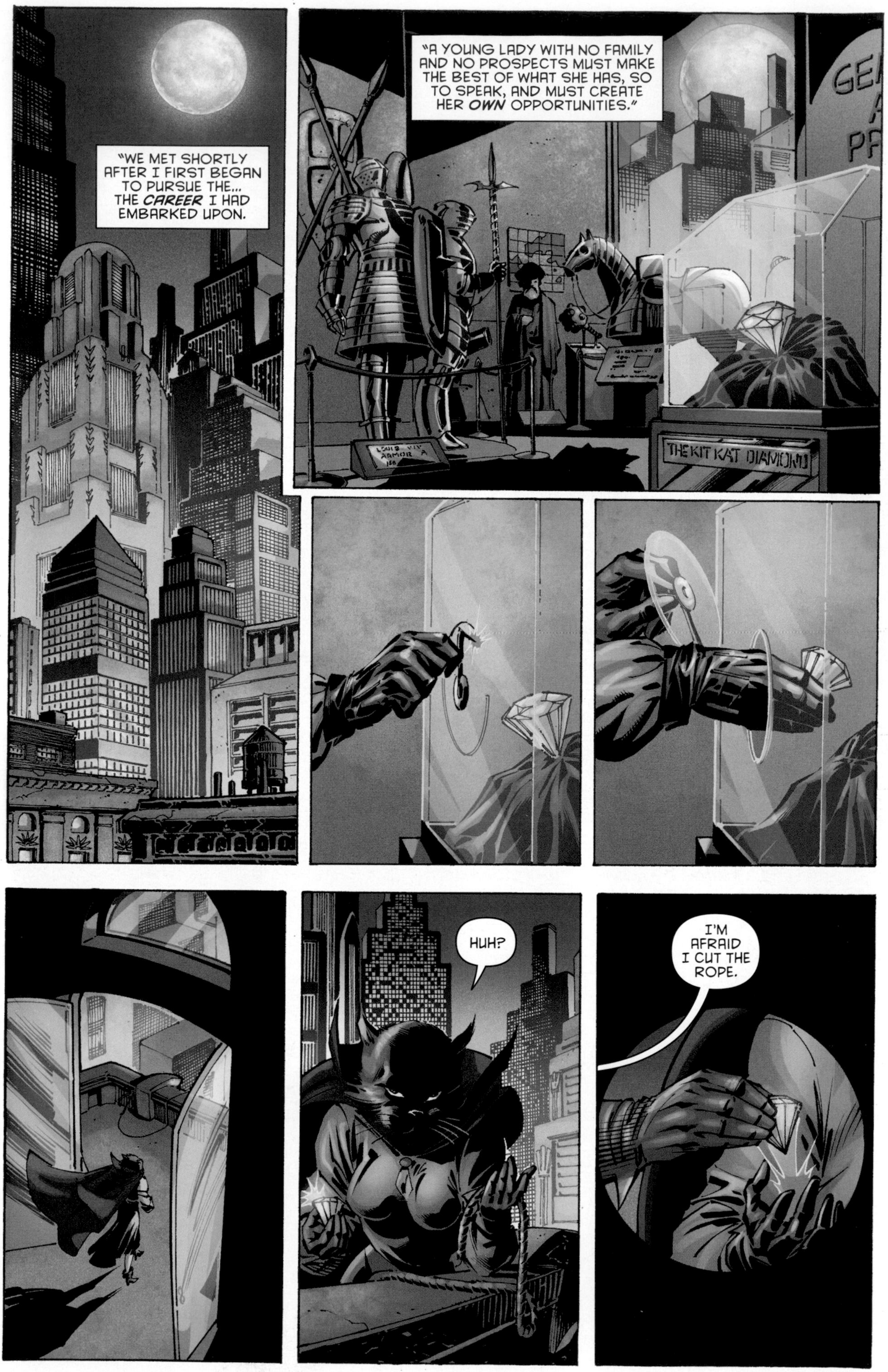
"WE MET SHORTLY AFTER I FIRST BEGAN TO PURSUE THE... THE *CAREER* I HAD EMBARKED UPON.
"A YOUNG LADY WITH NO FAMILY AND NO PROSPECTS MUST MAKE THE BEST OF WHAT SHE HAS, SO TO SPEAK, AND MUST CREATE HER *OWN* OPPORTUNITIES."
THE KIT KAT DIAMOND
HUH?
I'M AFRAID I CUT THE ROPE.

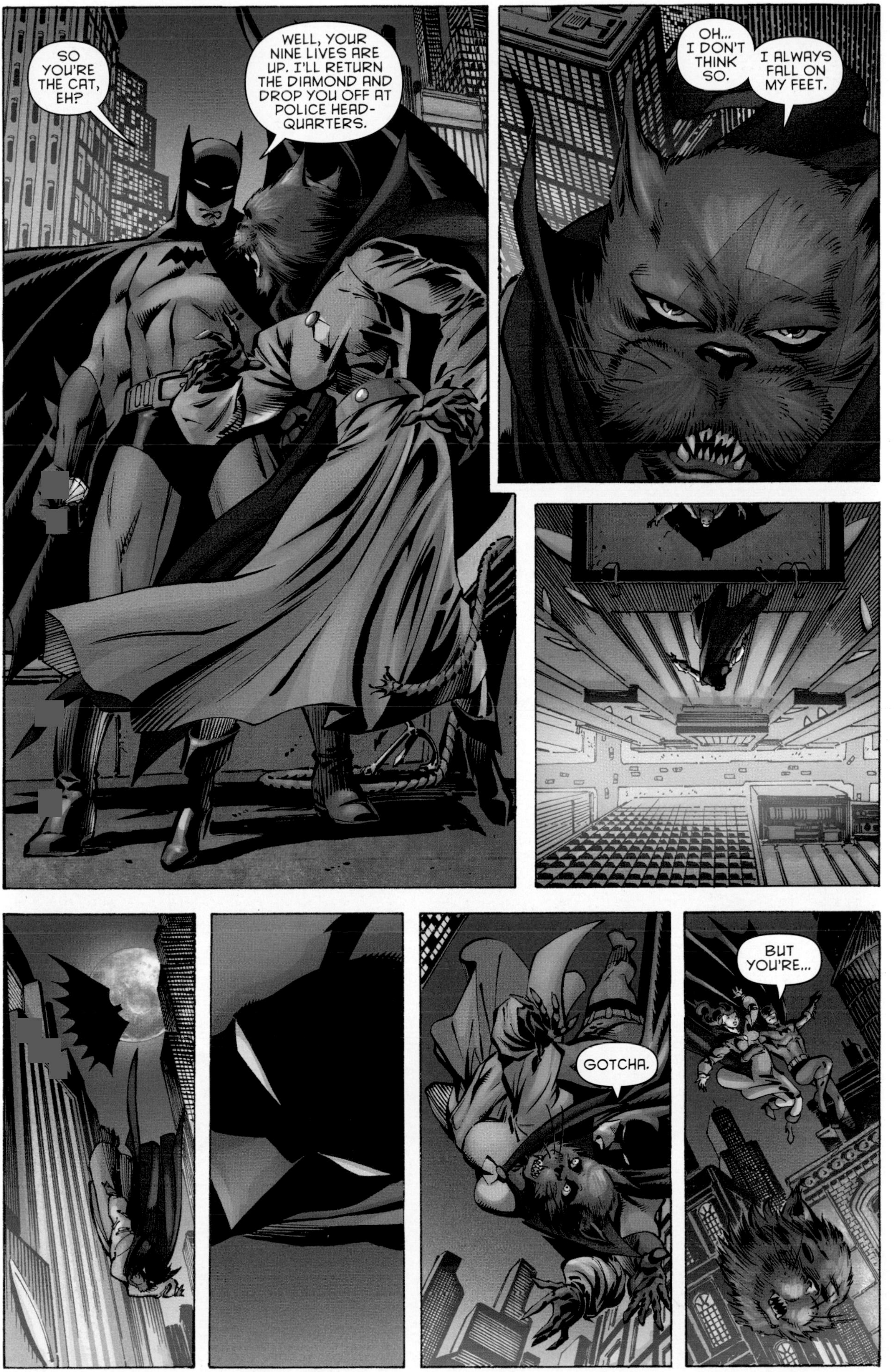
SO YOU'RE THE CAT, EH?
WELL, YOUR NINE LIVES ARE UP. I'LL RETURN THE DIAMOND AND DROP YOU OFF AT POLICE HEAD-QUARTERS.
OH... I DON'T THINK SO.
I ALWAYS FALL ON MY FEET.
GOTCHA.
BUT YOU'RE...

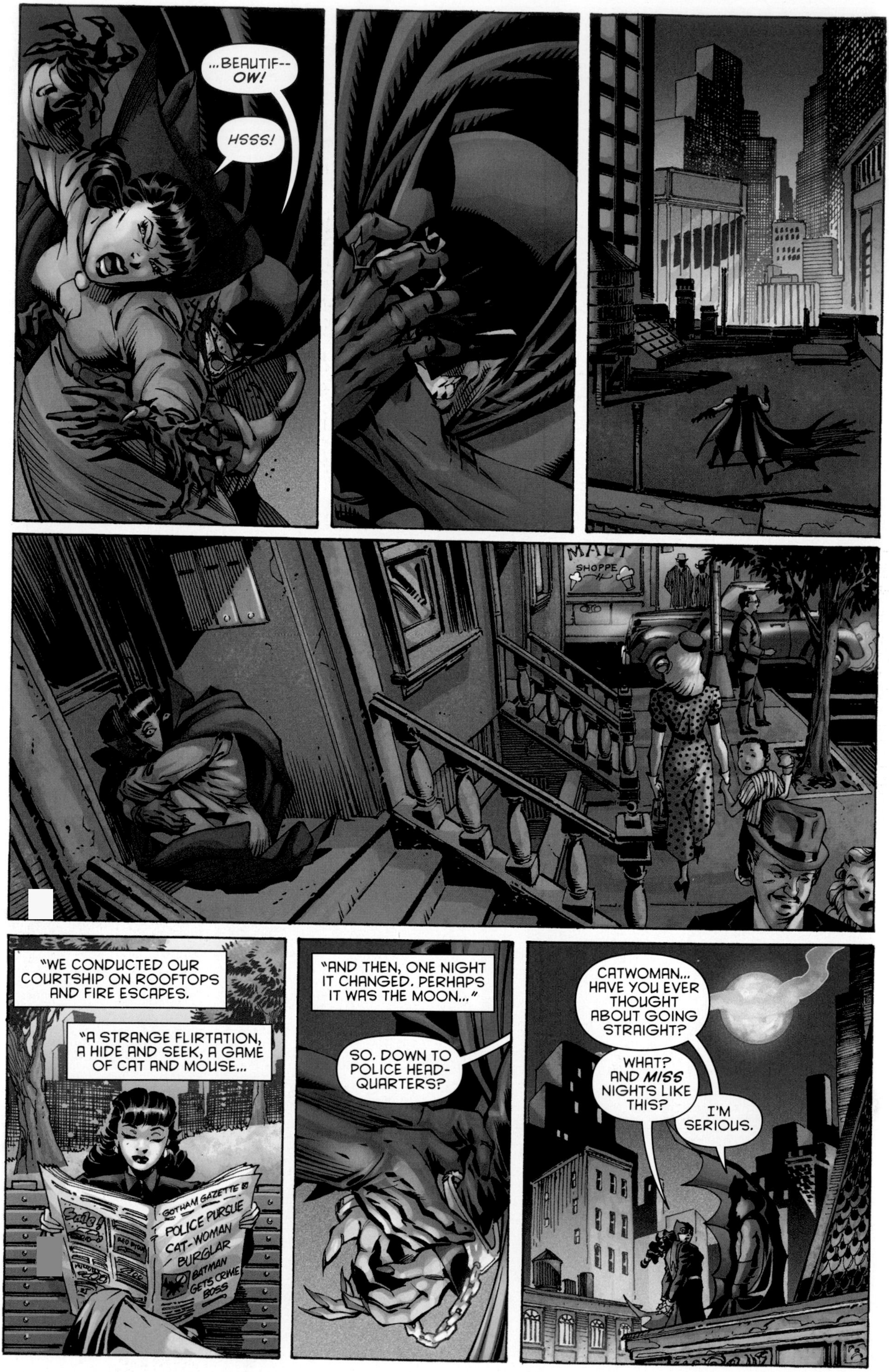
...BEAUTIF-- OW!
HSSS!
MALT SHOPPE
"WE CONDUCTED OUR COURTSHIP ON ROOFTOPS AND FIRE ESCAPES.
"A STRANGE FLIRTATION, A HIDE AND SEEK, A GAME OF CAT AND MOUSE...
GOTHAM GAZETTE
POLICE PURSUE CAT-WOMAN BURGLAR
BATMAN GETS CRIME BOSS
"AND THEN, ONE NIGHT IT CHANGED. PERHAPS IT WAS THE MOON..."
SO. DOWN TO POLICE HEAD-QUARTERS?
CATWOMAN... HAVE YOU EVER THOUGHT ABOUT GOING STRAIGHT?
WHAT? AND MISS NIGHTS LIKE THIS?
I'M SERIOUS.

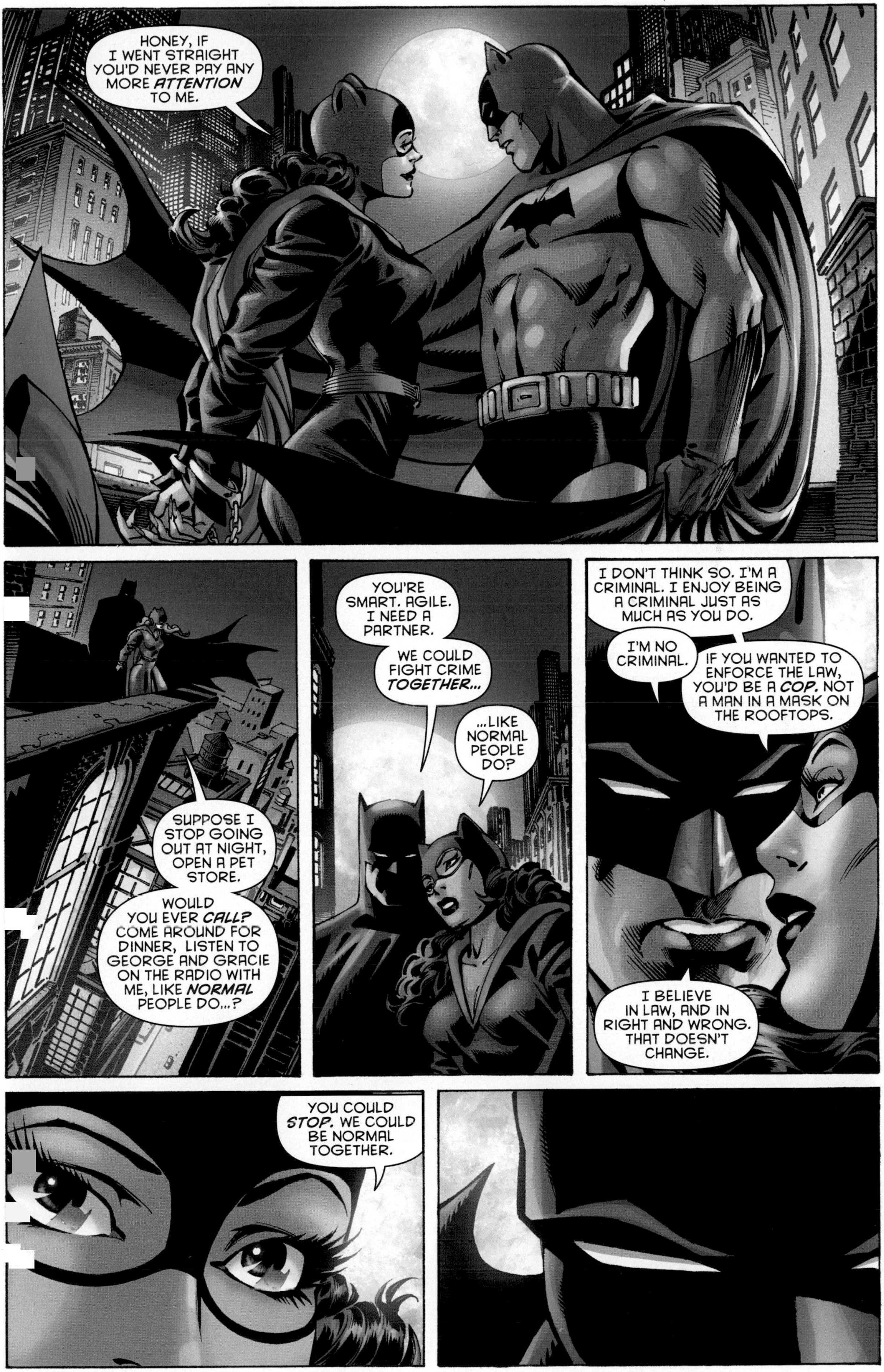
HONEY, IF I WENT STRAIGHT YOU'D NEVER PAY ANY MORE ATTENTION TO ME.
SUPPOSE I STOP GOING OUT AT NIGHT, OPEN A PET STORE.
WOULD YOU EVER CALL? COME AROUND FOR DINNER, LISTEN TO GEORGE AND GRACIE ON THE RADIO WITH ME, LIKE NORMAL PEOPLE DO...?
YOU'RE SMART. AGILE. I NEED A PARTNER.
WE COULD FIGHT CRIME TOGETHER...
...LIKE NORMAL PEOPLE DO?
I DON'T THINK SO. I'M A CRIMINAL. I ENJOY BEING A CRIMINAL JUST AS MUCH AS YOU DO.
I'M NO CRIMINAL.
IF YOU WANTED TO ENFORCE THE LAW, YOU'D BE A COP. NOT A MAN IN A MASK ON THE ROOFTOPS.
I BELIEVE IN LAW, AND IN RIGHT AND WRONG. THAT DOESN'T CHANGE.
YOU COULD STOP. WE COULD BE NORMAL TOGETHER.

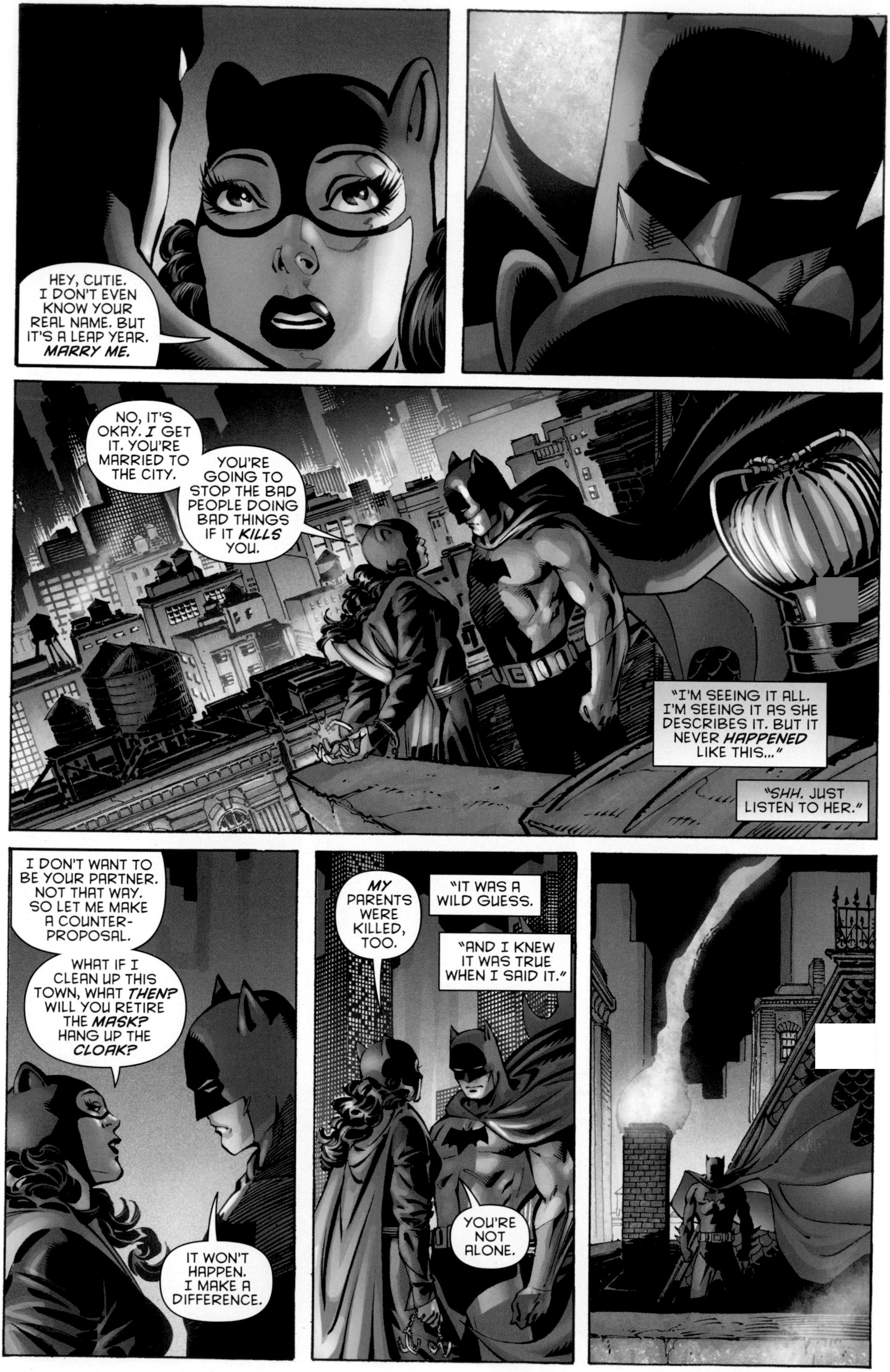
HEY, CUTIE. I DON'T EVEN KNOW YOUR REAL NAME. BUT IT'S A LEAP YEAR. MARRY ME.
NO, IT'S OKAY. I GET IT. YOU'RE MARRIED TO THE CITY.
YOU'RE GOING TO STOP THE BAD PEOPLE DOING BAD THINGS IF IT KILLS YOU.
"I'M SEEING IT ALL. I'M SEEING IT AS SHE DESCRIBES IT. BUT IT NEVER HAPPENED LIKE THIS..."
"SHH. JUST LISTEN TO HER."
I DON'T WANT TO BE YOUR PARTNER. NOT THAT WAY. SO LET ME MAKE A COUNTER-PROPOSAL.
WHAT IF I CLEAN UP THIS TOWN, WHAT THEN? WILL YOU RETIRE THE MASK? HANG UP THE CLOAK?
IT WON'T HAPPEN. I MAKE A DIFFERENCE.
MY PARENTS WERE KILLED, TOO.
"IT WAS A WILD GUESS.
"AND I KNEW IT WAS TRUE WHEN I SAID IT."
YOU'RE NOT ALONE.

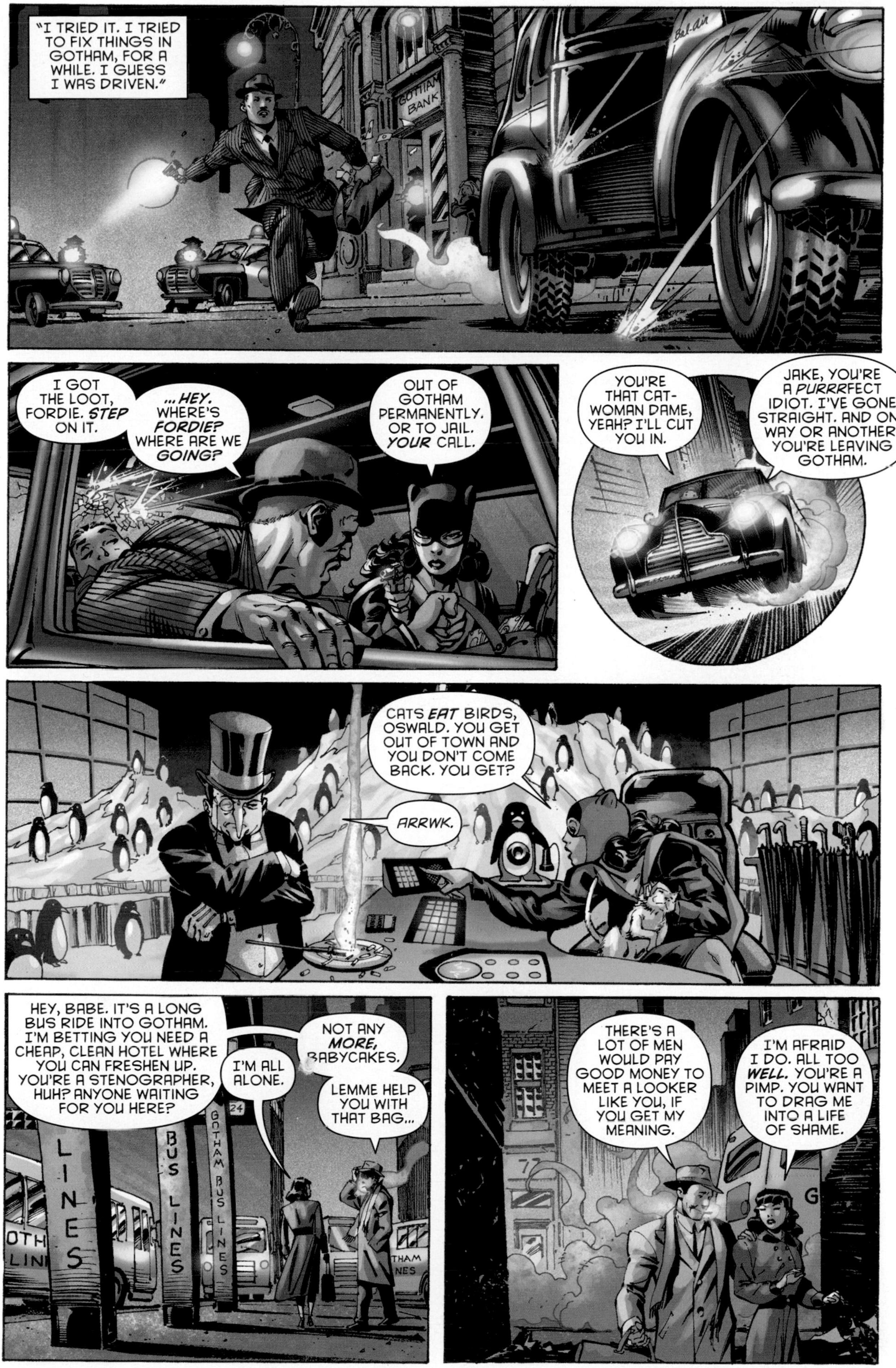
"I TRIED IT. I TRIED TO FIX THINGS IN GOTHAM, FOR A WHILE. I GUESS I WAS DRIVEN."
GOTHAM BANK
I GOT THE LOOT, FORDIE. STEP ON IT.
...HEY. WHERE'S FORDIE? WHERE ARE WE GOING?
OUT OF GOTHAM PERMANENTLY. OR TO JAIL. YOUR CALL.
YOU'RE THAT CAT-WOMAN DAME, YEAH? I'LL CUT YOU IN.
JAKE, YOU'RE A PURRRFECT IDIOT. I'VE GONE STRAIGHT. AND ONE WAY OR ANOTHER, YOU'RE LEAVING GOTHAM.
CATS EAT BIRDS, OSWALD. YOU GET OUT OF TOWN AND YOU DON'T COME BACK. YOU GET?
ARRWK.
HEY, BABE. IT'S A LONG BUS RIDE INTO GOTHAM. I'M BETTING YOU NEED A CHEAP, CLEAN HOTEL WHERE YOU CAN FRESHEN UP. YOU'RE A STENOGRAPHER, HUH? ANYONE WAITING FOR YOU HERE?
I'M ALL ALONE.
NOT ANY MORE, BABYCAKES.
LEMME HELP YOU WITH THAT BAG...
LINES
BUS LINES
GOTHAM BUS LINES
24
THERE'S A LOT OF MEN WOULD PAY GOOD MONEY TO MEET A LOOKER LIKE YOU, IF YOU GET MY MEANING.
I'M AFRAID I DO. ALL TOO WELL. YOU'RE A PIMP. YOU WANT TO DRAG ME INTO A LIFE OF SHAME.

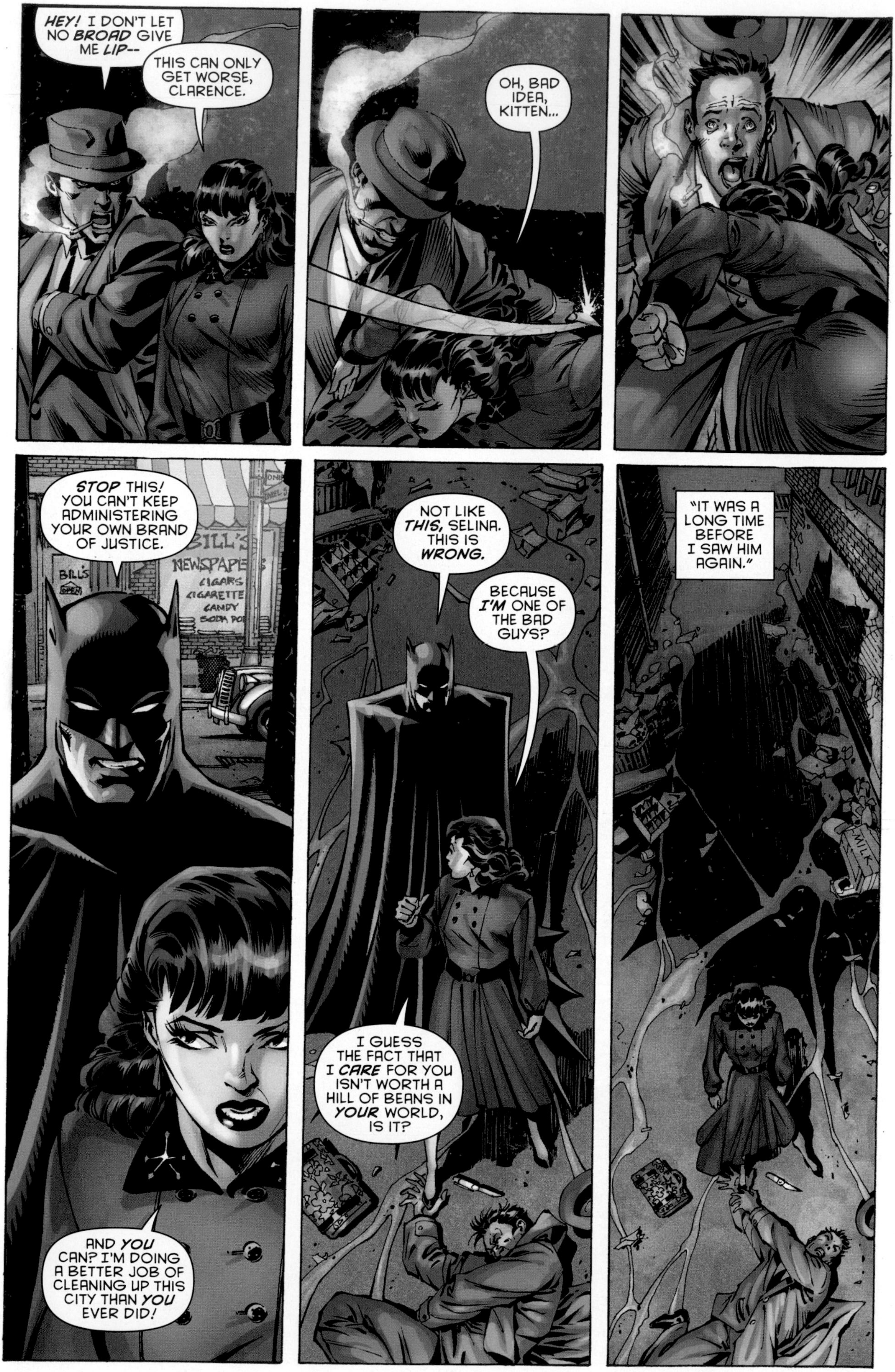
HEY! I DON'T LET NO BROAD GIVE ME LIP--
THIS CAN ONLY GET WORSE, CLARENCE.
OH, BAD IDEA, KITTEN...
STOP THIS! YOU CAN'T KEEP ADMINISTERING YOUR OWN BRAND OF JUSTICE.
BILL'S
NEWSPAPERS
CIGARS
CIGARETTES
CANDY
SODA POP
AND YOU CAN? I'M DOING A BETTER JOB OF CLEANING UP THIS CITY THAN YOU EVER DID!
NOT LIKE THIS, SELINA. THIS IS WRONG.
BECAUSE I'M ONE OF THE BAD GUYS?
I GUESS THE FACT THAT I CARE FOR YOU ISN'T WORTH A HILL OF BEANS IN YOUR WORLD, IS IT?
"IT WAS A LONG TIME BEFORE I SAW HIM AGAIN."
MILK

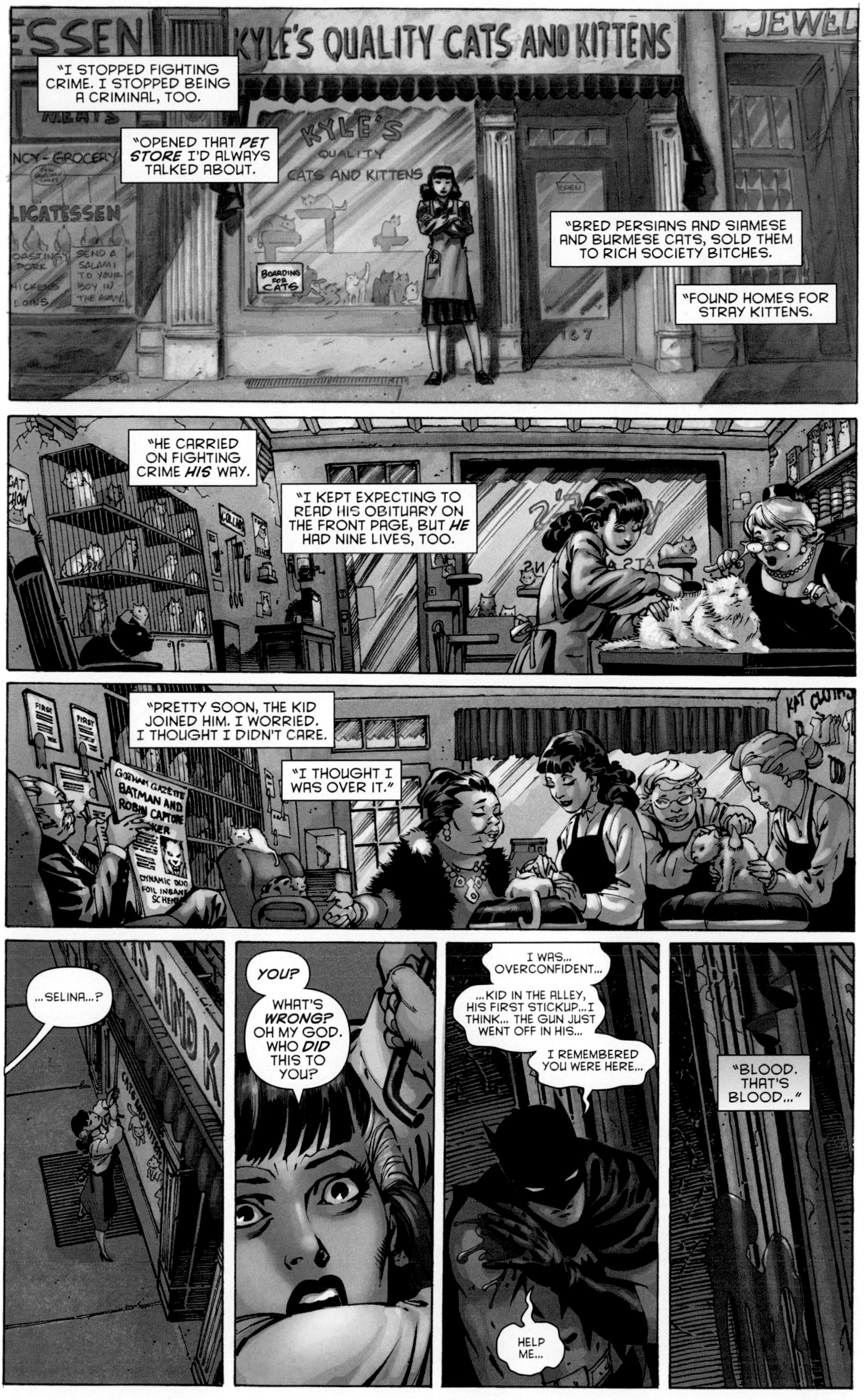
KYLE'S QUALITY CATS AND KITTENS
"I STOPPED FIGHTING CRIME. I STOPPED BEING A CRIMINAL, TOO.
"OPENED THAT PET STORE I'D ALWAYS TALKED ABOUT.
"BRED PERSIANS AND SIAMESE AND BURMESE CATS, SOLD THEM TO RICH SOCIETY BITCHES.
"FOUND HOMES FOR STRAY KITTENS.
"HE CARRIED ON FIGHTING CRIME HIS WAY.
"I KEPT EXPECTING TO READ HIS OBITUARY ON THE FRONT PAGE, BUT HE HAD NINE LIVES, TOO.
"PRETTY SOON, THE KID JOINED HIM. I WORRIED. I THOUGHT I DIDN'T CARE.
"I THOUGHT I WAS OVER IT."
GOTHAM GAZETTE
BATMAN AND ROBIN CAPTURE
DYNAMIC DUO FOIL INSANE SCHEME
...SELINA...?
YOU?
WHAT'S WRONG? OH MY GOD. WHO DID THIS TO YOU?
I WAS... OVERCONFIDENT...
...KID IN THE ALLEY, HIS FIRST STICKUP... I THINK... THE GUN JUST WENT OFF IN HIS...
I REMEMBERED YOU WERE HERE...
HELP ME...
"BLOOD. THAT'S BLOOD..."

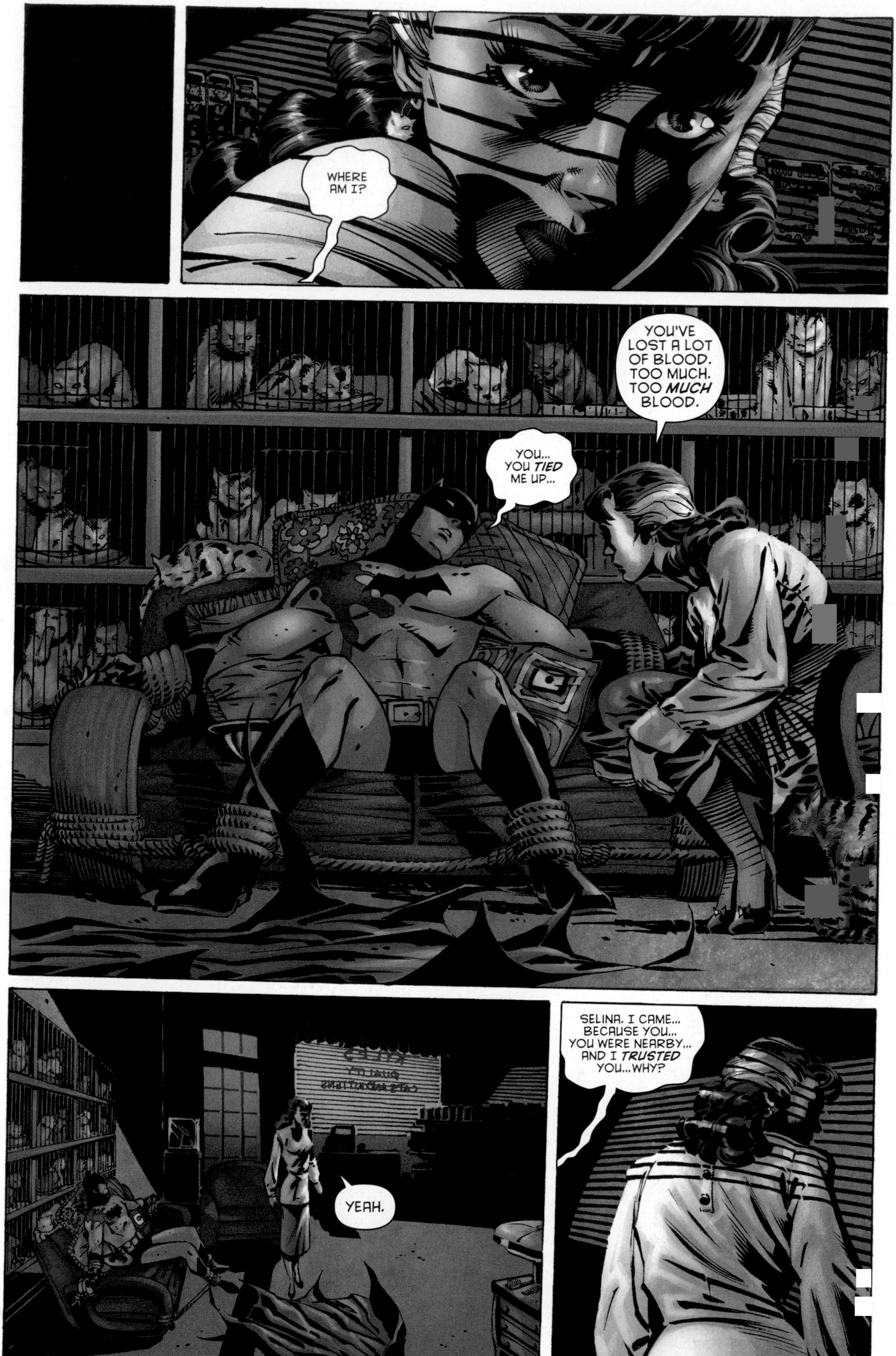
WHERE AM I?
YOU'VE LOST A LOT OF BLOOD. TOO MUCH. TOO *MUCH* BLOOD.
YOU... YOU *TIED* ME UP...
YEAH.
SELINA. I CAME... BECAUSE YOU... YOU WERE NEARBY... AND I *TRUSTED* YOU...WHY?

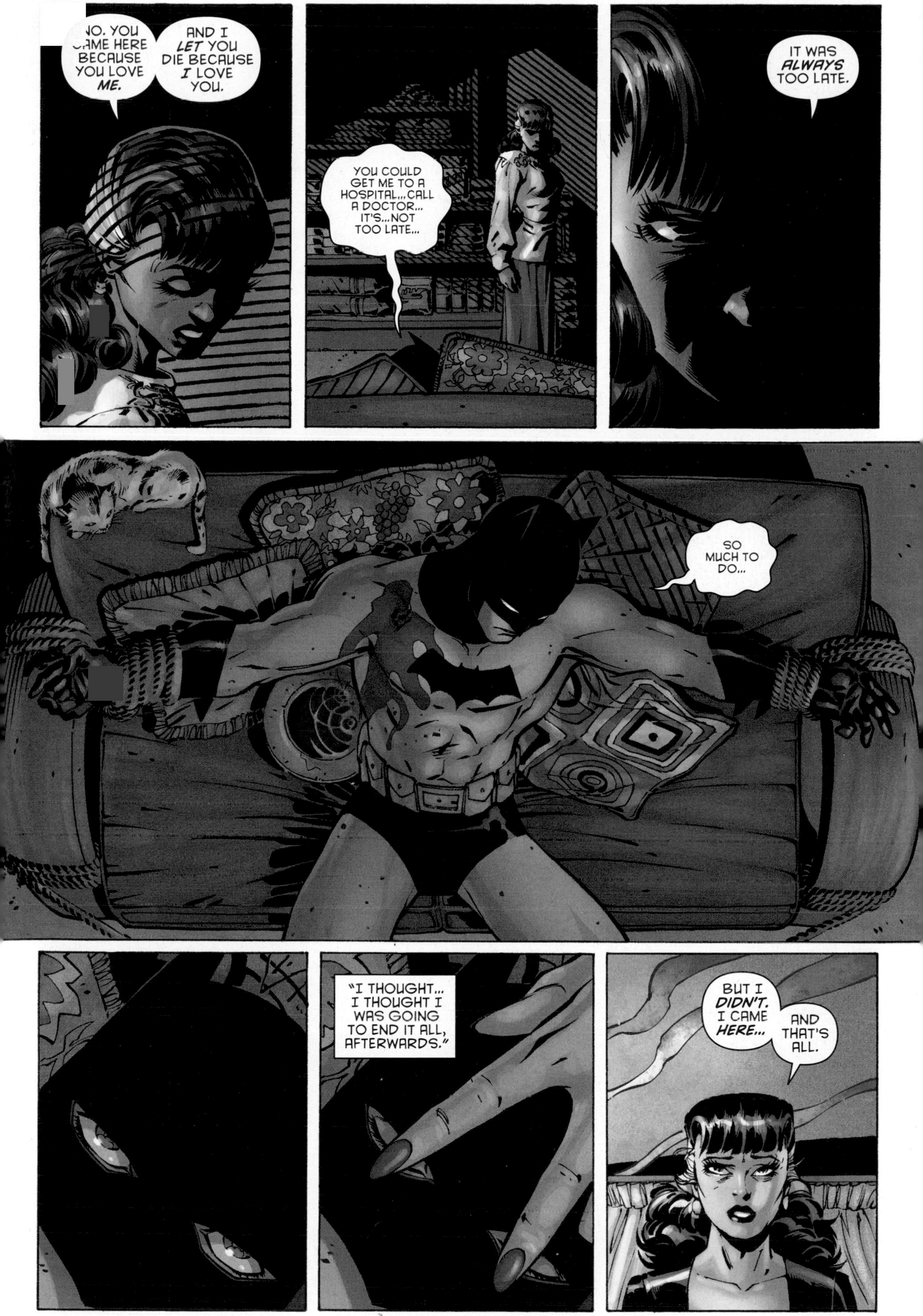
NO. YOU CAME HERE BECAUSE YOU LOVE ME.
AND I LET YOU DIE BECAUSE I LOVE YOU.
YOU COULD GET ME TO A HOSPITAL...CALL A DOCTOR... IT'S...NOT TOO LATE...
IT WAS ALWAYS TOO LATE.
SO MUCH TO DO...
"I THOUGHT... I THOUGHT I WAS GOING TO END IT ALL, AFTERWARDS."
BUT I DIDN'T. I CAME HERE...
AND THAT'S ALL.

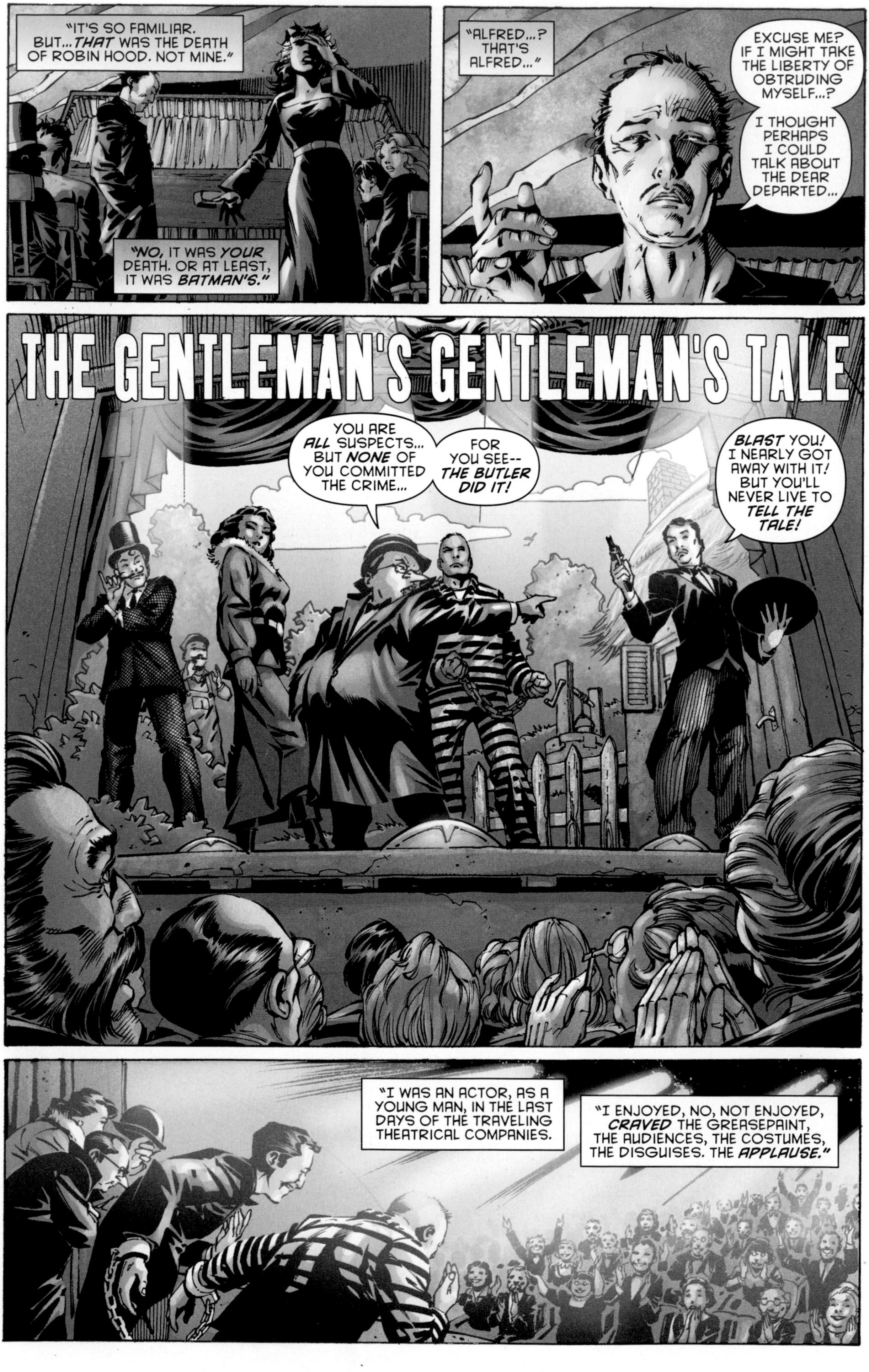
"IT'S SO FAMILIAR. BUT...THAT WAS THE DEATH OF ROBIN HOOD. NOT MINE."
"NO, IT WAS YOUR DEATH. OR AT LEAST, IT WAS BATMAN'S."
"ALFRED...? THAT'S ALFRED..."
EXCUSE ME? IF I MIGHT TAKE THE LIBERTY OF OBTRUDING MYSELF...?
I THOUGHT PERHAPS I COULD TALK ABOUT THE DEAR DEPARTED...
THE GENTLEMAN'S GENTLEMAN'S TALE
YOU ARE ALL SUSPECTS... BUT NONE OF YOU COMMITTED THE CRIME...
FOR YOU SEE-- THE BUTLER DID IT!
BLAST YOU! I NEARLY GOT AWAY WITH IT! BUT YOU'LL NEVER LIVE TO TELL THE TALE!
"I WAS AN ACTOR, AS A YOUNG MAN, IN THE LAST DAYS OF THE TRAVELING THEATRICAL COMPANIES.
"I ENJOYED, NO, NOT ENJOYED, CRAVED THE GREASEPAINT, THE AUDIENCES, THE COSTUMES, THE DISGUISES. THE APPLAUSE."

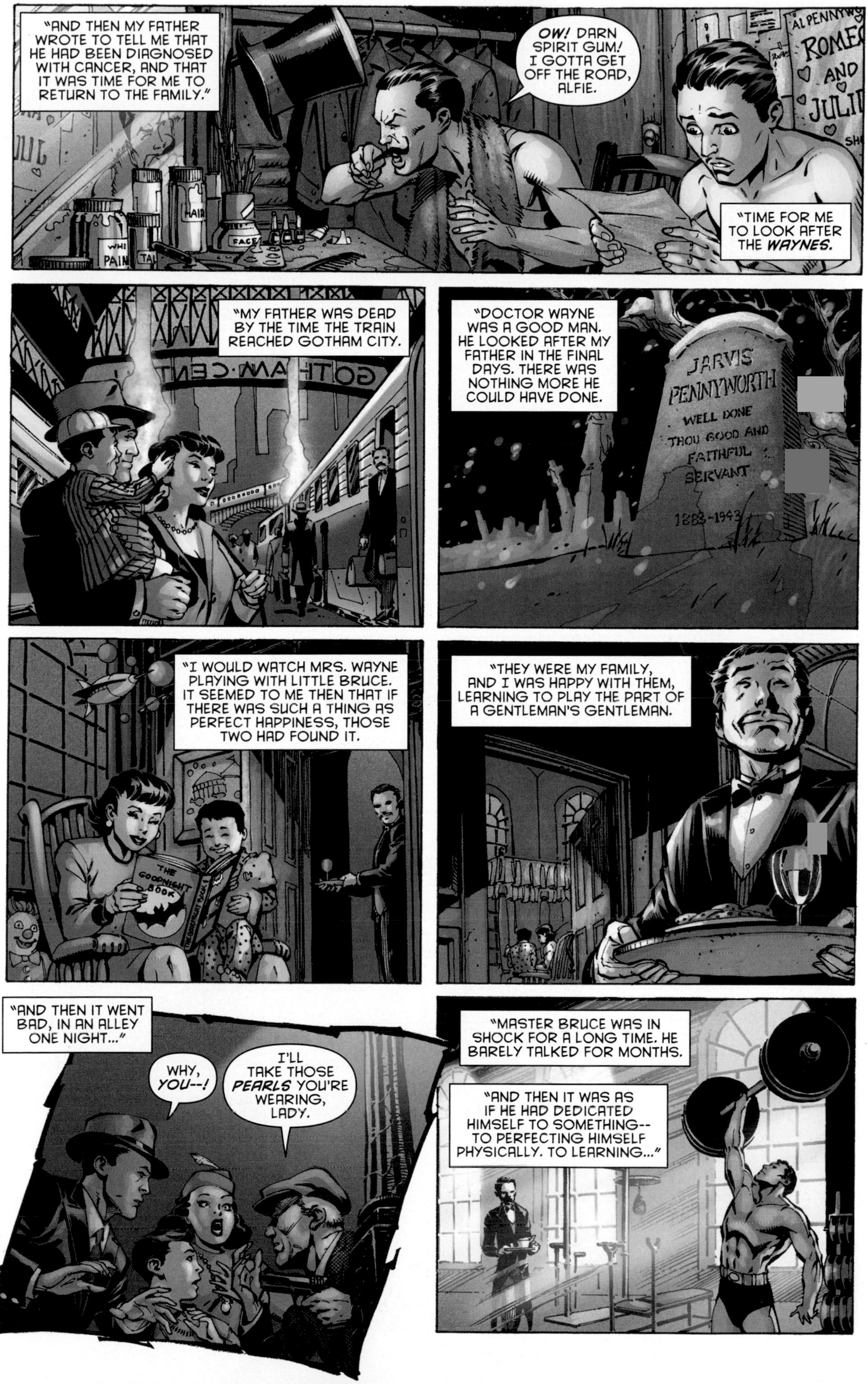
"AND THEN MY FATHER WROTE TO TELL ME THAT HE HAD BEEN DIAGNOSED WITH CANCER, AND THAT IT WAS TIME FOR ME TO RETURN TO THE FAMILY."
OW! DARN SPIRIT GUM! I GOTTA GET OFF THE ROAD, ALFIE.
ROMEO AND JULIET
"TIME FOR ME TO LOOK AFTER THE WAYNES.
"MY FATHER WAS DEAD BY THE TIME THE TRAIN REACHED GOTHAM CITY.
"DOCTOR WAYNE WAS A GOOD MAN. HE LOOKED AFTER MY FATHER IN THE FINAL DAYS. THERE WAS NOTHING MORE HE COULD HAVE DONE.
JARVIS PENNYWORTH WELL DONE THOU GOOD AND FAITHFUL SERVANT 1883-1943
"I WOULD WATCH MRS. WAYNE PLAYING WITH LITTLE BRUCE. IT SEEMED TO ME THEN THAT IF THERE WAS SUCH A THING AS PERFECT HAPPINESS, THOSE TWO HAD FOUND IT.
THE GOODNIGHT BOOK
"THEY WERE MY FAMILY, AND I WAS HAPPY WITH THEM, LEARNING TO PLAY THE PART OF A GENTLEMAN'S GENTLEMAN.
"AND THEN IT WENT BAD, IN AN ALLEY ONE NIGHT..."
WHY, YOU--!
I'LL TAKE THOSE PEARLS YOU'RE WEARING, LADY.
"MASTER BRUCE WAS IN SHOCK FOR A LONG TIME. HE BARELY TALKED FOR MONTHS.
"AND THEN IT WAS AS IF HE HAD DEDICATED HIMSELF TO SOMETHING-- TO PERFECTING HIMSELF PHYSICALLY. TO LEARNING..."

"THE YEARS FLEW BY. I WAS THERE THE FIRST TIME HE RODE OUT AS A MASKED VIGILANTE."

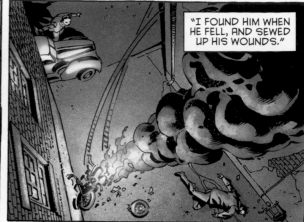

"I FOUND HIM WHEN HE FELL, AND SEWED UP HIS WOUNDS."

AND THEN HE BEGAN DRESSING AS A *BAT...*

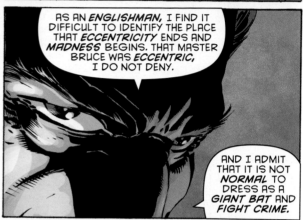

AS AN *ENGLISHMAN,* I FIND IT DIFFICULT TO IDENTIFY THE PLACE THAT *ECCENTRICITY* ENDS AND *MADNESS* BEGINS. THAT MASTER BRUCE WAS *ECCENTRIC,* I DO NOT DENY.

AND I ADMIT THAT IT IS NOT *NORMAL* TO DRESS AS A *GIANT BAT* AND *FIGHT CRIME.*

"BUT DOING IT MADE HIM *HAPPIER* THAN I HAD SEEN HIM IN A LONG, LONG TIME."

"THE BLACK MOODS THAT HAD STARTED WHEN HIS PARENTS WERE KILLED *RECEDED.*"

"HE *SMILED,* SOMETIMES."

"AND THEN THE SMILE BEGAN TO FADE. HE *STILL* WENT OUT AT NIGHT. SOMETIMES HE FOUND CRIMINALS IN THE ACT OF COMMITTING CRIMES, AND STOPPED THEM."

"MOSTLY, HE DID *NOT.*"

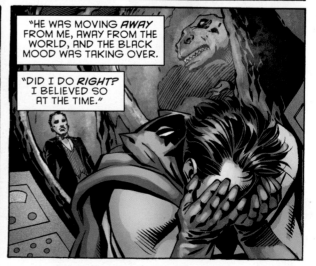

"HE WAS MOVING *AWAY* FROM ME, AWAY FROM THE WORLD, AND THE BLACK MOOD WAS TAKING OVER.

"DID I DO *RIGHT?* I BELIEVED SO AT THE TIME."

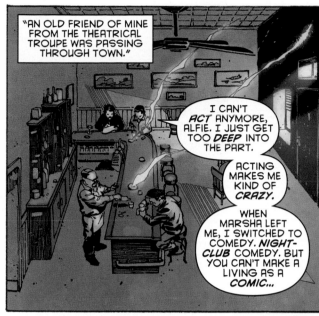

"AN OLD FRIEND OF MINE FROM THE THEATRICAL TROUPE WAS PASSING THROUGH TOWN."
I CAN'T ACT ANYMORE, ALFIE. I JUST GET TOO DEEP INTO THE PART.
ACTING MAKES ME KIND OF CRAZY.
WHEN MARSHA LEFT ME, I SWITCHED TO COMEDY. NIGHT-CLUB COMEDY. BUT YOU CAN'T MAKE A LIVING AS A COMIC...
EDDIE. I NEED A FAVOR.
SURE. NAME IT.
I NEED SOME-THING TO INTRIGUE MASTER BRUCE. SOMETHING CRIME-RELATED. I WAS THINKING ABOUT RIDDLES. WOULD YOU DELIVER THEM?
Carlsson
Gotham
YOU WANT ME TO PLAY A MASTER CRIMINAL? ONE THAT TELLS RIDDLES?
IF YOU'RE WILLING, YES.
"A PLANE RISES TO TURN. A RIVER RUNS BETWEEN. WHAT AM I?" "A BANK!" YEAH...I CAN DO THAT!
WE CAN WORK ON THE MATERIAL.
CROSSWORD
"THE RIDDLES WERE MY IDEA. THE COSTUME WAS HIS."
HOW DO I LOOK?
REMARKABLE.
I--THE "RIDDLE-MASTER"--WILL CHALLENGE THIS BAT-MAN TO A DUEL OF WITS. I'LL LEAVE CLUES EVERY-WHERE. IT'S A COMPULSION.
"RIDDLER", I THINK. IT'S MORE MEMORABLE.
"MASTER BRUCE WAS A NEW MAN.
"AND WHEN THE BLACK MOOD CAME UPON HIM, I WOULD CALL IN FRIENDS, AND IT WOULD HELP, FOR A WHILE.
"IT HELPED. IT DID NOT HELP ENOUGH."

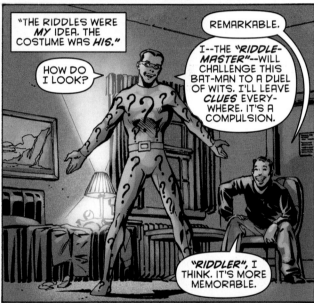

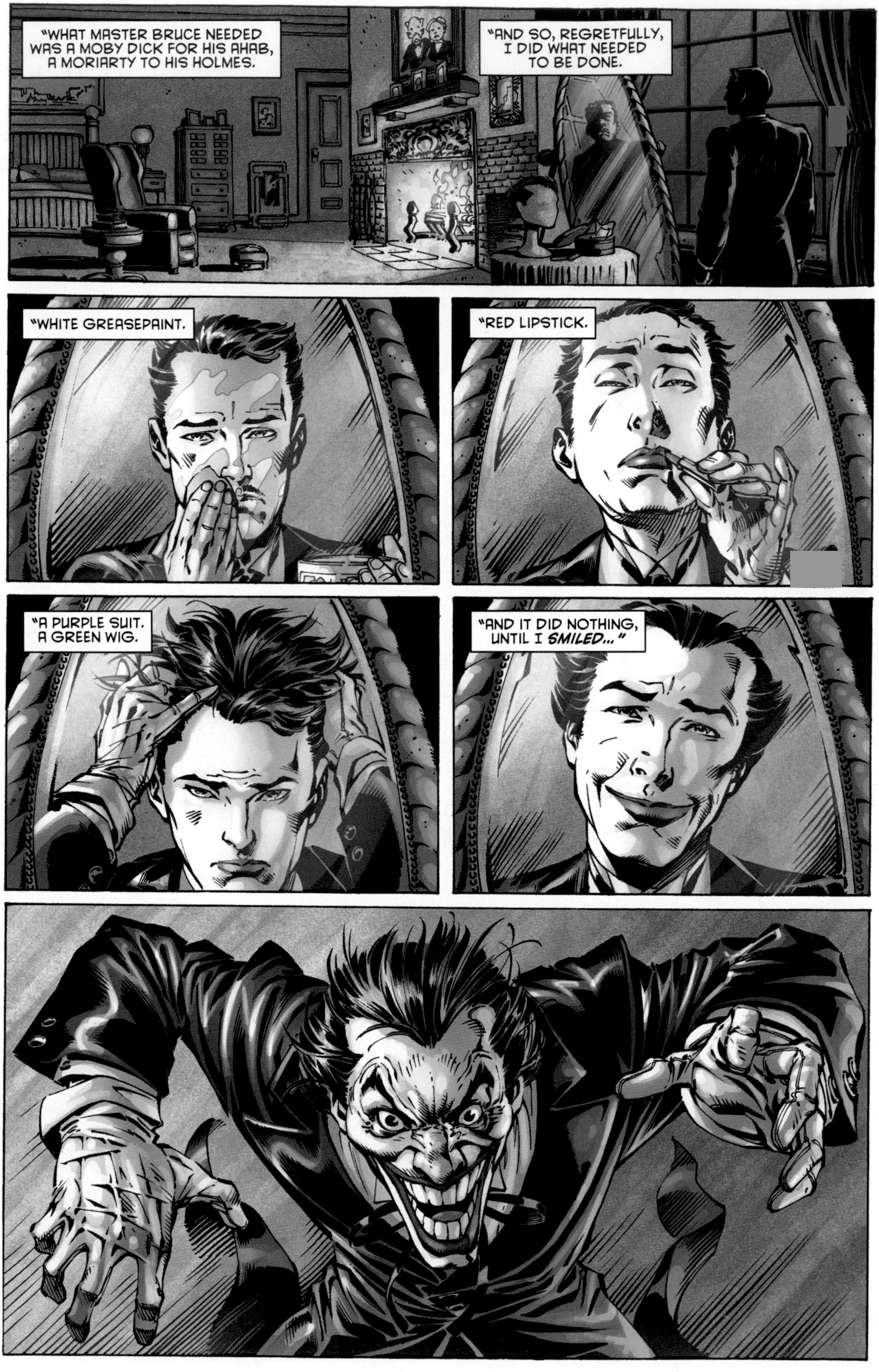
"WHAT MASTER BRUCE NEEDED WAS A MOBY DICK FOR HIS AHAB, A MORIARTY TO HIS HOLMES.
"AND SO, REGRETFULLY, I DID WHAT NEEDED TO BE DONE.
"WHITE GREASEPAINT.
"RED LIPSTICK.
"A PURPLE SUIT. A GREEN WIG.
"AND IT DID NOTHING, UNTIL I *SMILED...*"

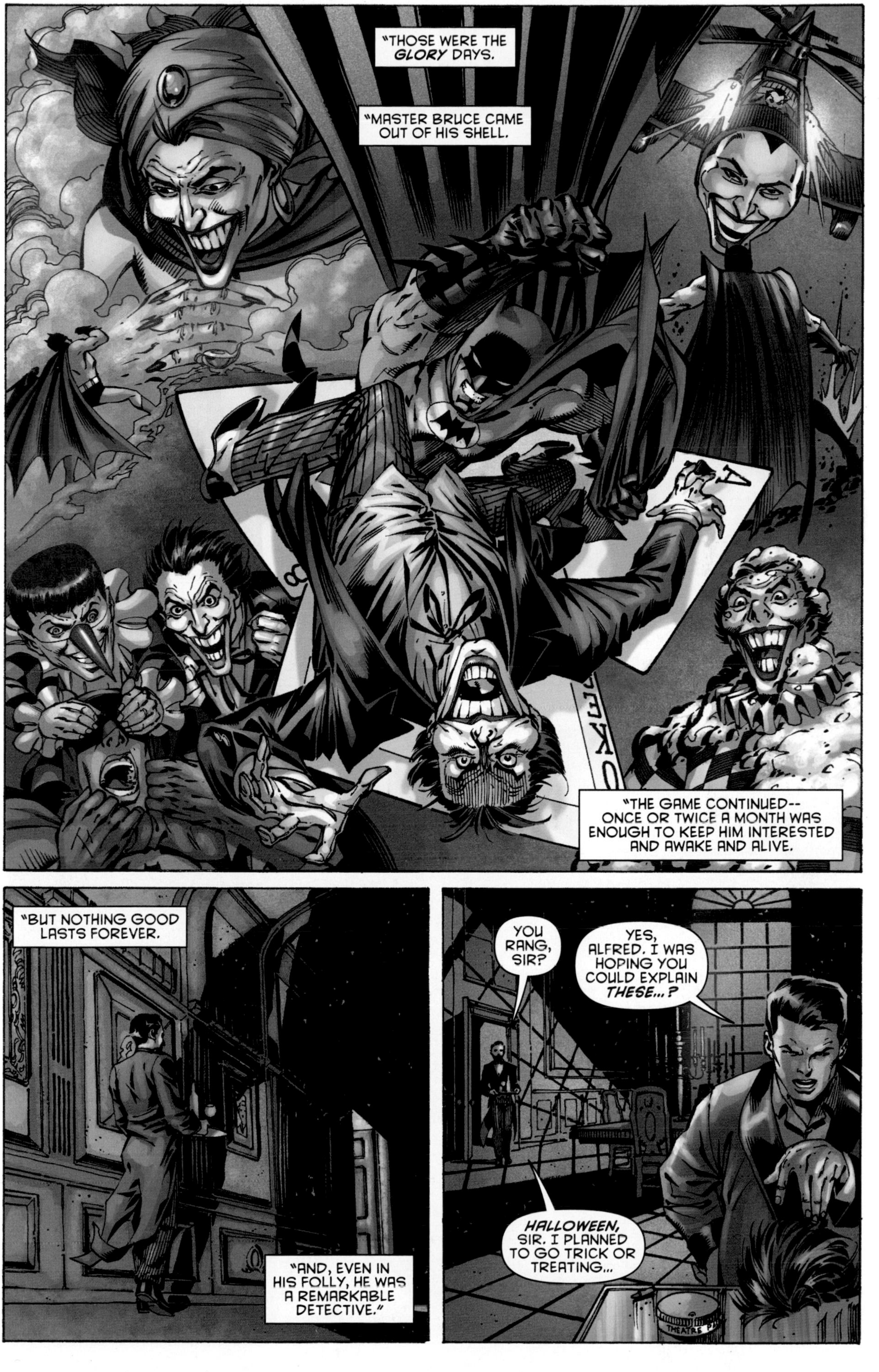
"THOSE WERE THE *GLORY* DAYS.
"MASTER BRUCE CAME OUT OF HIS SHELL.
"THE GAME CONTINUED-- ONCE OR TWICE A MONTH WAS ENOUGH TO KEEP HIM INTERESTED AND AWAKE AND ALIVE.
"BUT NOTHING GOOD LASTS FOREVER.
"AND, EVEN IN HIS FOLLY, HE WAS A REMARKABLE DETECTIVE."
YOU RANG, SIR?
YES, ALFRED. I WAS HOPING YOU COULD EXPLAIN *THESE...?*
HALLOWEEN, SIR. I PLANNED TO GO TRICK OR TREATING...

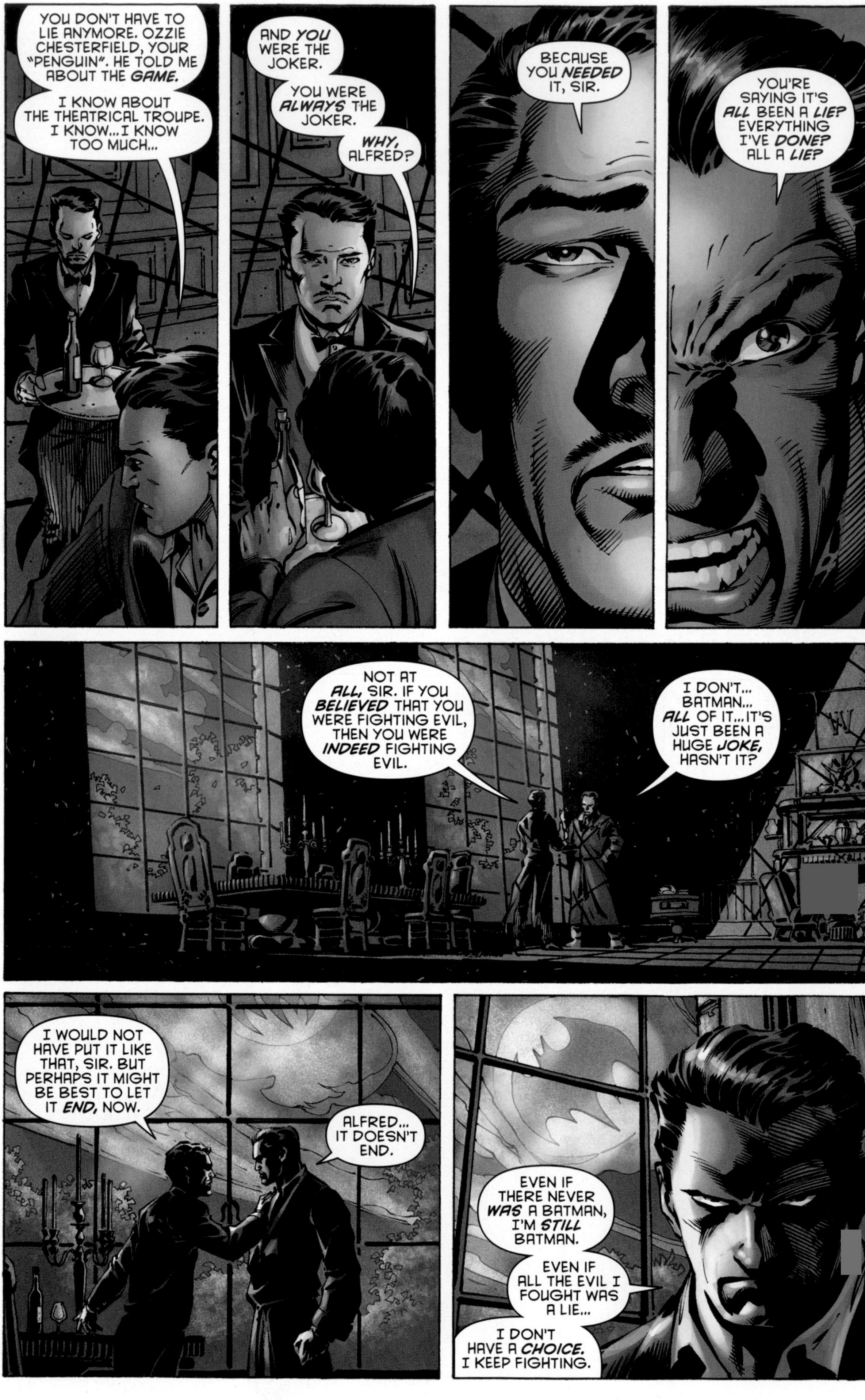
YOU DON'T HAVE TO LIE ANYMORE. OZZIE CHESTERFIELD, YOUR "PENGUIN". HE TOLD ME ABOUT THE GAME.
I KNOW ABOUT THE THEATRICAL TROUPE. I KNOW...I KNOW TOO MUCH...
AND YOU WERE THE JOKER.
YOU WERE ALWAYS THE JOKER.
WHY, ALFRED?
BECAUSE YOU NEEDED IT, SIR.
YOU'RE SAYING IT'S ALL BEEN A LIE? EVERYTHING I'VE DONE? ALL A LIE?
NOT AT ALL, SIR. IF YOU BELIEVED THAT YOU WERE FIGHTING EVIL, THEN YOU WERE INDEED FIGHTING EVIL.
I DON'T... BATMAN... ALL OF IT...IT'S JUST BEEN A HUGE JOKE, HASN'T IT?
I WOULD NOT HAVE PUT IT LIKE THAT, SIR. BUT PERHAPS IT MIGHT BE BEST TO LET IT END, NOW.
ALFRED... IT DOESN'T END.
EVEN IF THERE NEVER WAS A BATMAN, I'M STILL BATMAN.
EVEN IF ALL THE EVIL I FOUGHT WAS A LIE...
I DON'T HAVE A CHOICE. I KEEP FIGHTING.

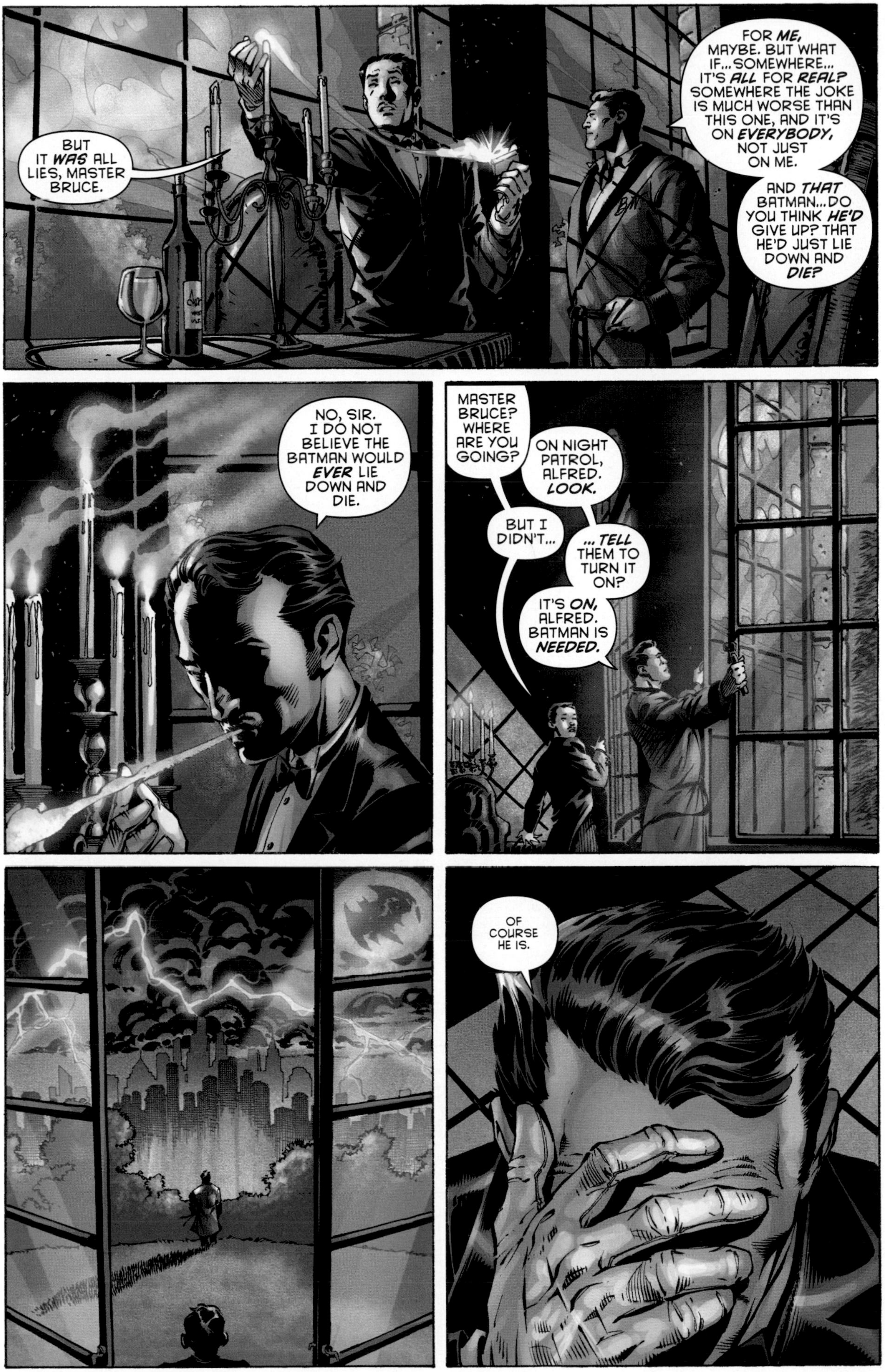
BUT IT WAS ALL LIES, MASTER BRUCE.
FOR ME, MAYBE. BUT WHAT IF... SOMEWHERE... IT'S ALL FOR REAL? SOMEWHERE THE JOKE IS MUCH WORSE THAN THIS ONE, AND IT'S ON EVERYBODY, NOT JUST ON ME.
AND THAT BATMAN... DO YOU THINK HE'D GIVE UP? THAT HE'D JUST LIE DOWN AND DIE?
NO, SIR. I DO NOT BELIEVE THE BATMAN WOULD EVER LIE DOWN AND DIE.
MASTER BRUCE? WHERE ARE YOU GOING?
ON NIGHT PATROL, ALFRED. LOOK.
BUT I DIDN'T...
...TELL THEM TO TURN IT ON?
IT'S ON, ALFRED. BATMAN IS NEEDED.
OF COURSE HE IS.

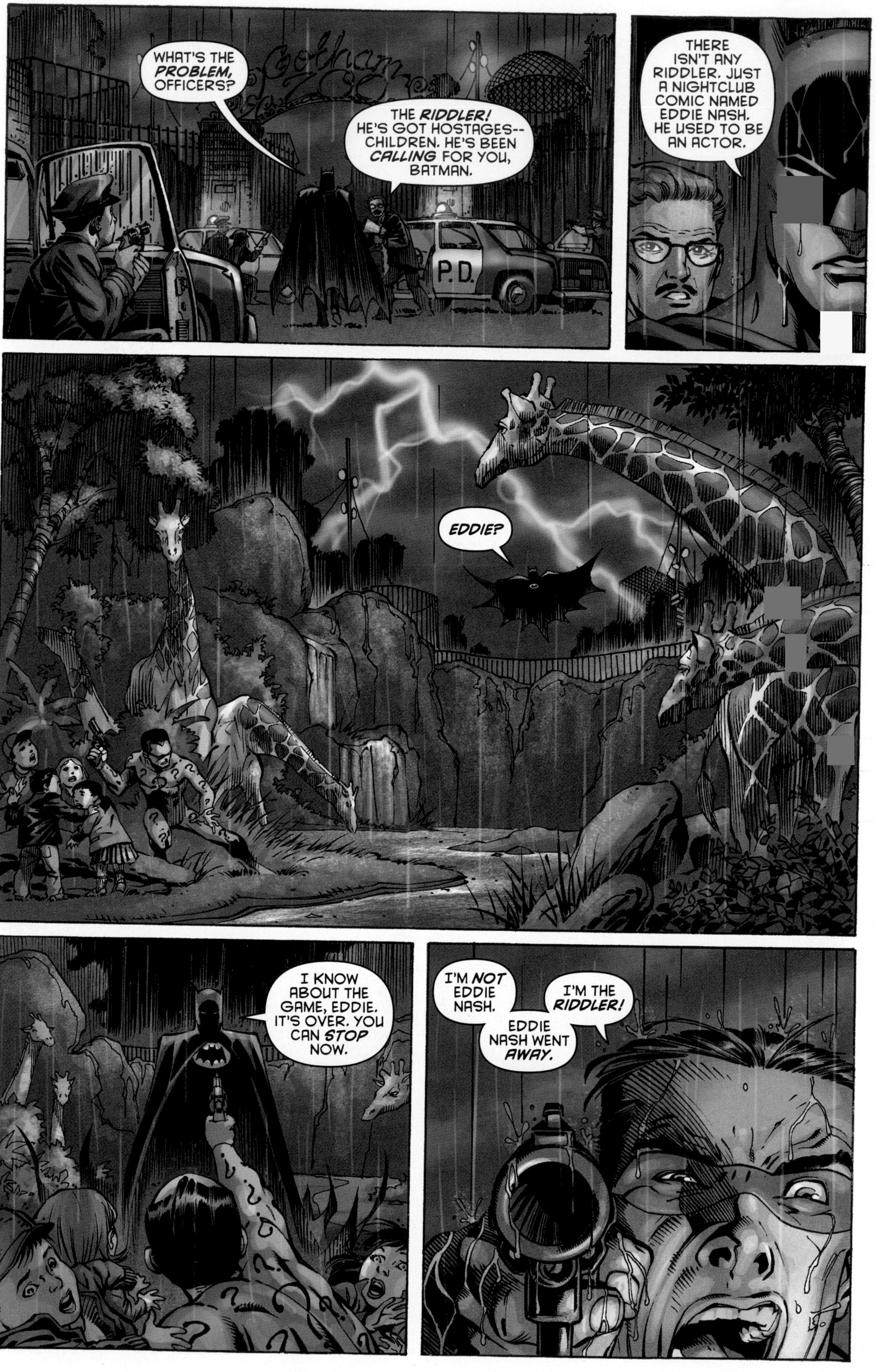

Gotham Zoo
WHAT'S THE *PROBLEM,* OFFICERS?
THE *RIDDLER!* HE'S GOT HOSTAGES-- CHILDREN. HE'S BEEN *CALLING* FOR YOU, BATMAN.
P.D.
THERE ISN'T ANY RIDDLER. JUST A NIGHTCLUB COMIC NAMED EDDIE NASH. HE USED TO BE AN ACTOR.
EDDIE?
I KNOW ABOUT THE GAME, EDDIE. IT'S OVER. YOU CAN *STOP* NOW.
I'M *NOT* EDDIE NASH.
I'M THE *RIDDLER!*
EDDIE NASH WENT *AWAY.*

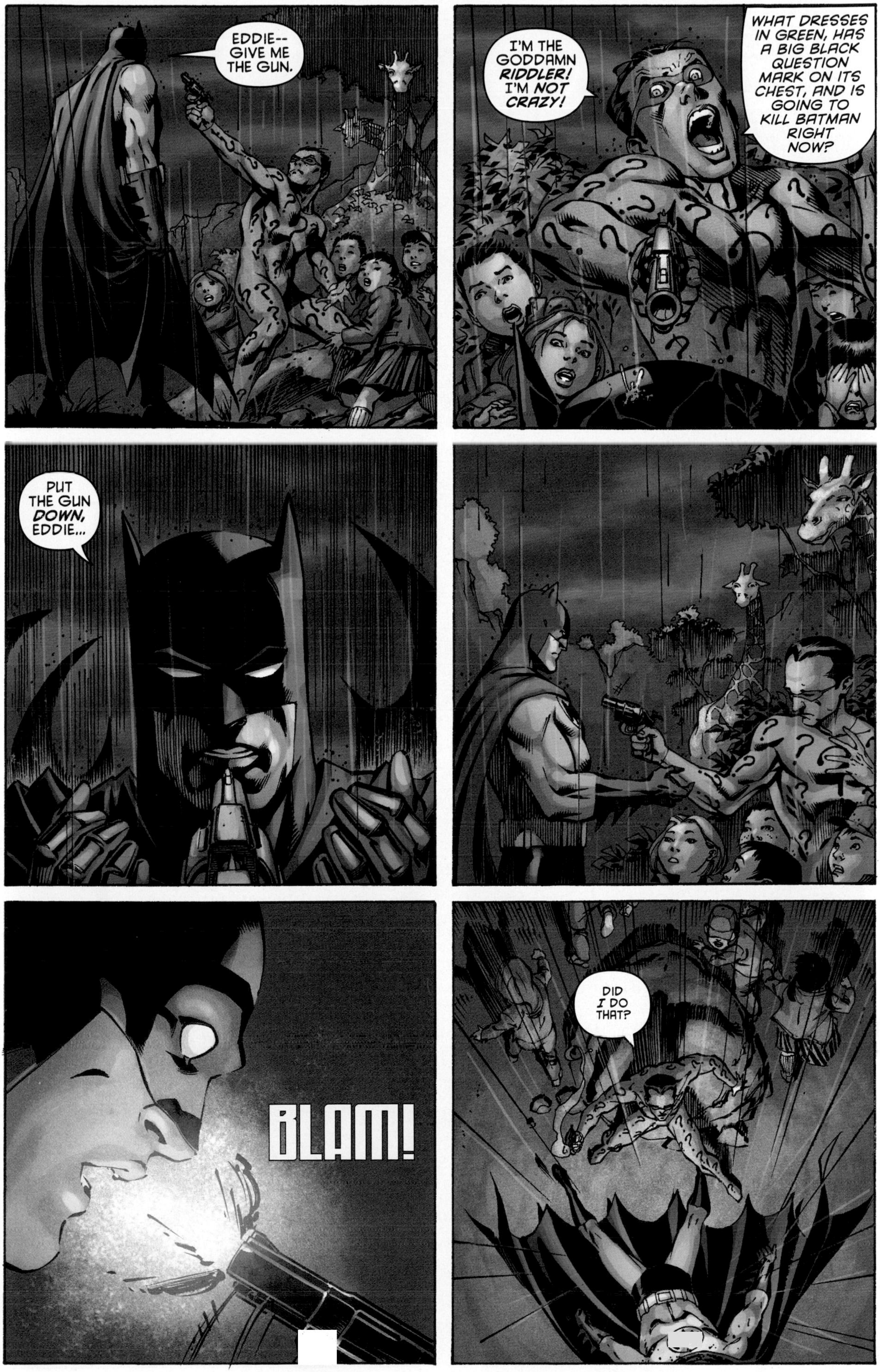
EDDIE-- GIVE ME THE GUN.
I'M THE GODDAMN RIDDLER! I'M NOT CRAZY!
WHAT DRESSES IN GREEN, HAS A BIG BLACK QUESTION MARK ON ITS CHEST, AND IS GOING TO KILL BATMAN RIGHT NOW?
PUT THE GUN DOWN, EDDIE...
BLAM!
DID I DO THAT?

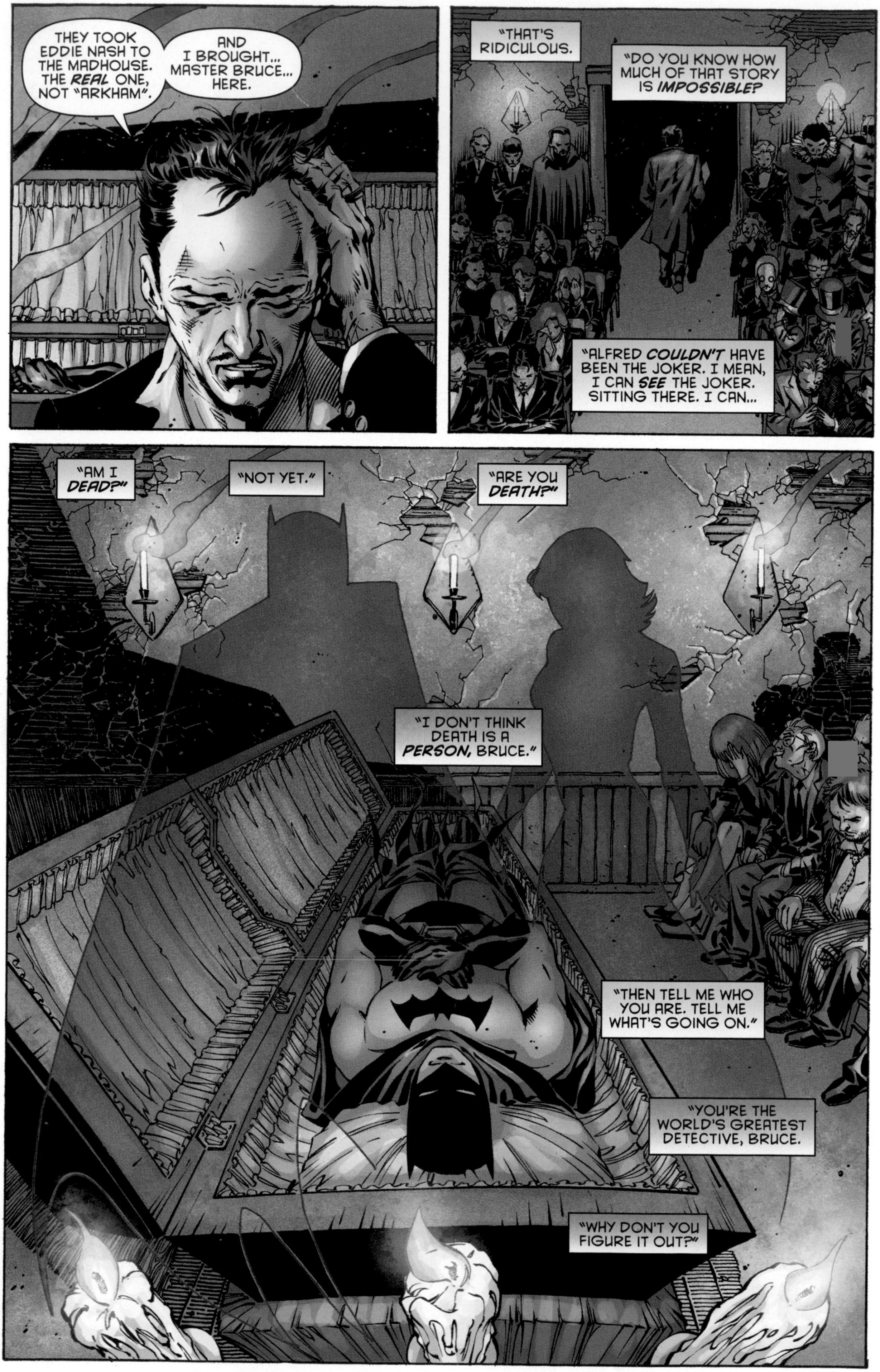
THEY TOOK EDDIE NASH TO THE MADHOUSE. THE *REAL* ONE, NOT "ARKHAM".
AND I BROUGHT... MASTER BRUCE... HERE.
"THAT'S RIDICULOUS.
"DO YOU KNOW HOW MUCH OF THAT STORY IS *IMPOSSIBLE?*
"ALFRED *COULDN'T* HAVE BEEN THE JOKER. I MEAN, I CAN *SEE* THE JOKER. SITTING THERE. I CAN...
"AM I *DEAD?*"
"NOT YET."
"ARE YOU *DEATH?*"
"I DON'T THINK DEATH IS A *PERSON,* BRUCE."
"THEN TELL ME WHO YOU ARE. TELL ME WHAT'S GOING ON."
"YOU'RE THE WORLD'S GREATEST DETECTIVE, BRUCE.
"WHY DON'T YOU FIGURE IT OUT?"

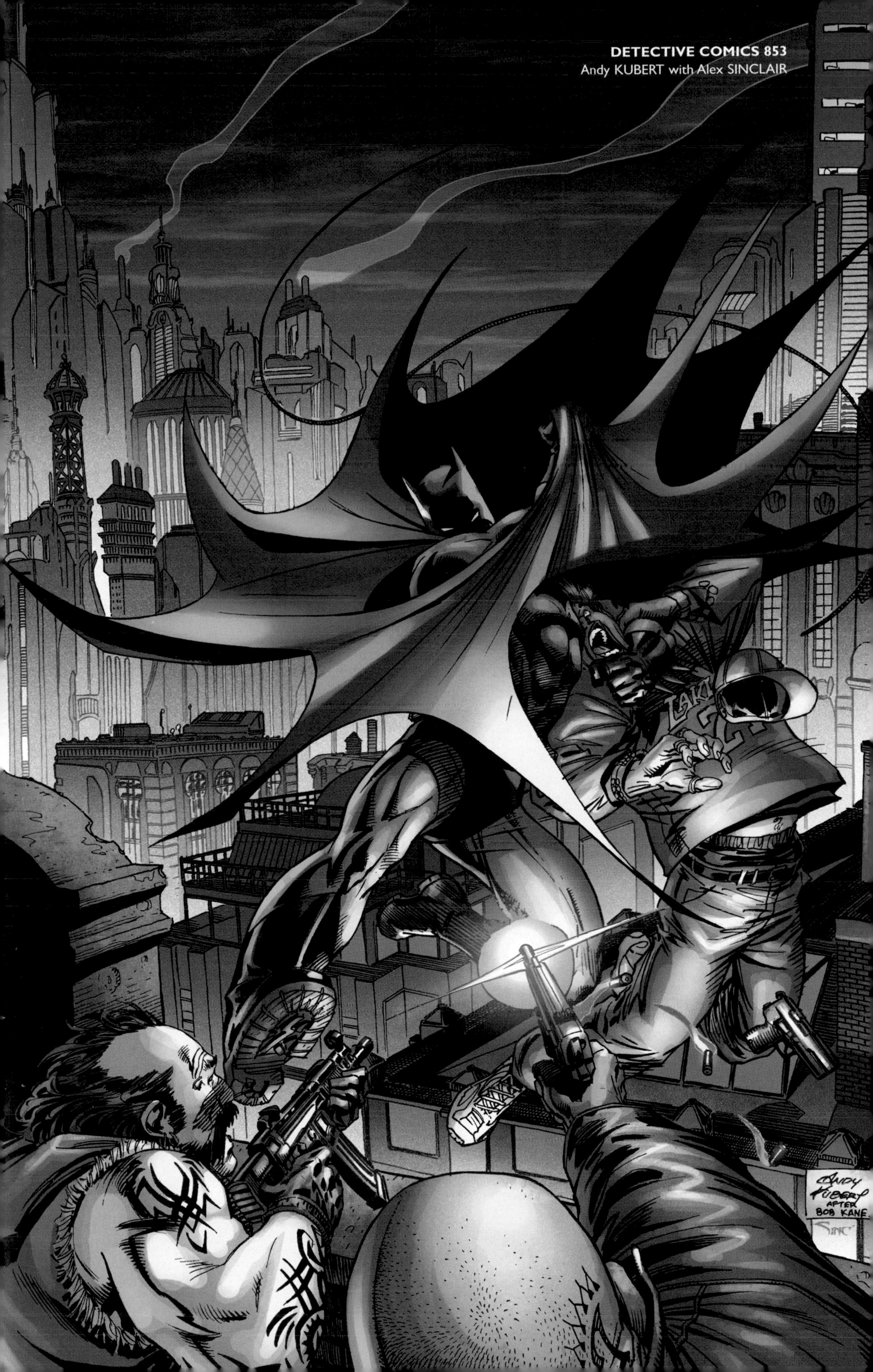
ANDY KUBERT AFTER BOB KANE.
SINC

DETECTIVE COMICS 853
Andy KUBERT with Alex SINCLAIR

WHATEVER HAPPENED TO THE CAPED CRUSADER?

Part 2 of 2

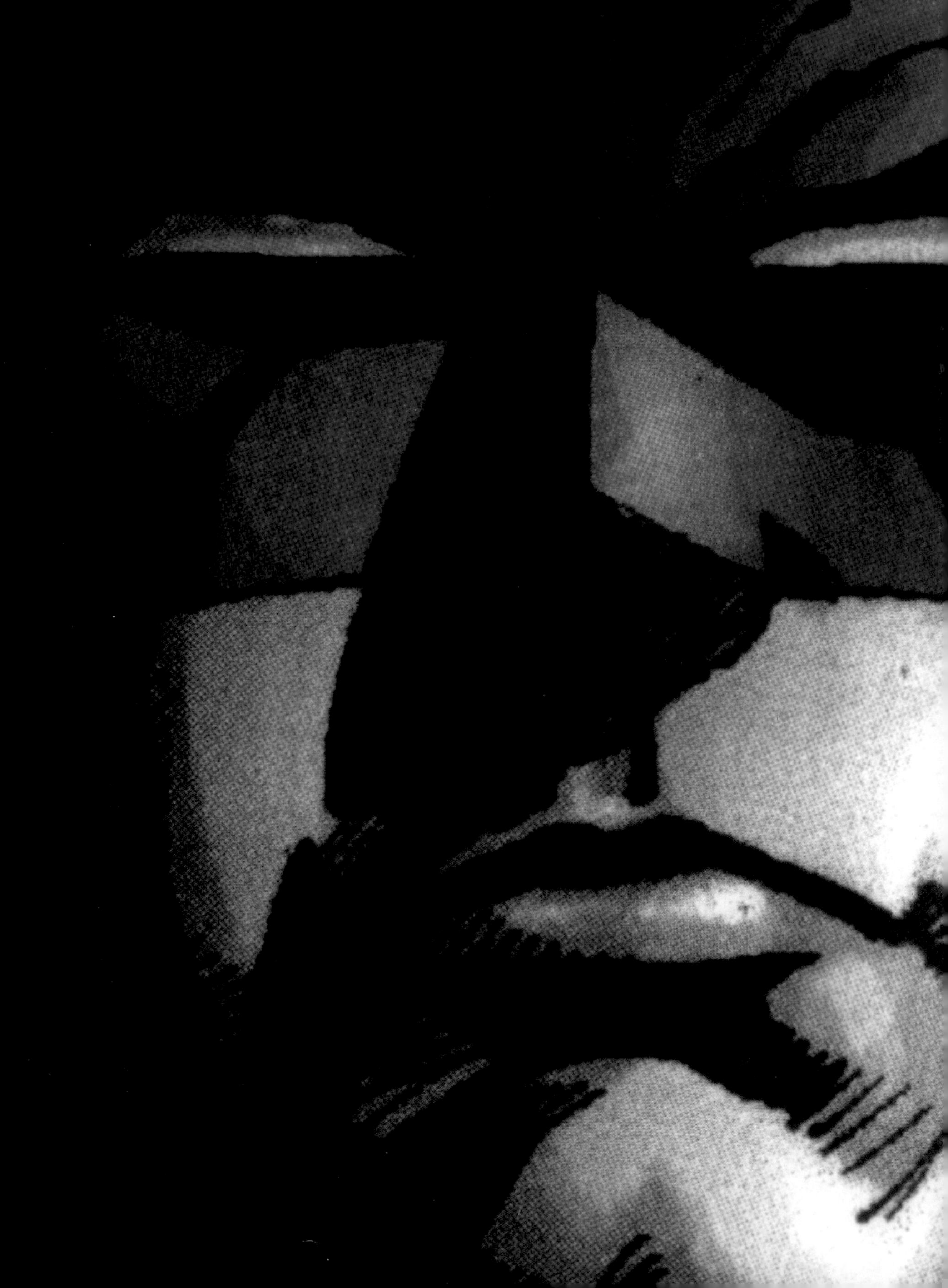

"I AM ATTENDING...

"I *SEEM* TO BE ATTENDING...

"MY OWN FUNERAL.

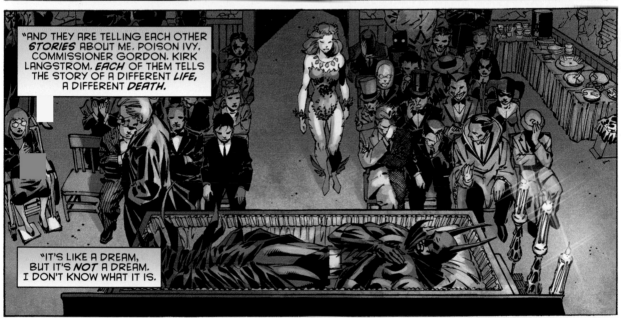

"AND THEY ARE TELLING EACH OTHER *STORIES* ABOUT ME. POISON IVY, COMMISSIONER GORDON. KIRK LANGSTROM. *EACH* OF THEM TELLS THE STORY OF A DIFFERENT *LIFE*, A DIFFERENT *DEATH.*

"IT'S LIKE A DREAM, BUT IT'S *NOT* A DREAM. I DON'T KNOW WHAT IT IS.

"AND I'M NOT *ALONE.*

"THERE'S SOMEONE HERE *WITH* ME. A *WOMAN.* I CAN'T SEE HER. IT'S AS IF SHE'S STANDING JUST BESIDE ME, OR ALL AROUND ME, *TALKING* TO ME...

"SHE SAYS I'M NOT *DEAD.*

"I'M NOT CERTAIN THAT I *BELIEVE* HER."

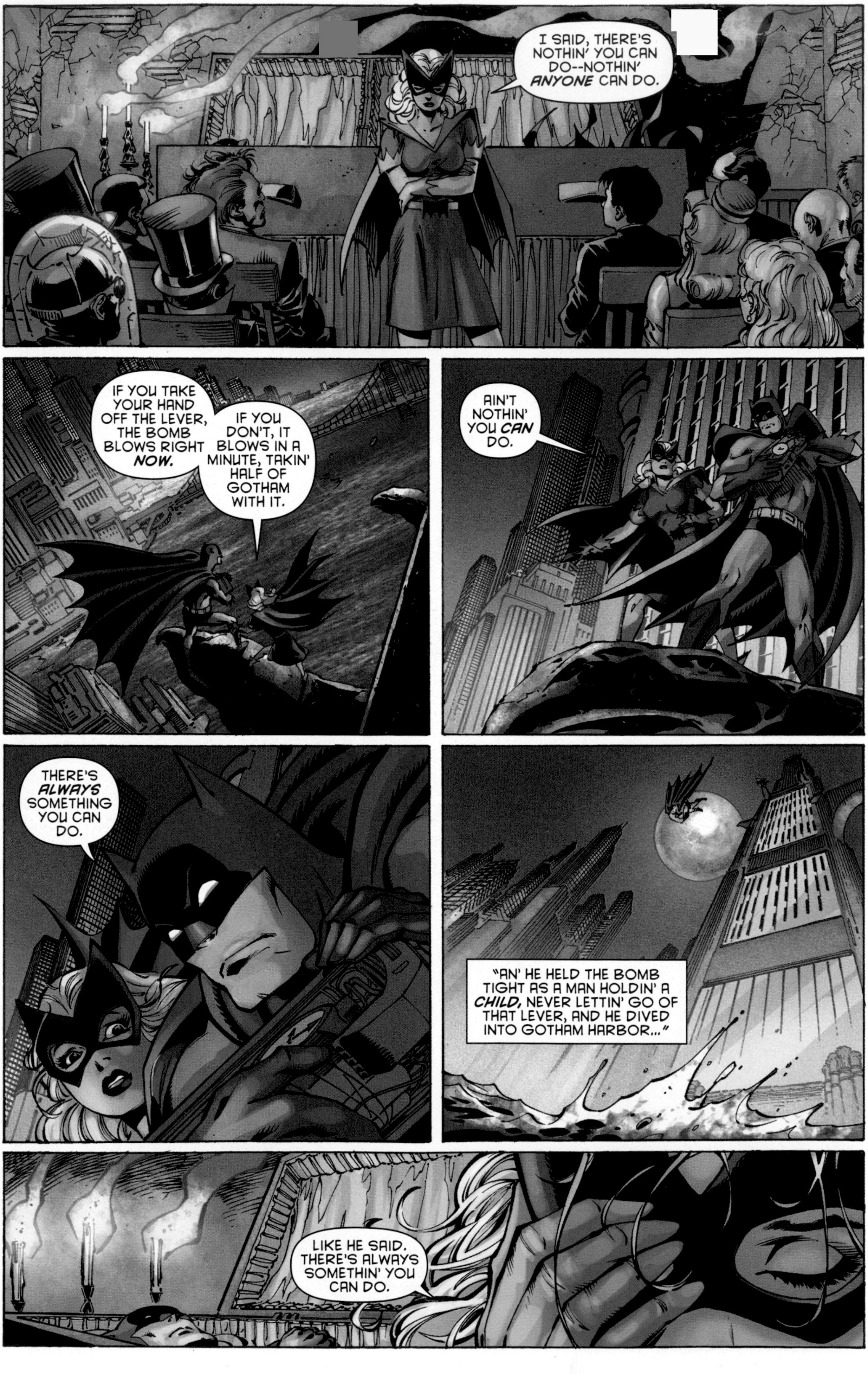
I SAID, THERE'S NOTHIN' YOU CAN DO--NOTHIN' ANYONE CAN DO.
IF YOU TAKE YOUR HAND OFF THE LEVER, THE BOMB BLOWS RIGHT NOW.
IF YOU DON'T, IT BLOWS IN A MINUTE, TAKIN' HALF OF GOTHAM WITH IT.
AIN'T NOTHIN' YOU CAN DO.
THERE'S ALWAYS SOMETHING YOU CAN DO.
"AN' HE HELD THE BOMB TIGHT AS A MAN HOLDIN' A CHILD, NEVER LETTIN' GO OF THAT LEVER, AND HE DIVED INTO GOTHAM HARBOR..."
LIKE HE SAID. THERE'S ALWAYS SOMETHIN' YOU CAN DO.

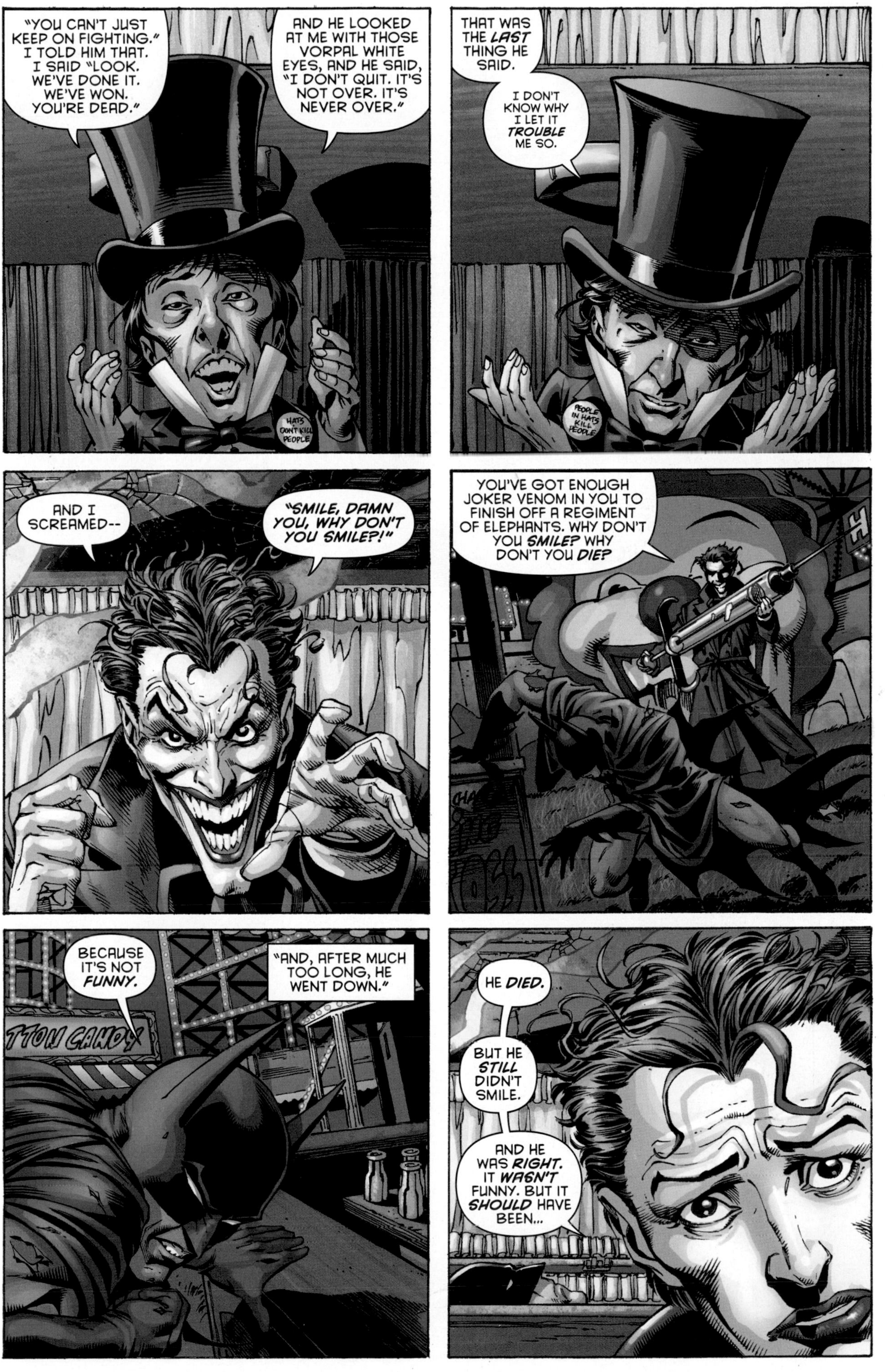
"YOU CAN'T JUST KEEP ON FIGHTING." I TOLD HIM THAT. I SAID "LOOK. WE'VE DONE IT. WE'VE WON. YOU'RE DEAD."
AND HE LOOKED AT ME WITH THOSE VORPAL WHITE EYES, AND HE SAID, "I DON'T QUIT. IT'S NOT OVER. IT'S NEVER OVER."
HATS DON'T KILL PEOPLE
THAT WAS THE LAST THING HE SAID.
I DON'T KNOW WHY I LET IT TROUBLE ME SO.
PEOPLE IN HATS KILL PEOPLE
AND I SCREAMED--
"SMILE, DAMN YOU, WHY DON'T YOU SMILE?!"
YOU'VE GOT ENOUGH JOKER VENOM IN YOU TO FINISH OFF A REGIMENT OF ELEPHANTS. WHY DON'T YOU SMILE? WHY DON'T YOU DIE?
BECAUSE IT'S NOT FUNNY.
"AND, AFTER MUCH TOO LONG, HE WENT DOWN."
TTON CANDY
HE DIED.
BUT HE STILL DIDN'T SMILE.
AND HE WAS RIGHT. IT WASN'T FUNNY. BUT IT SHOULD HAVE BEEN...

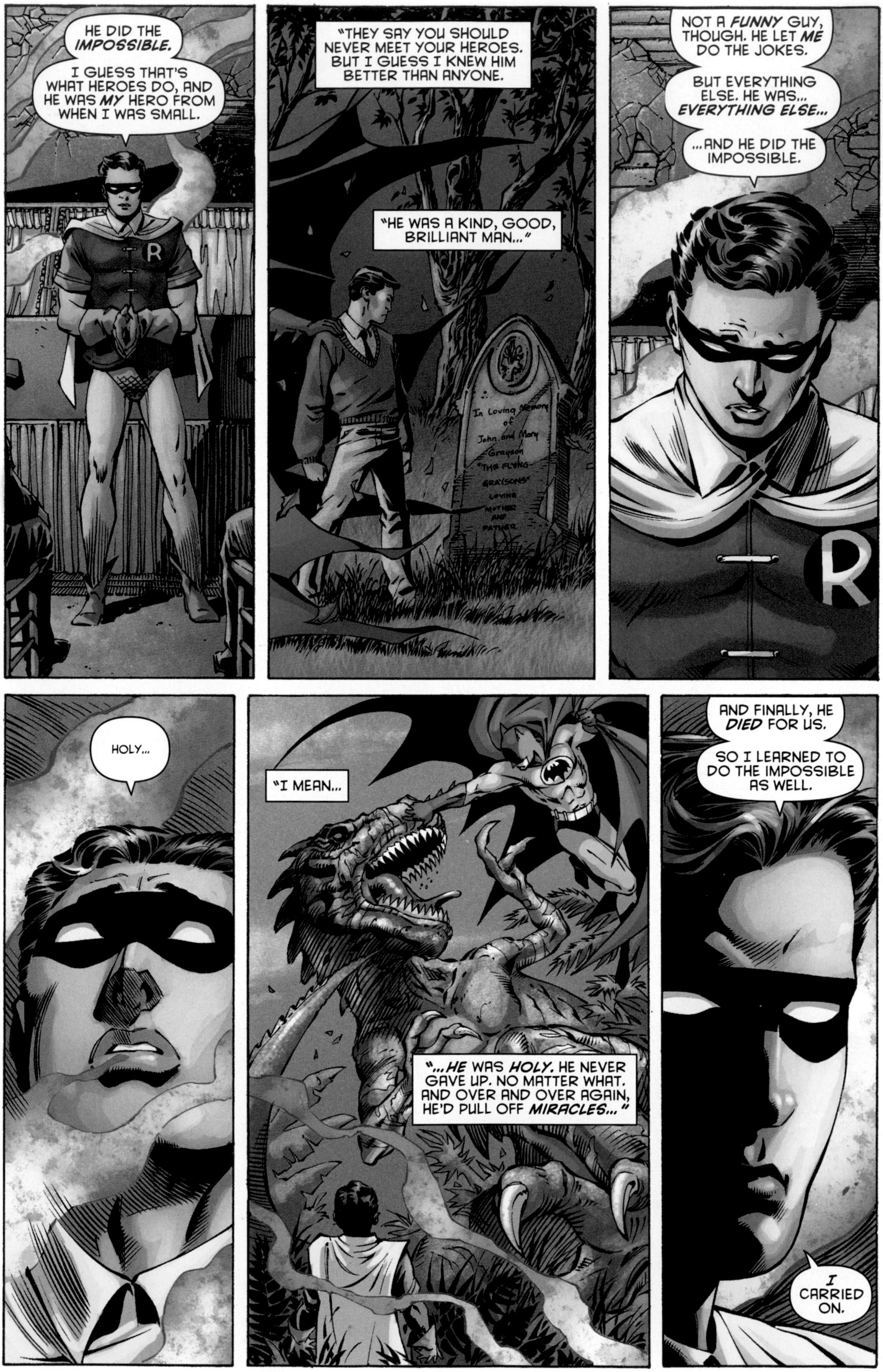
HE DID THE IMPOSSIBLE.
I GUESS THAT'S WHAT HEROES DO, AND HE WAS MY HERO FROM WHEN I WAS SMALL.
"THEY SAY YOU SHOULD NEVER MEET YOUR HEROES. BUT I GUESS I KNEW HIM BETTER THAN ANYONE.
"HE WAS A KIND, GOOD, BRILLIANT MAN..."
In Loving Memory of John and Mary Grayson "THE FLYING GRAYSONS" LOVING MOTHER AND FATHER
NOT A FUNNY GUY, THOUGH. HE LET ME DO THE JOKES.
BUT EVERYTHING ELSE. HE WAS... EVERYTHING ELSE...
...AND HE DID THE IMPOSSIBLE.
HOLY...
"I MEAN...
"...HE WAS HOLY. HE NEVER GAVE UP. NO MATTER WHAT. AND OVER AND OVER AGAIN, HE'D PULL OFF MIRACLES..."
AND FINALLY, HE DIED FOR US.
SO I LEARNED TO DO THE IMPOSSIBLE AS WELL.
I CARRIED ON.

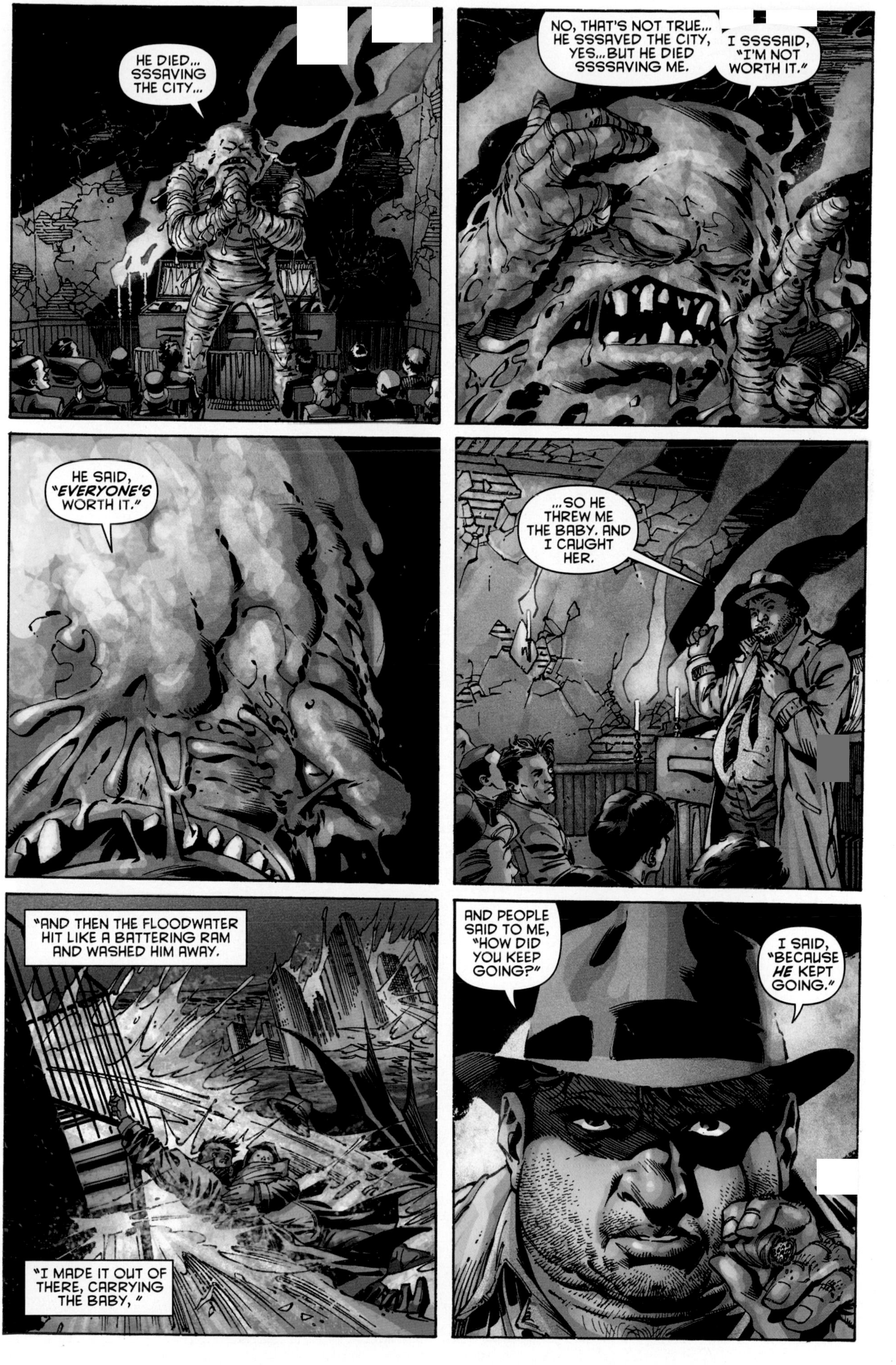
HE DIED... SSSAVING THE CITY...
NO, THAT'S NOT TRUE... HE SSSAVED THE CITY, YES...BUT HE DIED SSSSAVING ME.
I SSSSAID, "I'M NOT WORTH IT."
HE SAID, "EVERYONE'S WORTH IT."
...SO HE THREW ME THE BABY. AND I CAUGHT HER.
"AND THEN THE FLOODWATER HIT LIKE A BATTERING RAM AND WASHED HIM AWAY.
"I MADE IT OUT OF THERE, CARRYING THE BABY,"
AND PEOPLE SAID TO ME, "HOW DID YOU KEEP GOING?"
I SAID, "BECAUSE HE KEPT GOING."

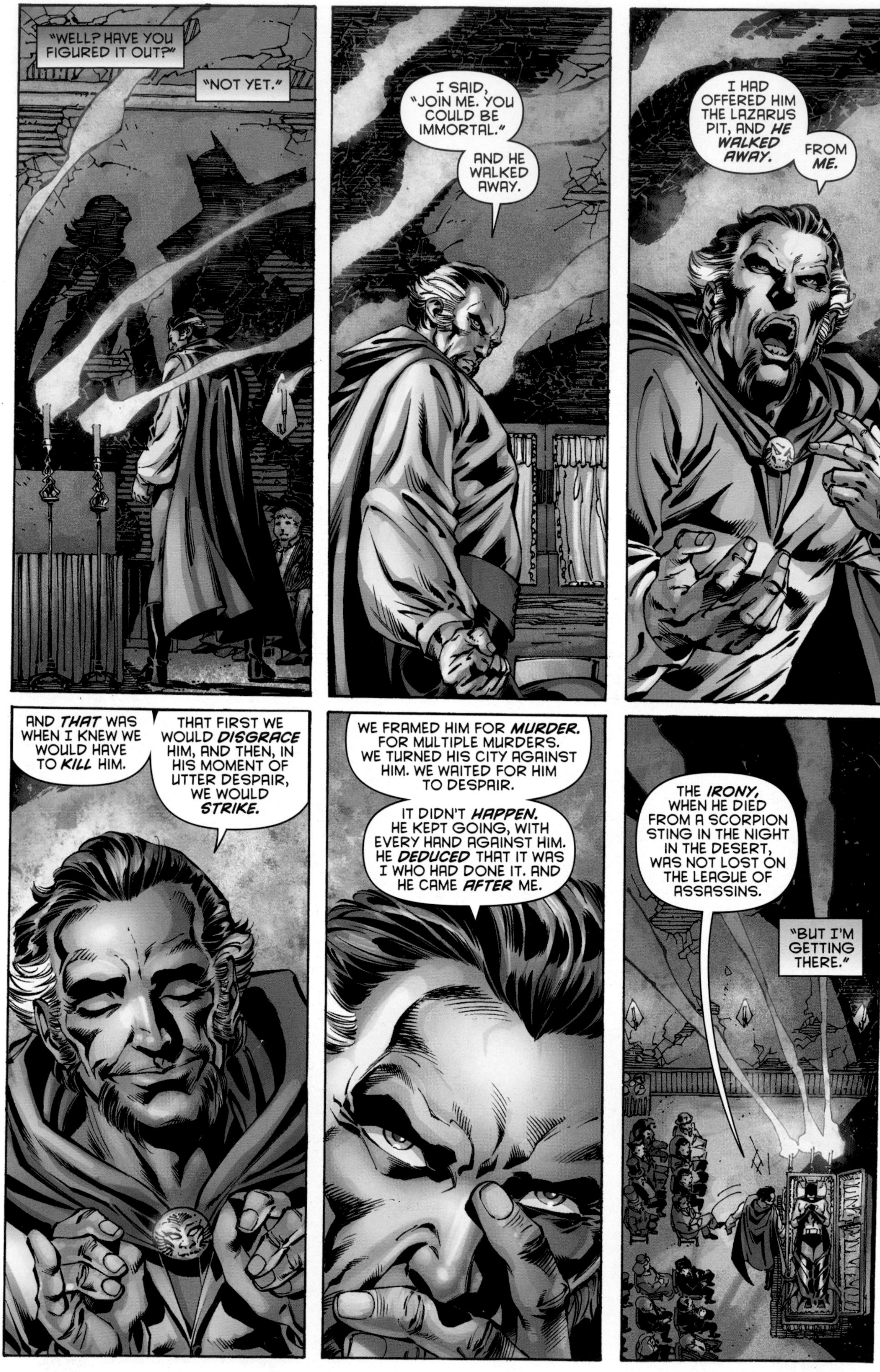
"WELL? HAVE YOU FIGURED IT OUT?"
"NOT YET."
I SAID, "JOIN ME. YOU COULD BE IMMORTAL."
AND HE WALKED AWAY.
I HAD OFFERED HIM THE LAZARUS PIT, AND HE WALKED AWAY.
FROM ME.
AND THAT WAS WHEN I KNEW WE WOULD HAVE TO KILL HIM.
THAT FIRST WE WOULD DISGRACE HIM, AND THEN, IN HIS MOMENT OF UTTER DESPAIR, WE WOULD STRIKE.
WE FRAMED HIM FOR MURDER. FOR MULTIPLE MURDERS. WE TURNED HIS CITY AGAINST HIM. WE WAITED FOR HIM TO DESPAIR.
IT DIDN'T HAPPEN. HE KEPT GOING, WITH EVERY HAND AGAINST HIM. HE DEDUCED THAT IT WAS I WHO HAD DONE IT. AND HE CAME AFTER ME.
THE IRONY, WHEN HE DIED FROM A SCORPION STING IN THE NIGHT IN THE DESERT, WAS NOT LOST ON THE LEAGUE OF ASSASSINS.
"BUT I'M GETTING THERE."

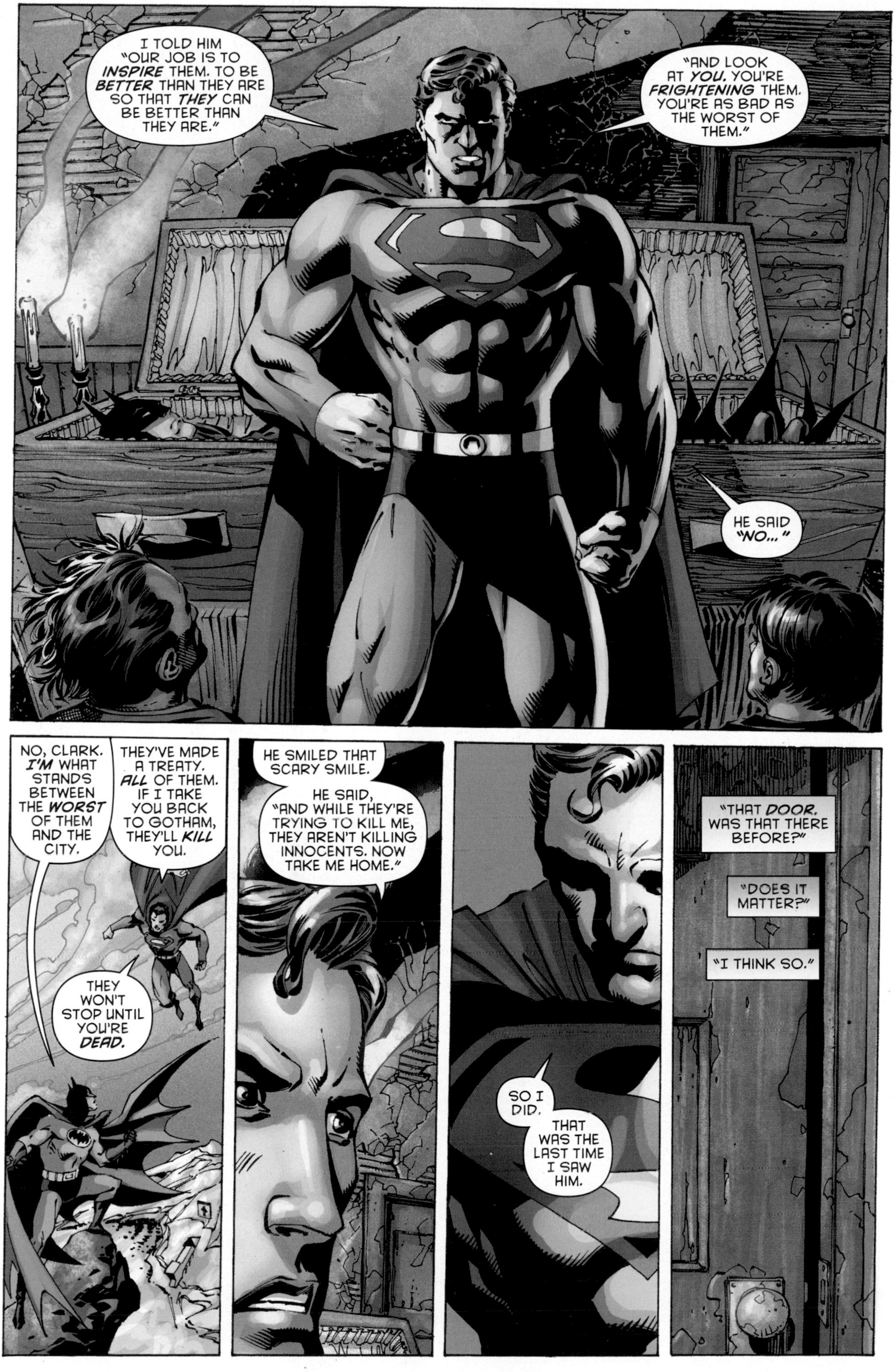
I TOLD HIM "OUR JOB IS TO INSPIRE THEM. TO BE BETTER THAN THEY ARE SO THAT THEY CAN BE BETTER THAN THEY ARE."
"AND LOOK AT YOU. YOU'RE FRIGHTENING THEM. YOU'RE AS BAD AS THE WORST OF THEM."
HE SAID "NO..."
NO, CLARK. I'M WHAT STANDS BETWEEN THE WORST OF THEM AND THE CITY.
THEY'VE MADE A TREATY. ALL OF THEM. IF I TAKE YOU BACK TO GOTHAM, THEY'LL KILL YOU.
THEY WON'T STOP UNTIL YOU'RE DEAD.
HE SMILED THAT SCARY SMILE.
HE SAID, "AND WHILE THEY'RE TRYING TO KILL ME, THEY AREN'T KILLING INNOCENTS. NOW TAKE ME HOME."
SO I DID.
THAT WAS THE LAST TIME I SAW HIM.
"THAT DOOR. WAS THAT THERE BEFORE?"
"DOES IT MATTER?"
"I THINK SO."

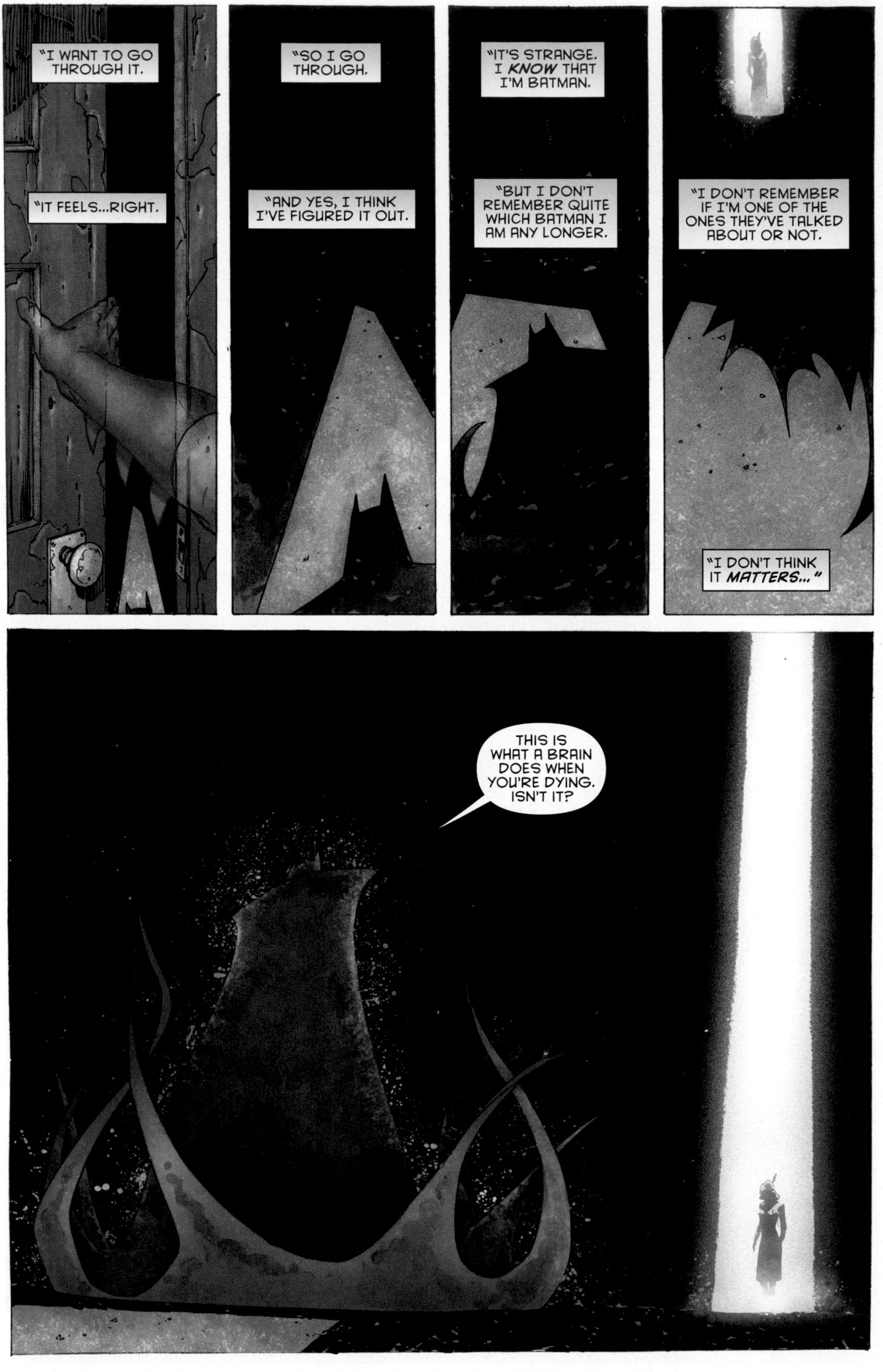
"I WANT TO GO THROUGH IT.
"IT FEELS...RIGHT.
"SO I GO THROUGH.
"AND YES, I THINK I'VE FIGURED IT OUT.
"IT'S STRANGE. I *KNOW* THAT I'M BATMAN.
"BUT I DON'T REMEMBER QUITE WHICH BATMAN I AM ANY LONGER.
"I DON'T REMEMBER IF I'M ONE OF THE ONES THEY'VE TALKED ABOUT OR NOT.
"I DON'T THINK IT *MATTERS...*"
THIS IS WHAT A BRAIN DOES WHEN YOU'RE DYING. ISN'T IT?

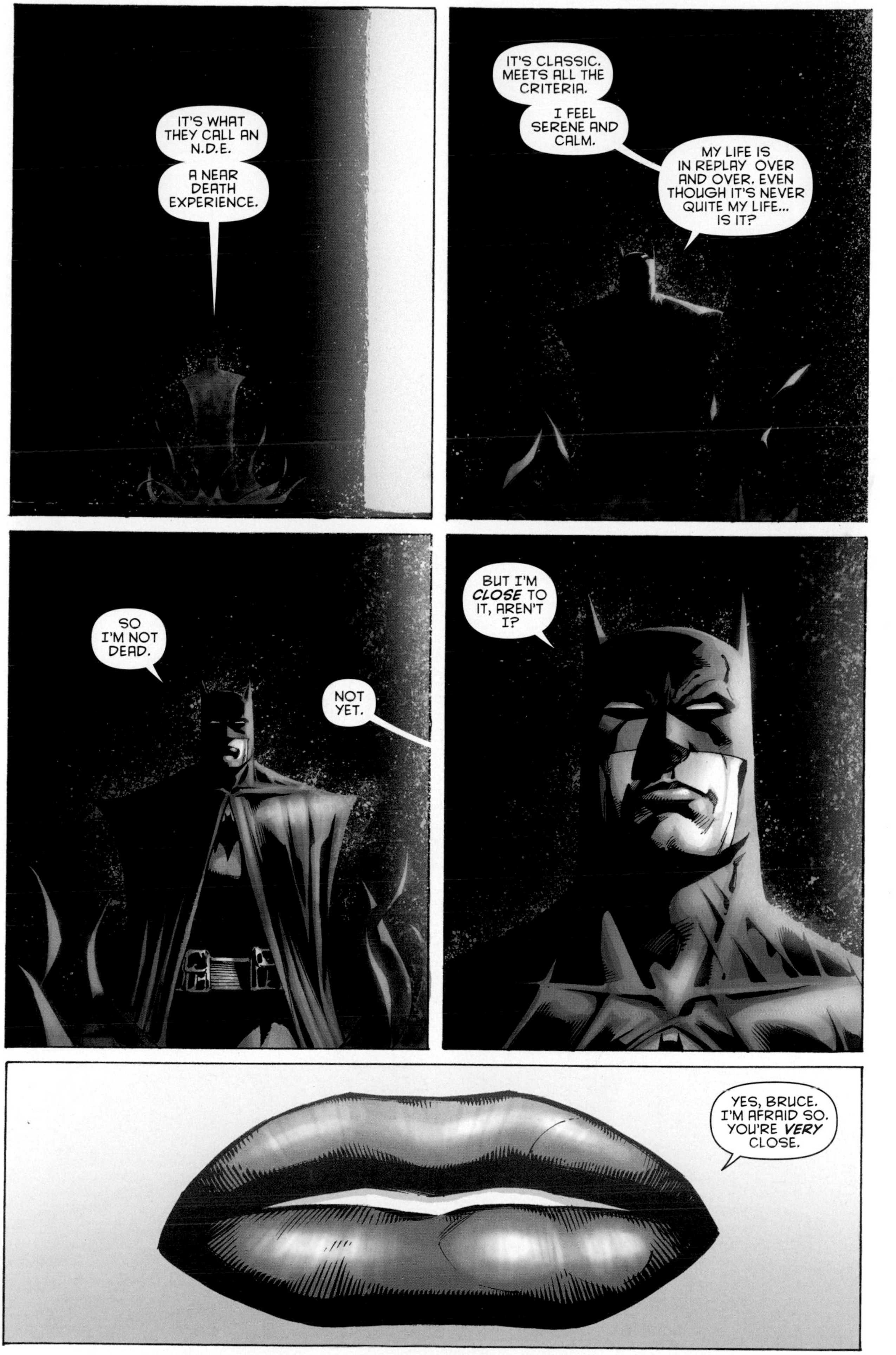
IT'S WHAT THEY CALL AN N.D.E.
A NEAR DEATH EXPERIENCE.
IT'S CLASSIC. MEETS ALL THE CRITERIA.
I FEEL SERENE AND CALM.
MY LIFE IS IN REPLAY OVER AND OVER. EVEN THOUGH IT'S NEVER QUITE MY LIFE... IS IT?
SO I'M NOT DEAD.
NOT YET.
BUT I'M CLOSE TO IT, AREN'T I?
YES, BRUCE. I'M AFRAID SO. YOU'RE VERY CLOSE.

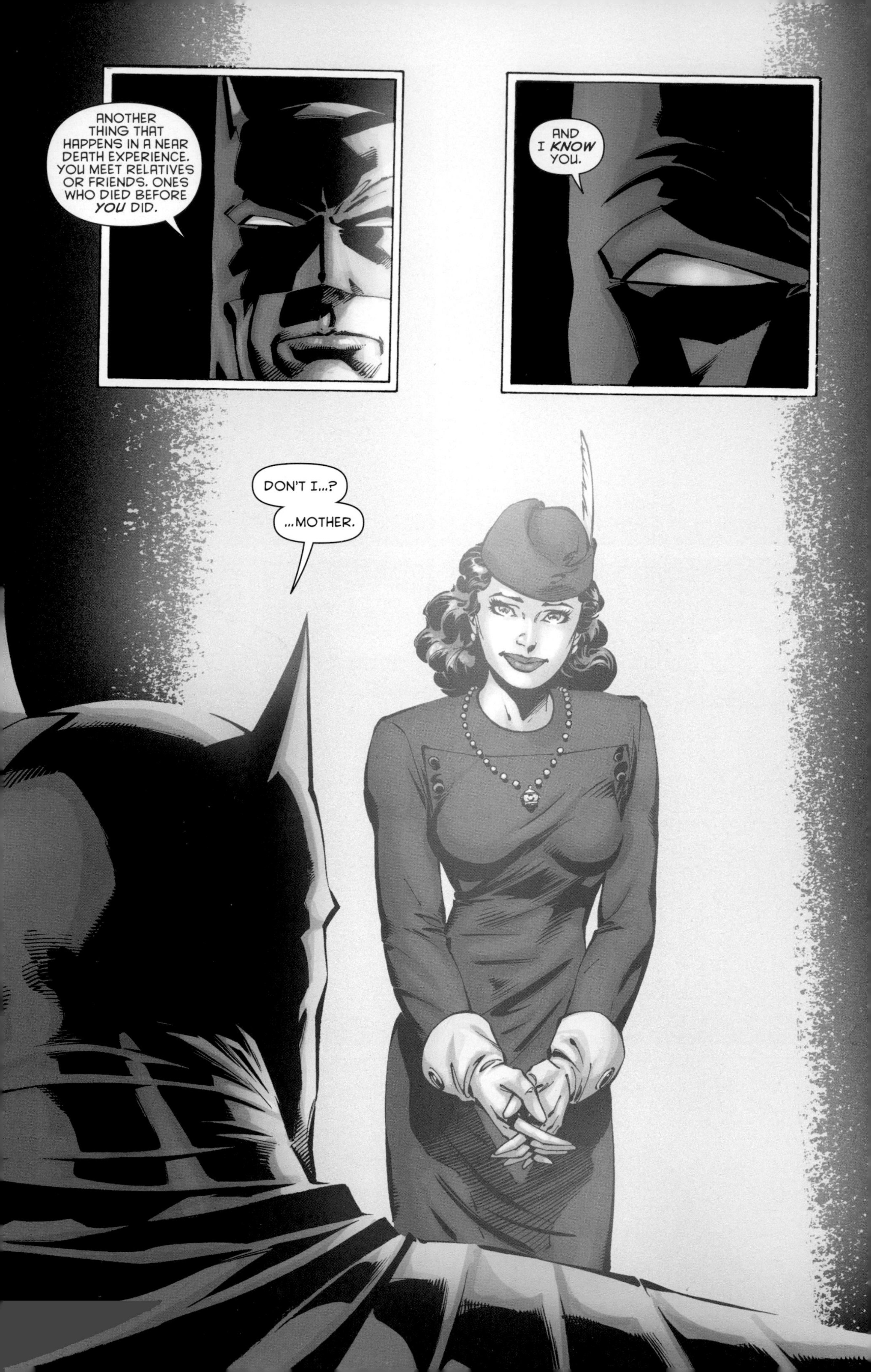
ANOTHER THING THAT HAPPENS IN A NEAR DEATH EXPERIENCE. YOU MEET RELATIVES OR FRIENDS. ONES WHO DIED BEFORE *YOU* DID.
AND I *KNOW* YOU.
DON'T I...?
...MOTHER.

YES, YOU DO, BRUCE.

SO ARE YOU *REAL?*

OR JUST SOMETHING *ELSE* THAT'S HAPPENING IN MY HEAD, BEFORE THE END?

IS THERE ANY *DIFFERENCE,* AT THIS POINT?

I GUESS *NOT.* IT'S TOO SUBJECTIVE.

EXACTLY. SO WHAT HAVE YOU LEARNED FROM YOUR FUNERAL, BRUCE?

LEARNED?

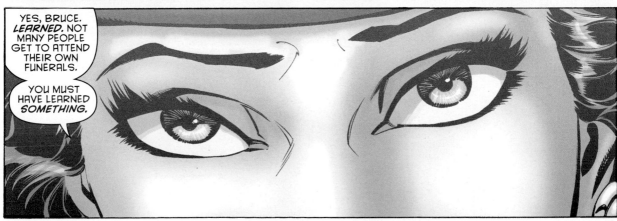

YES, BRUCE. *LEARNED.* NOT MANY PEOPLE GET TO ATTEND THEIR OWN FUNERALS.

YOU MUST HAVE LEARNED *SOMETHING.*

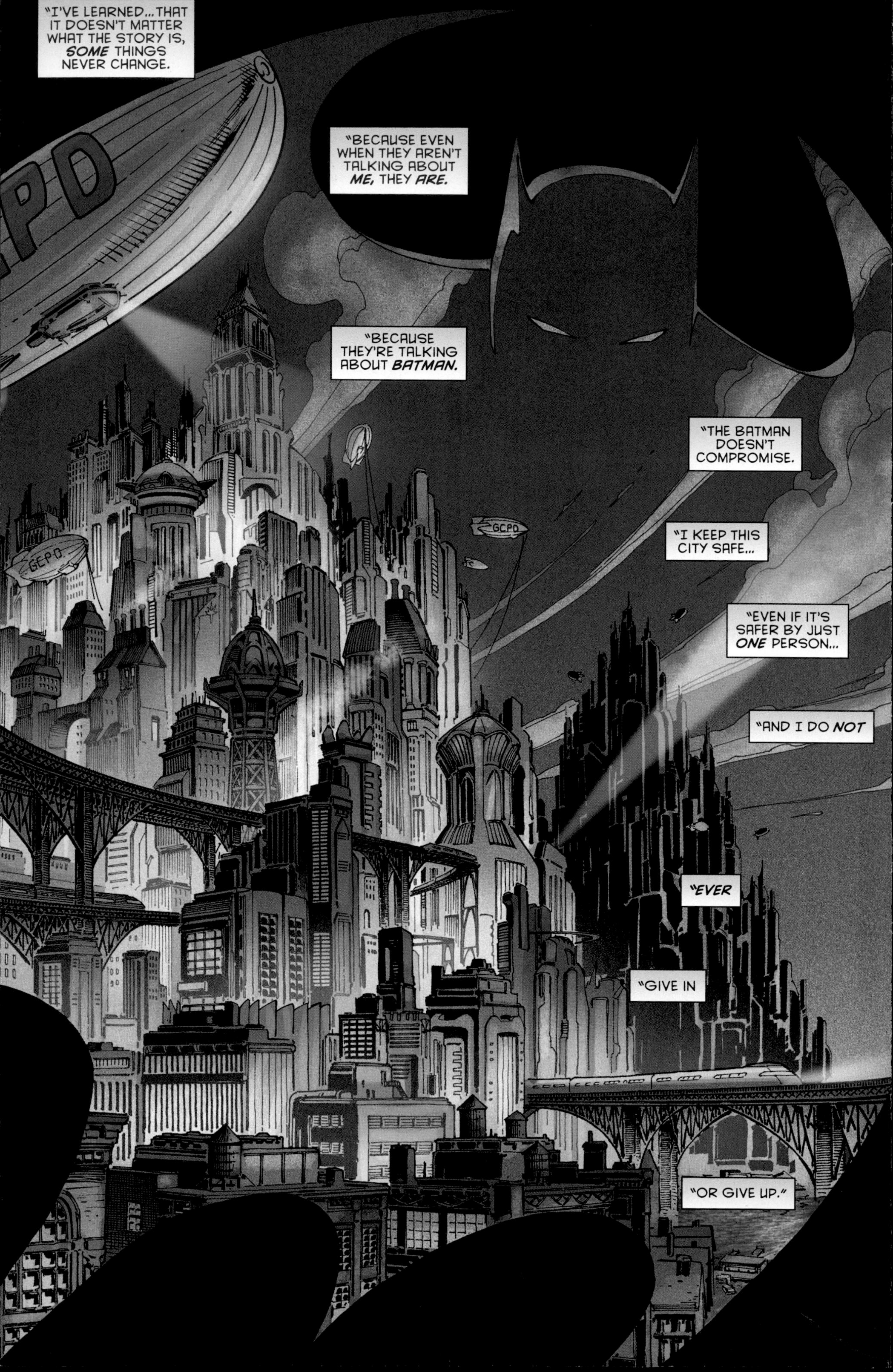
"I'VE LEARNED... THAT IT DOESN'T MATTER WHAT THE STORY IS, SOME THINGS NEVER CHANGE.
GCPD
"BECAUSE EVEN WHEN THEY AREN'T TALKING ABOUT ME, THEY ARE.
"BECAUSE THEY'RE TALKING ABOUT BATMAN.
"THE BATMAN DOESN'T COMPROMISE.
GCPD
"I KEEP THIS CITY SAFE...
GCPD
"EVEN IF IT'S SAFER BY JUST ONE PERSON...
"AND I DO NOT
"EVER
"GIVE IN
"OR GIVE UP."

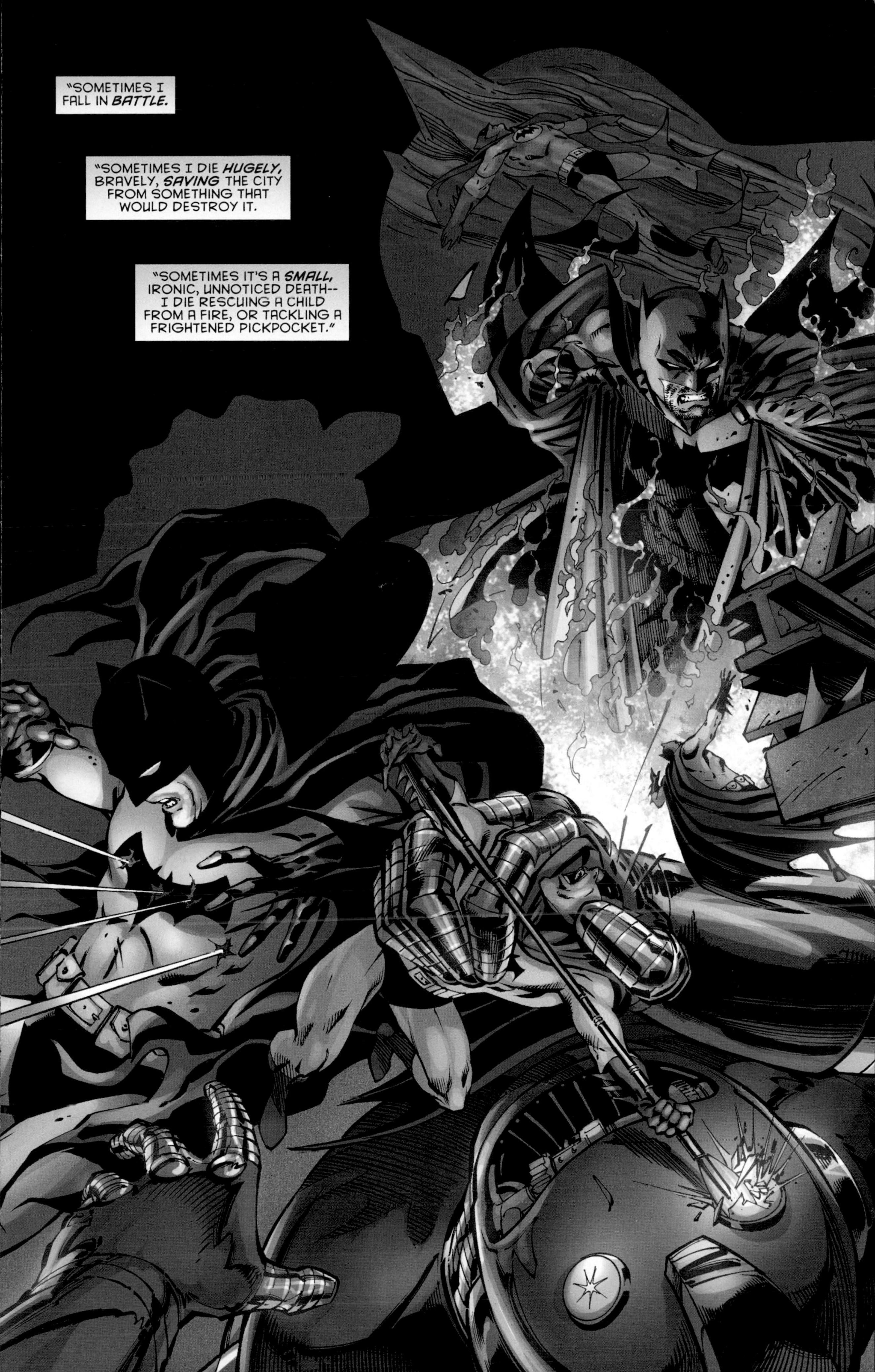
"SOMETIMES I FALL IN *BATTLE.*
"SOMETIMES I DIE *HUGELY,* BRAVELY, *SAVING* THE CITY FROM SOMETHING THAT WOULD DESTROY IT.
"SOMETIMES IT'S A *SMALL,* IRONIC, UNNOTICED DEATH-- I DIE RESCUING A CHILD FROM A FIRE, OR TACKLING A FRIGHTENED PICKPOCKET."

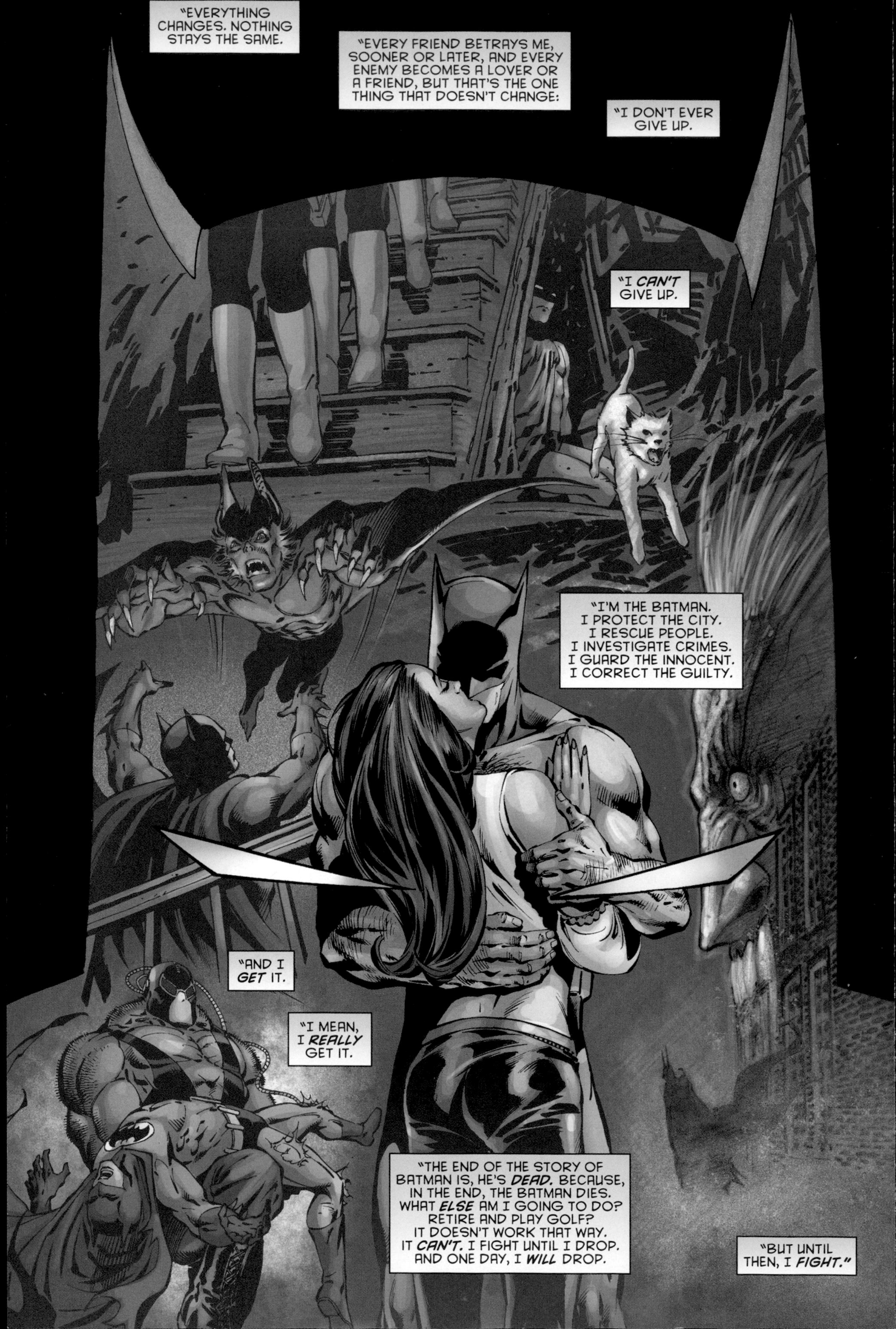
"EVERYTHING CHANGES. NOTHING STAYS THE SAME.
"EVERY FRIEND BETRAYS ME, SOONER OR LATER, AND EVERY ENEMY BECOMES A LOVER OR A FRIEND, BUT THAT'S THE ONE THING THAT DOESN'T CHANGE:
"I DON'T EVER GIVE UP.
"I *CAN'T* GIVE UP.
"I'M THE BATMAN. I PROTECT THE CITY. I RESCUE PEOPLE. I INVESTIGATE CRIMES. I GUARD THE INNOCENT. I CORRECT THE GUILTY.
"AND I *GET* IT.
"I MEAN, I *REALLY* GET IT.
"THE END OF THE STORY OF BATMAN IS, HE'S *DEAD.* BECAUSE, IN THE END, THE BATMAN DIES. WHAT *ELSE* AM I GOING TO DO? RETIRE AND PLAY GOLF? IT DOESN'T WORK THAT WAY. IT *CAN'T.* I FIGHT UNTIL I DROP. AND ONE DAY, I *WILL* DROP.
"BUT UNTIL THEN, I *FIGHT.*"

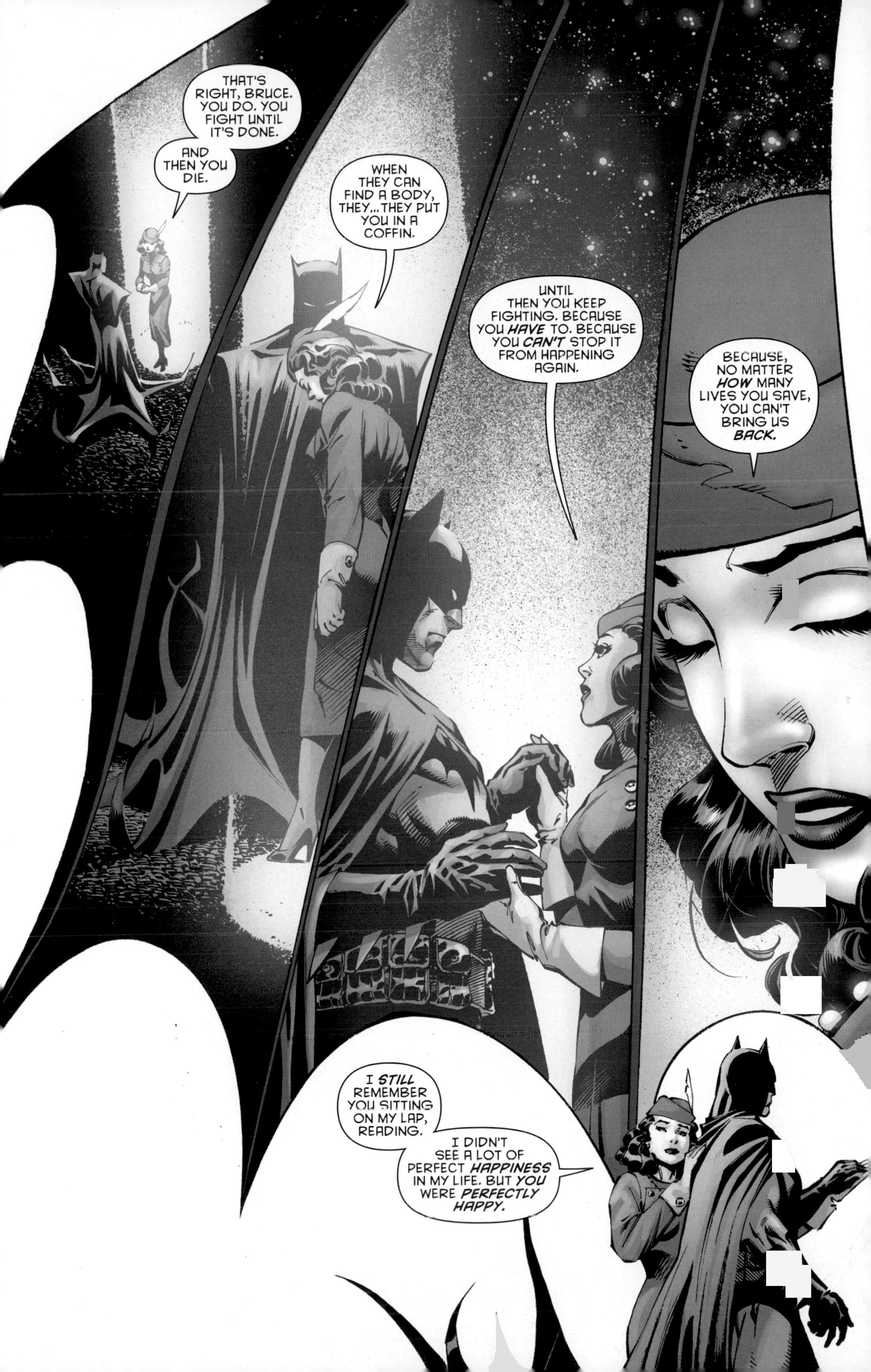
THAT'S RIGHT, BRUCE. YOU DO. YOU FIGHT UNTIL IT'S DONE.
AND THEN YOU DIE.
WHEN THEY CAN FIND A BODY, THEY... THEY PUT YOU IN A COFFIN.
UNTIL THEN YOU KEEP FIGHTING. BECAUSE YOU HAVE TO. BECAUSE YOU CAN'T STOP IT FROM HAPPENING AGAIN.
BECAUSE, NO MATTER HOW MANY LIVES YOU SAVE, YOU CAN'T BRING US BACK.
I STILL REMEMBER YOU SITTING ON MY LAP, READING.
I DIDN'T SEE A LOT OF PERFECT HAPPINESS IN MY LIFE. BUT YOU WERE PERFECTLY HAPPY.

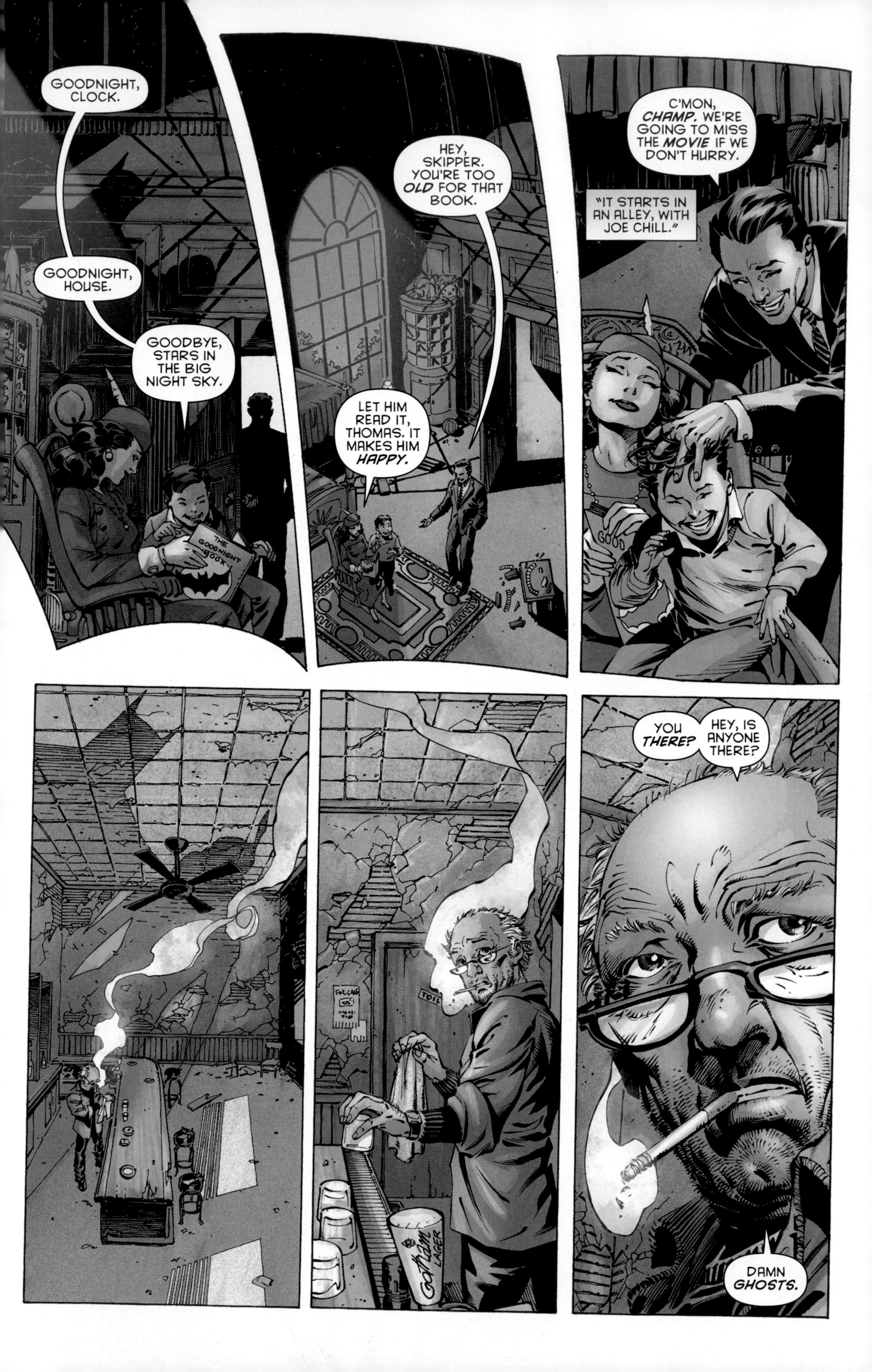
GOODNIGHT, CLOCK.
GOODNIGHT, HOUSE.
GOODBYE, STARS IN THE BIG NIGHT SKY.
THE GOODNIGHT BOOK
HEY, SKIPPER. YOU'RE TOO OLD FOR THAT BOOK.
LET HIM READ IT, THOMAS. IT MAKES HIM HAPPY.
C'MON, CHAMP. WE'RE GOING TO MISS THE MOVIE IF WE DON'T HURRY.
"IT STARTS IN AN ALLEY, WITH JOE CHILL."
Gotham LAGER
HEY, IS ANYONE THERE?
YOU THERE?
DAMN GHOSTS.

HE WAS SO *BRAVE*, MOMMY.

IT WAS MORE VIOLENT THAN I WAS EXPECTING...

WELL, I *LOVED* IT. GOOD OLD-FASHIONED HEROICS NEVER GO OUT OF STYLE--

I'LL TAKE THAT PEARL NECKLACE YOU'RE WEARIN', LADY!

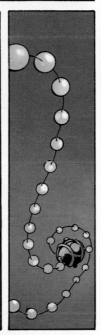

GET *AWAY* FROM HER...

"PLEASE. GET *AWAY* FROM HER.

"JUST THIS ONCE. TURN AROUND, LET IT GO."

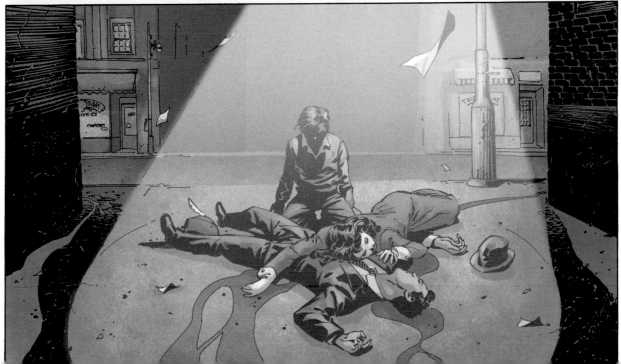

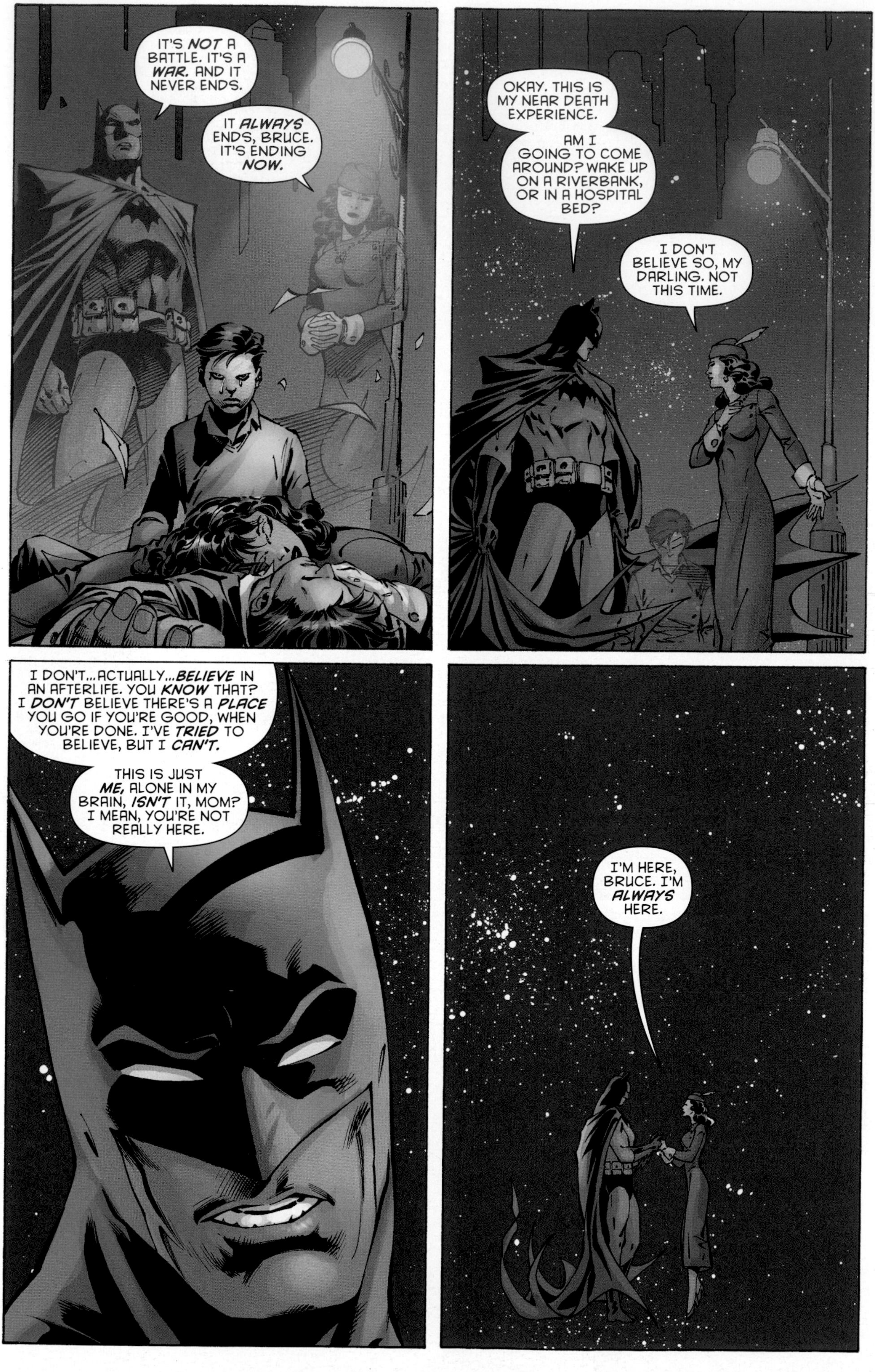
IT'S NOT A BATTLE. IT'S A WAR. AND IT NEVER ENDS.
IT ALWAYS ENDS, BRUCE. IT'S ENDING NOW.
OKAY. THIS IS MY NEAR DEATH EXPERIENCE.
AM I GOING TO COME AROUND? WAKE UP ON A RIVERBANK, OR IN A HOSPITAL BED?
I DON'T BELIEVE SO, MY DARLING. NOT THIS TIME.
I DON'T...ACTUALLY...BELIEVE IN AN AFTERLIFE. YOU KNOW THAT? I DON'T BELIEVE THERE'S A PLACE YOU GO IF YOU'RE GOOD, WHEN YOU'RE DONE. I'VE TRIED TO BELIEVE, BUT I CAN'T.
THIS IS JUST ME, ALONE IN MY BRAIN, ISN'T IT, MOM? I MEAN, YOU'RE NOT REALLY HERE.
I'M HERE, BRUCE. I'M ALWAYS HERE.

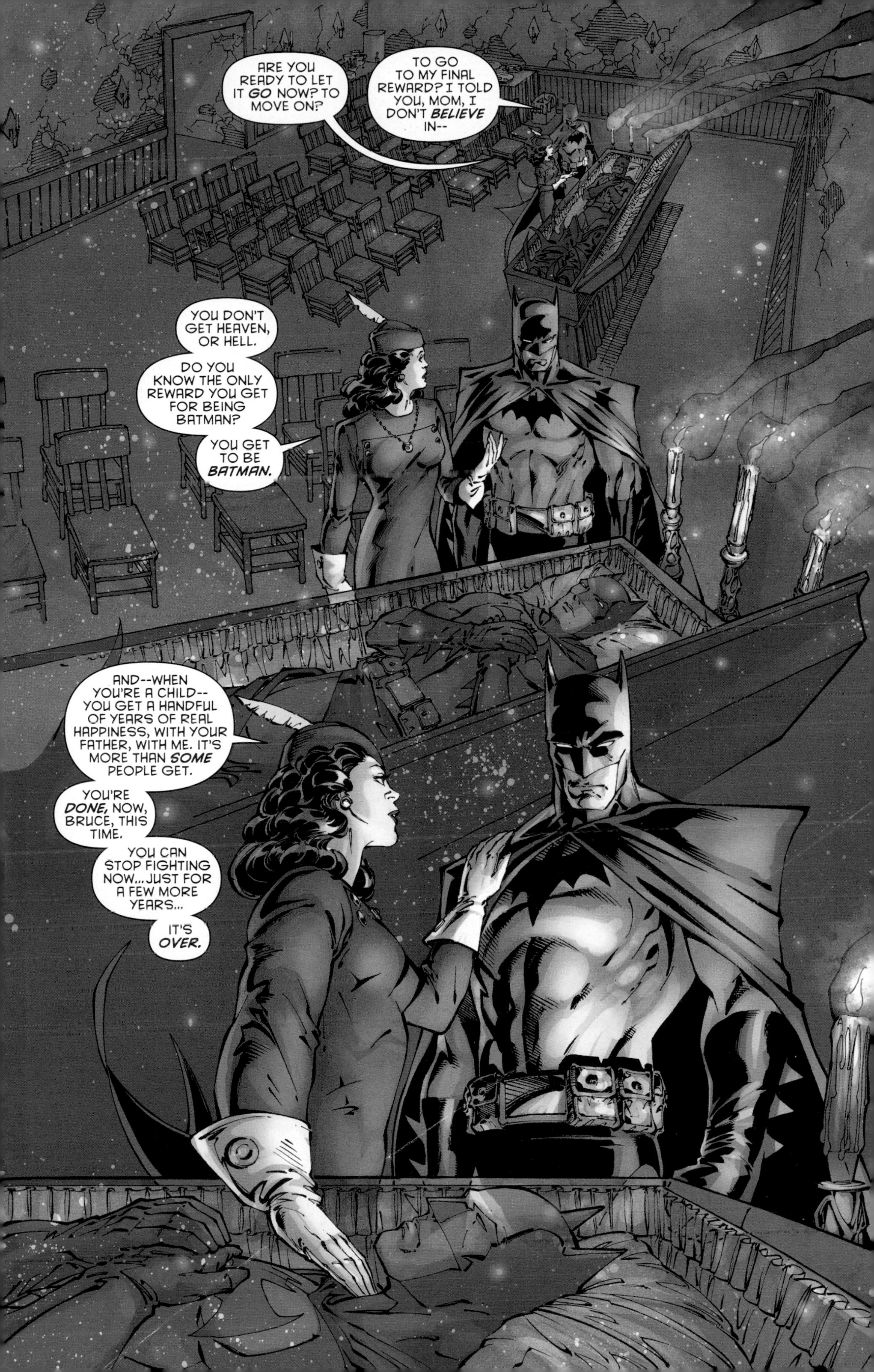
ARE YOU READY TO LET IT GO NOW? TO MOVE ON?
TO GO TO MY FINAL REWARD? I TOLD YOU, MOM, I DON'T BELIEVE IN--
YOU DON'T GET HEAVEN, OR HELL.
DO YOU KNOW THE ONLY REWARD YOU GET FOR BEING BATMAN?
YOU GET TO BE BATMAN.
AND--WHEN YOU'RE A CHILD--YOU GET A HANDFUL OF YEARS OF REAL HAPPINESS, WITH YOUR FATHER, WITH ME. IT'S MORE THAN SOME PEOPLE GET.
YOU'RE DONE, NOW, BRUCE, THIS TIME.
YOU CAN STOP FIGHTING NOW... JUST FOR A FEW MORE YEARS...
IT'S OVER.

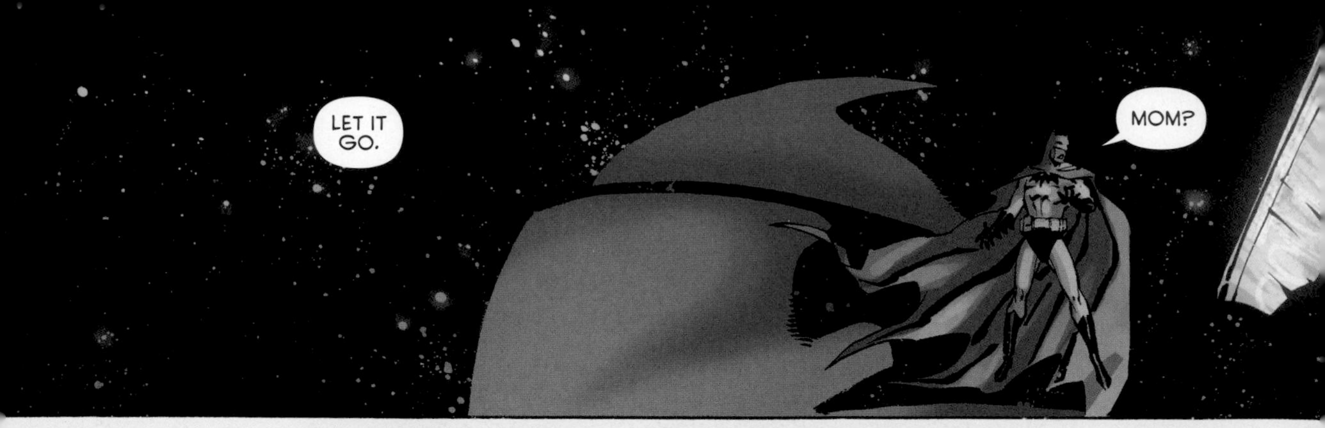
LET IT GO.
MOM?
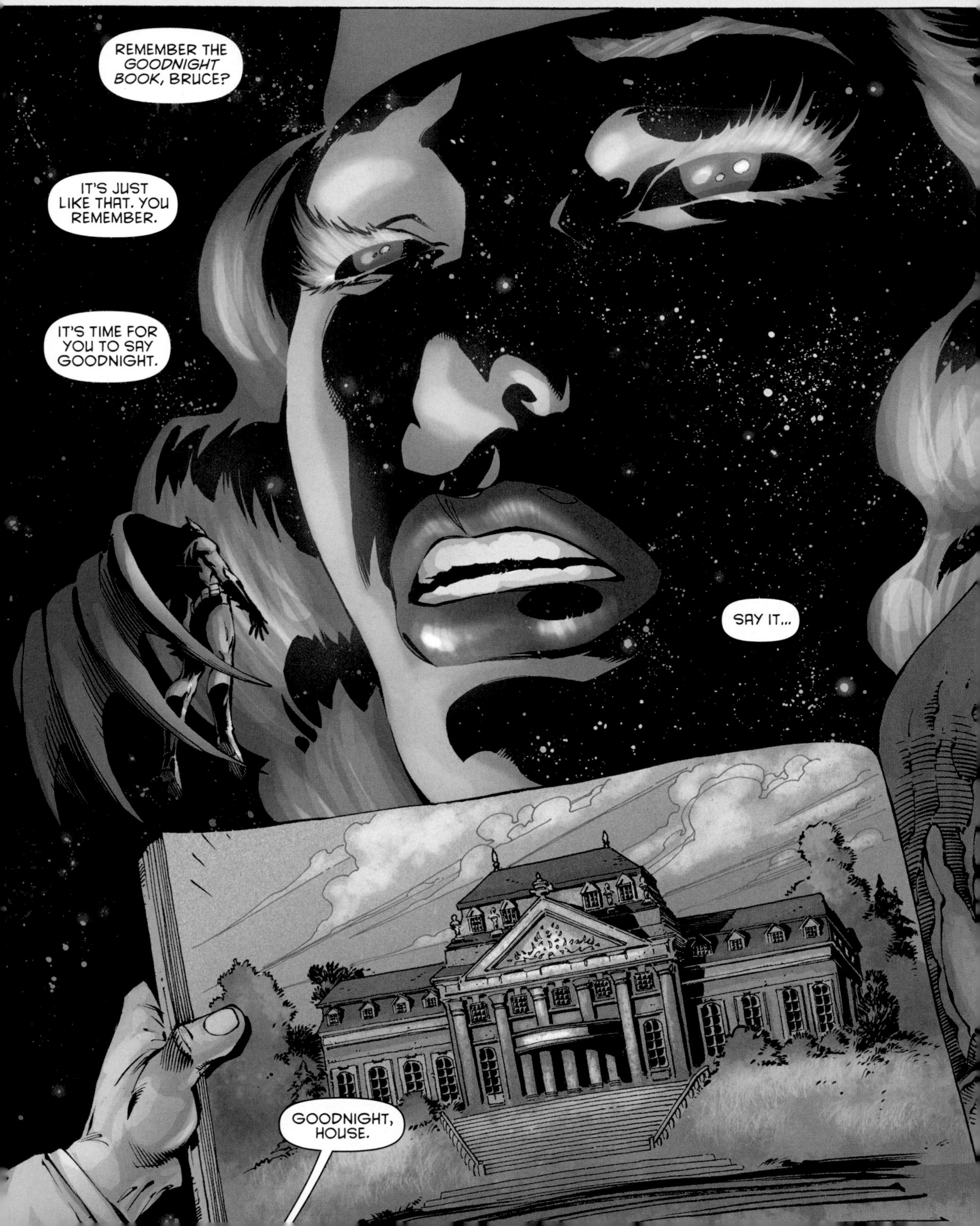
REMEMBER THE *GOODNIGHT BOOK*, BRUCE?
IT'S JUST LIKE THAT. YOU REMEMBER.
IT'S TIME FOR YOU TO SAY GOODNIGHT.
SAY IT...
GOODNIGHT, HOUSE.

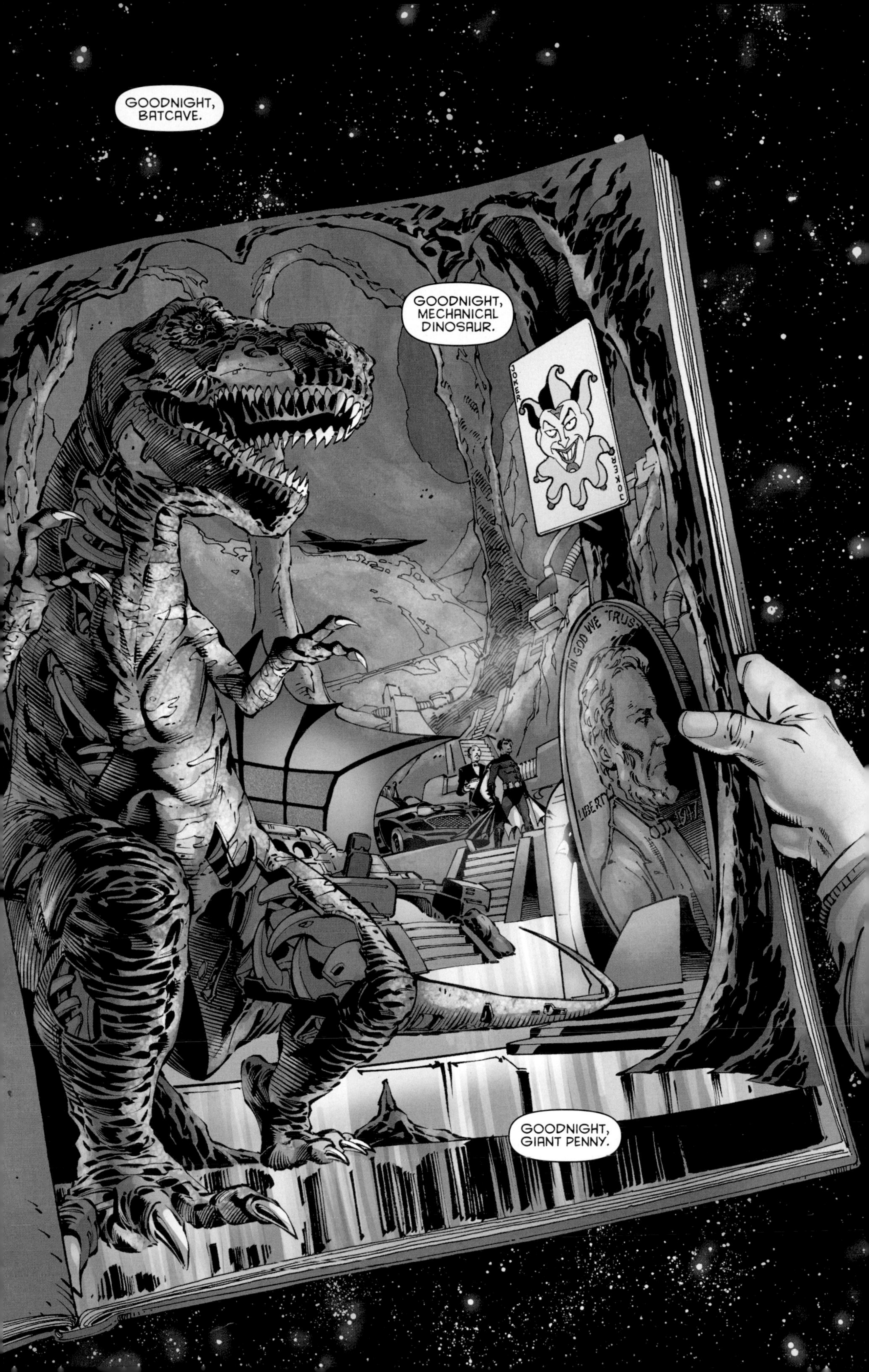
GOODNIGHT, BATCAVE.
GOODNIGHT, MECHANICAL DINOSAUR.
JOKER
GOODNIGHT, GIANT PENNY.

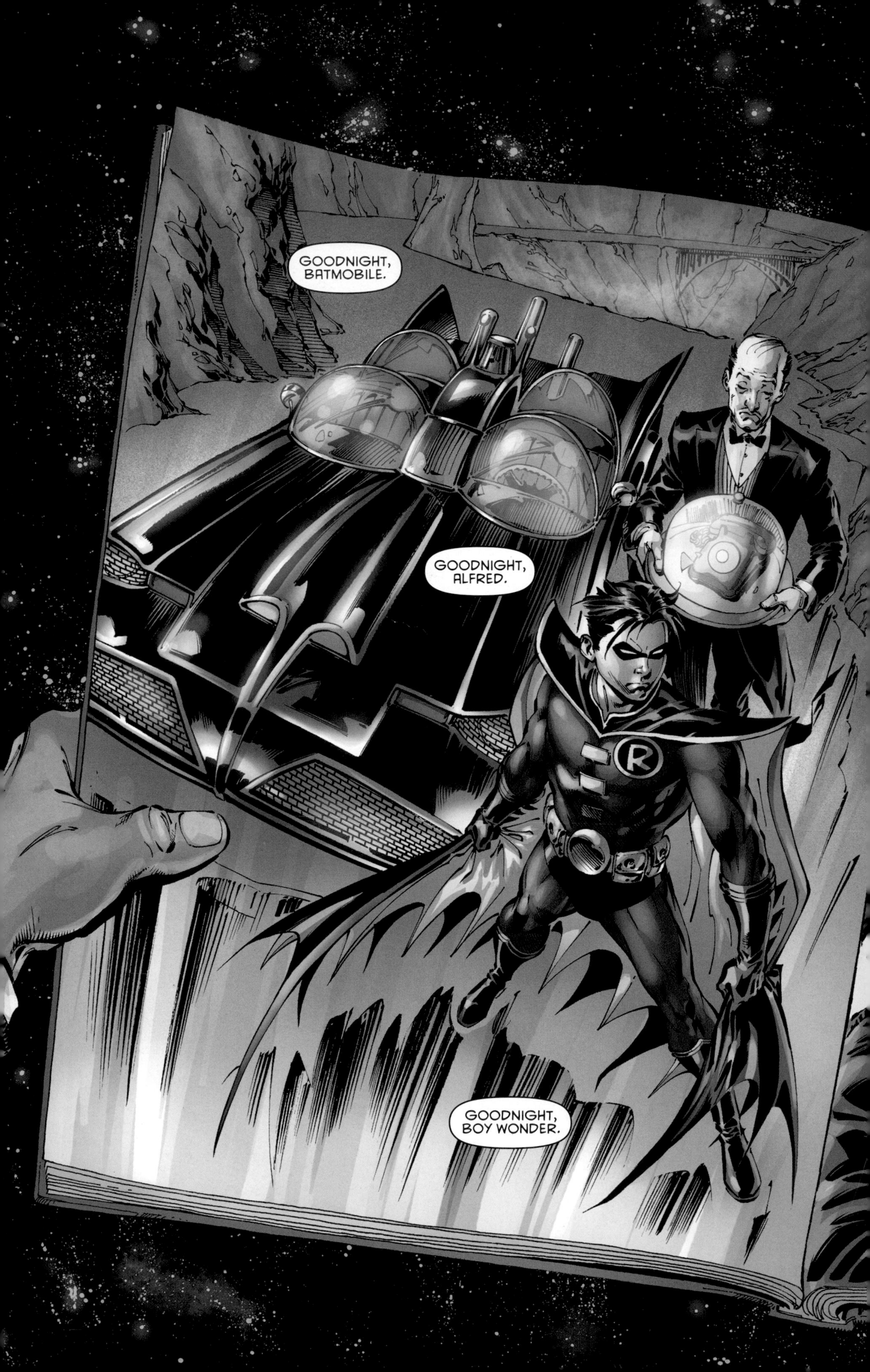
GOODNIGHT, BATMOBILE.
GOODNIGHT, ALFRED.
GOODNIGHT, BOY WONDER.

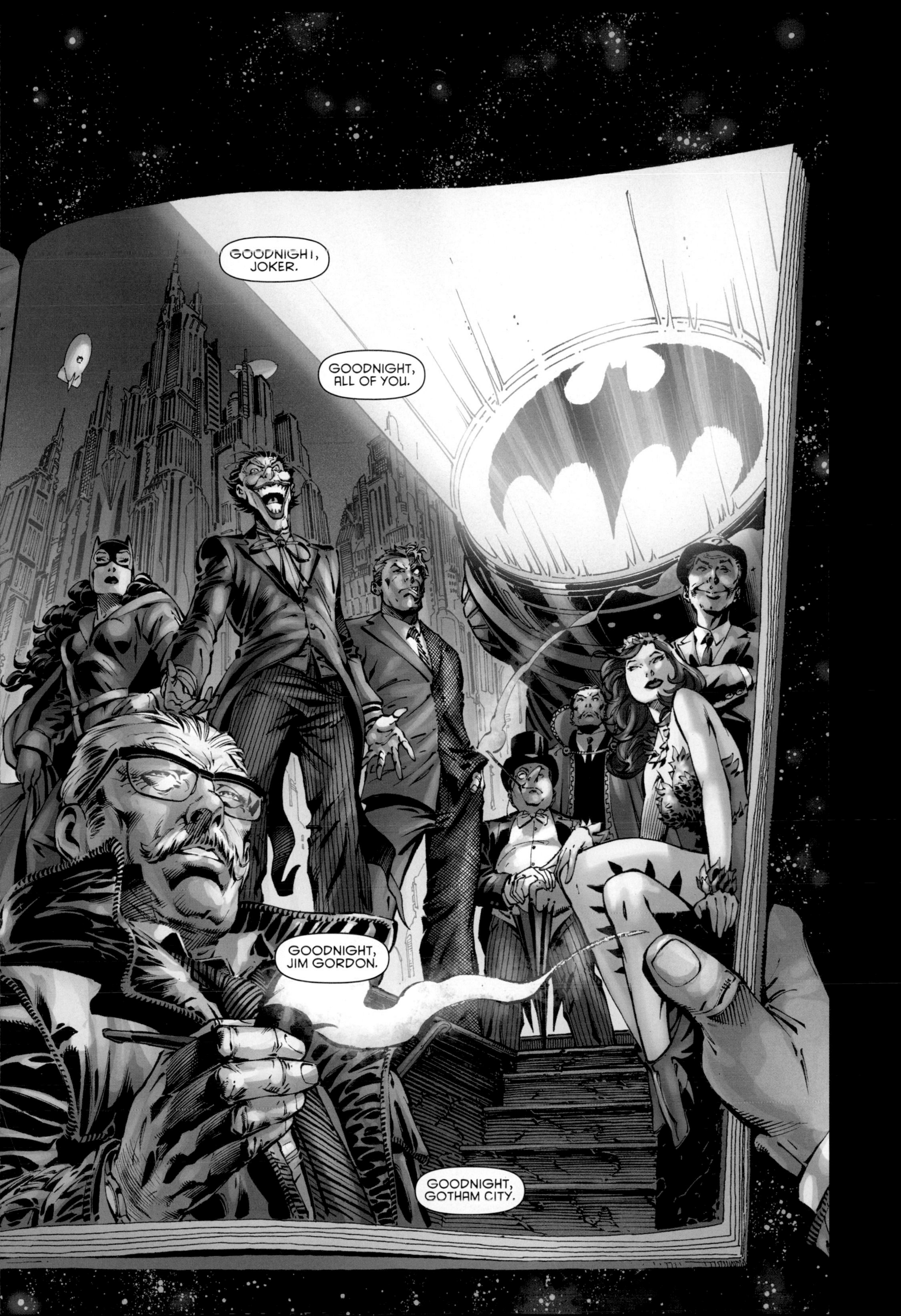
GOODNIGHT, JOKER.
GOODNIGHT, ALL OF YOU.
GOODNIGHT, JIM GORDON.
GOODNIGHT, GOTHAM CITY.

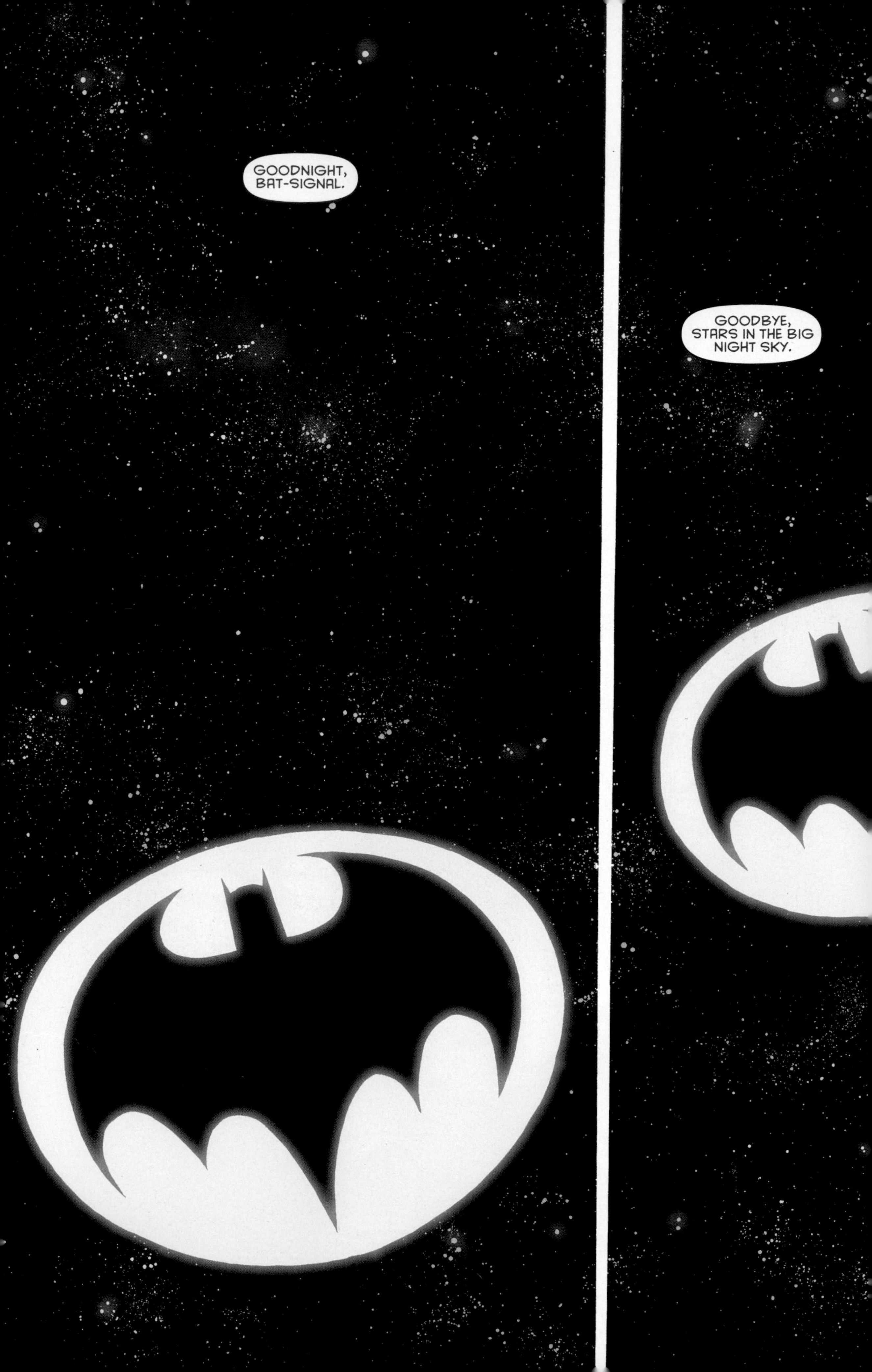
GOODNIGHT, BAT-SIGNAL.
GOODBYE, STARS IN THE BIG NIGHT SKY.

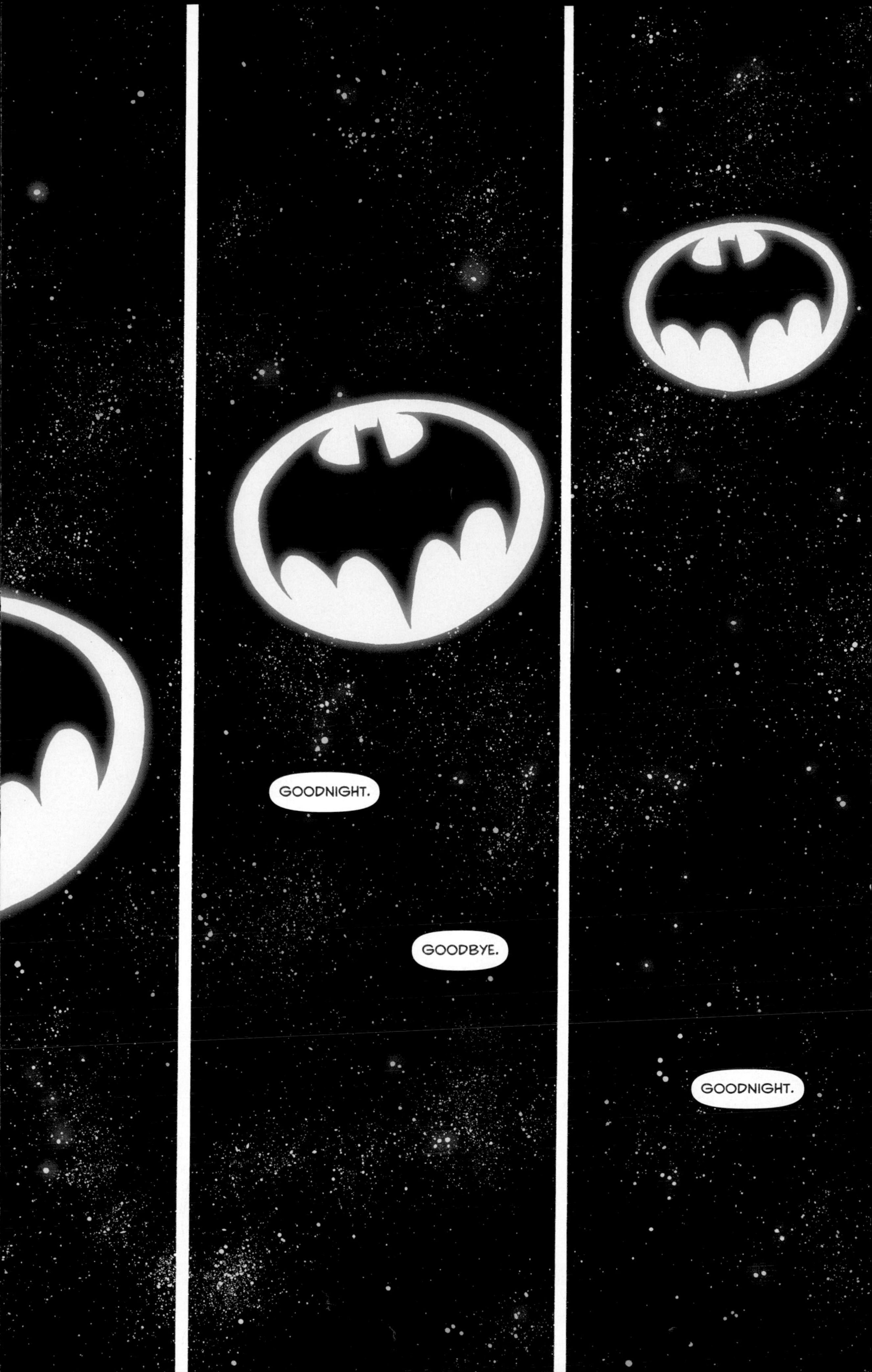
GOODNIGHT.
GOODBYE.
GOODNIGHT.

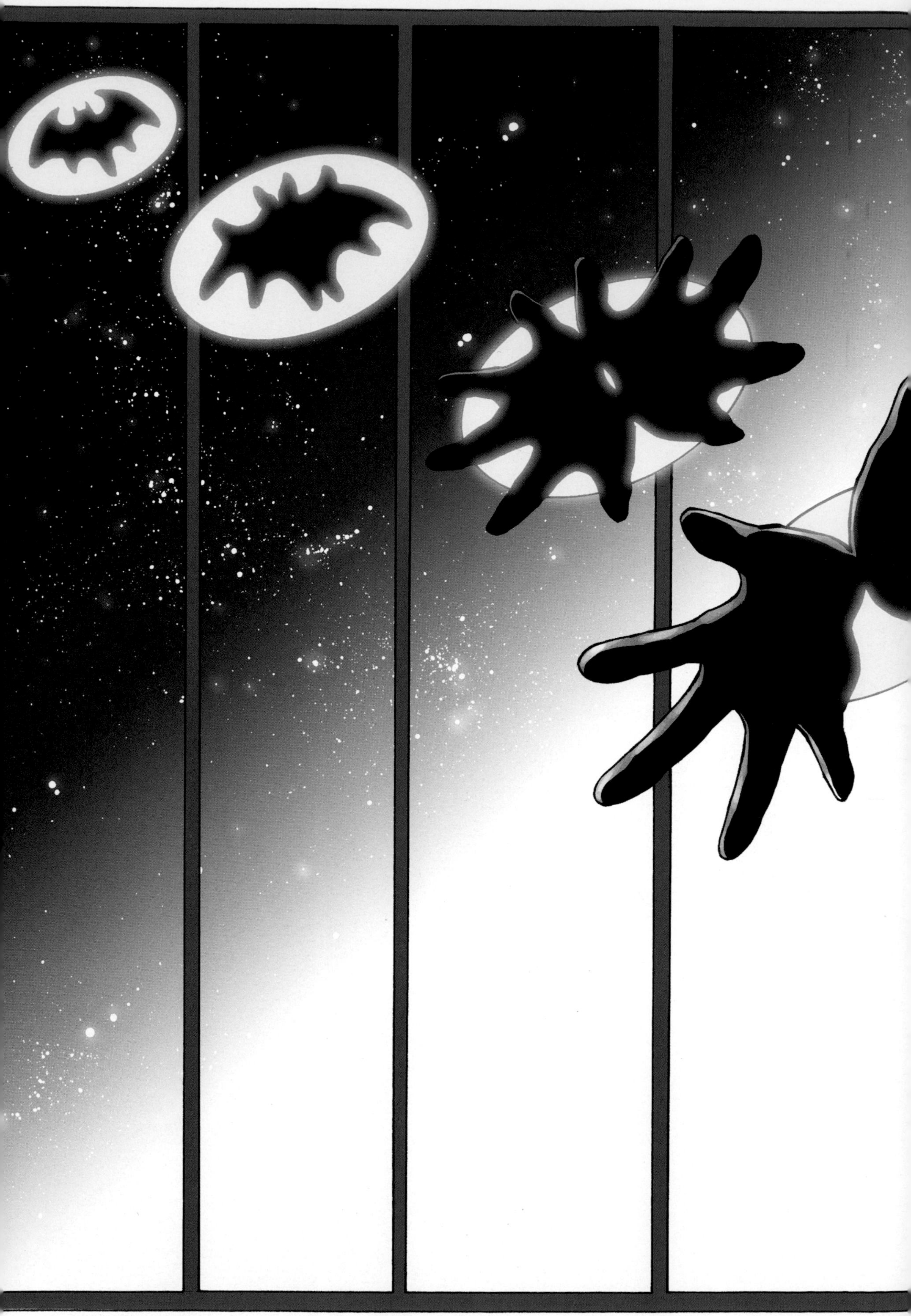

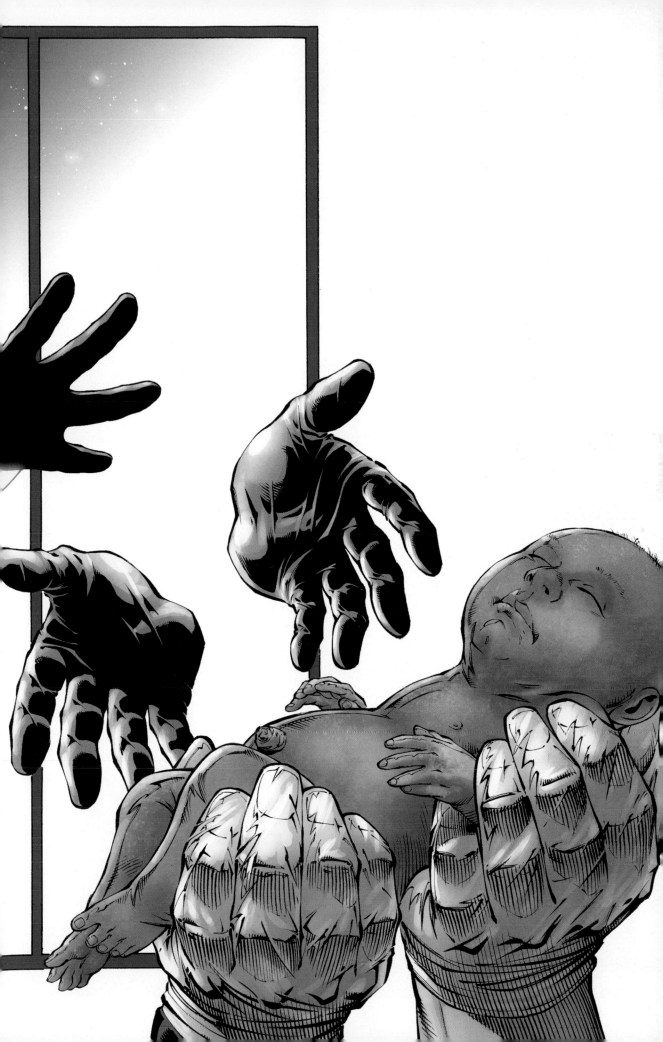

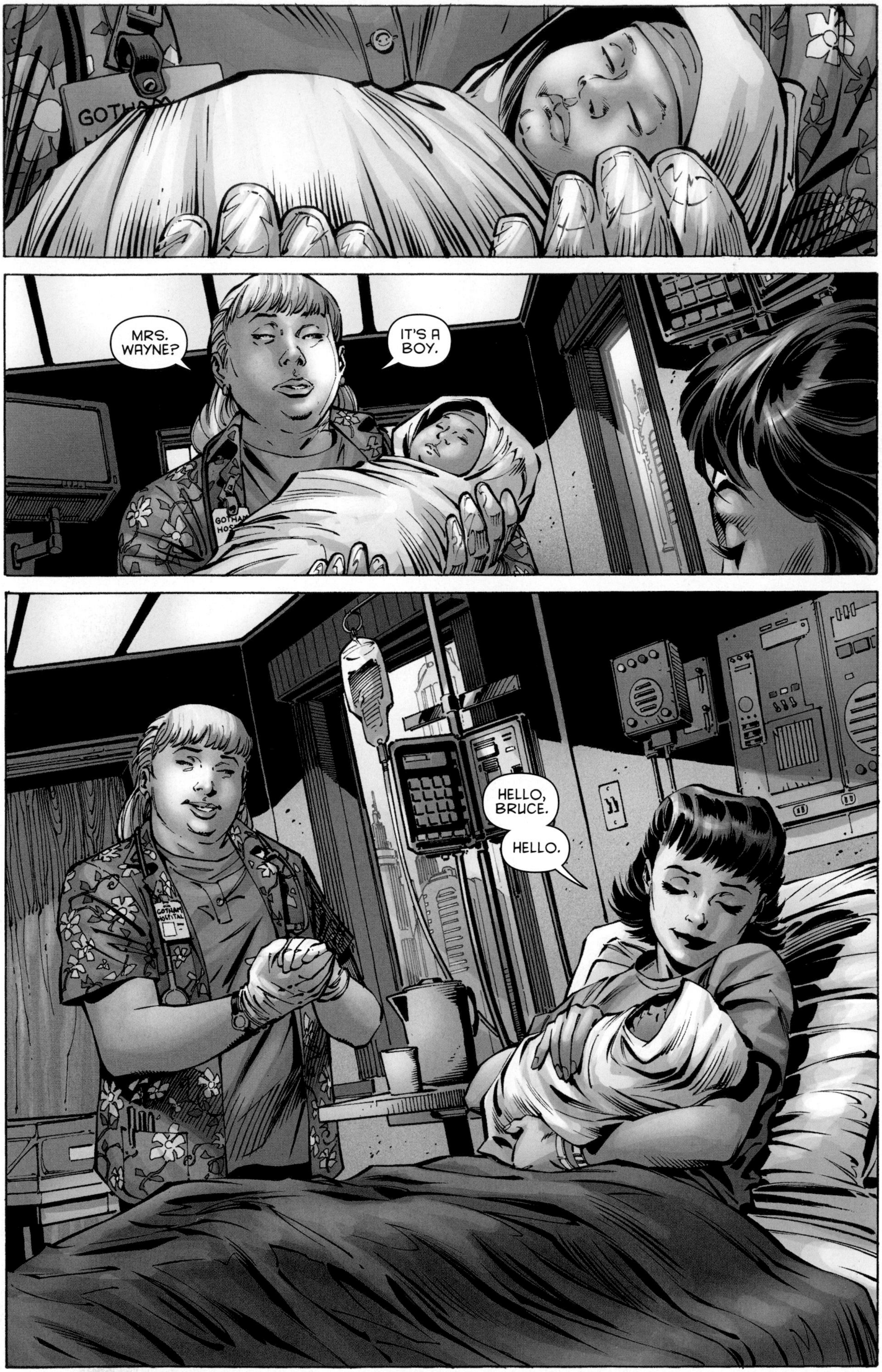
GOTHAM
MRS. WAYNE?
IT'S A BOY.
GOTHAM HOSPITAL
HELLO, BRUCE.
HELLO.

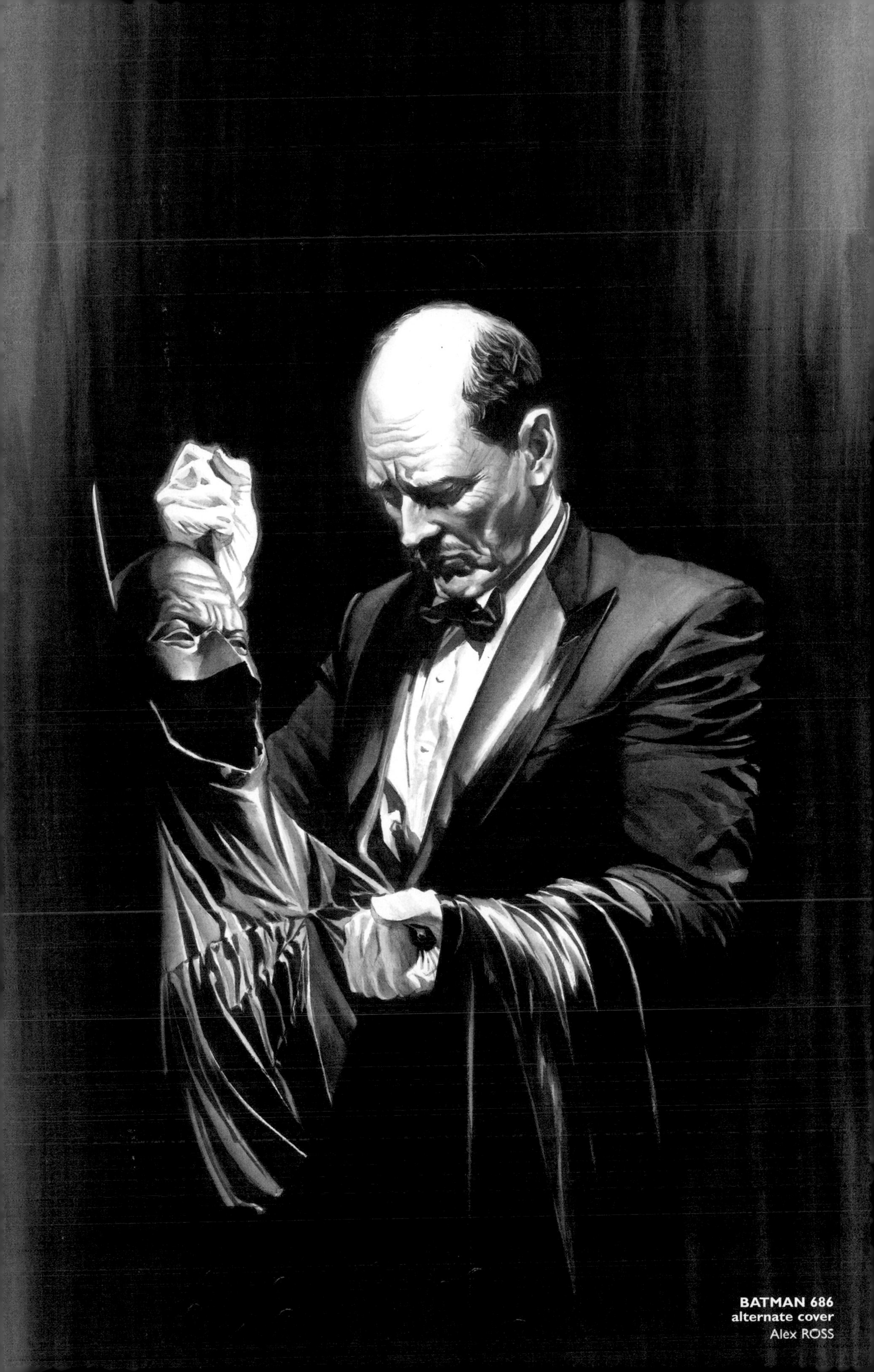

BATMAN 686
alternate cover
Alex ROSS

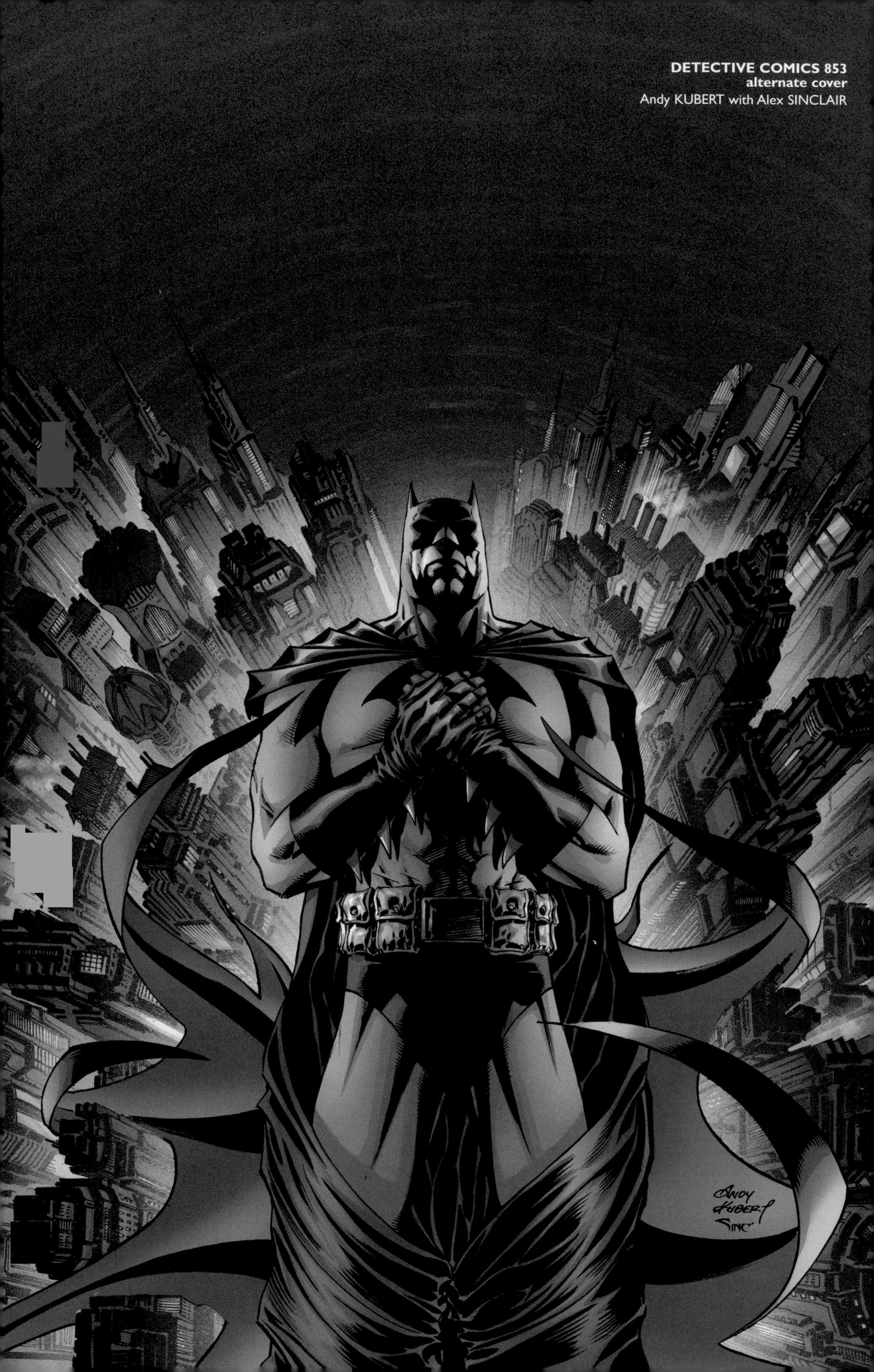
ANDY KUBERT SINC'

DETECTIVE COMICS 853
alternate cover
Andy KUBERT with Alex SINCLAIR

WHATEVER HAPPENED TO THE CAPED CRUSADER? Sketchbook By Andy Kubert

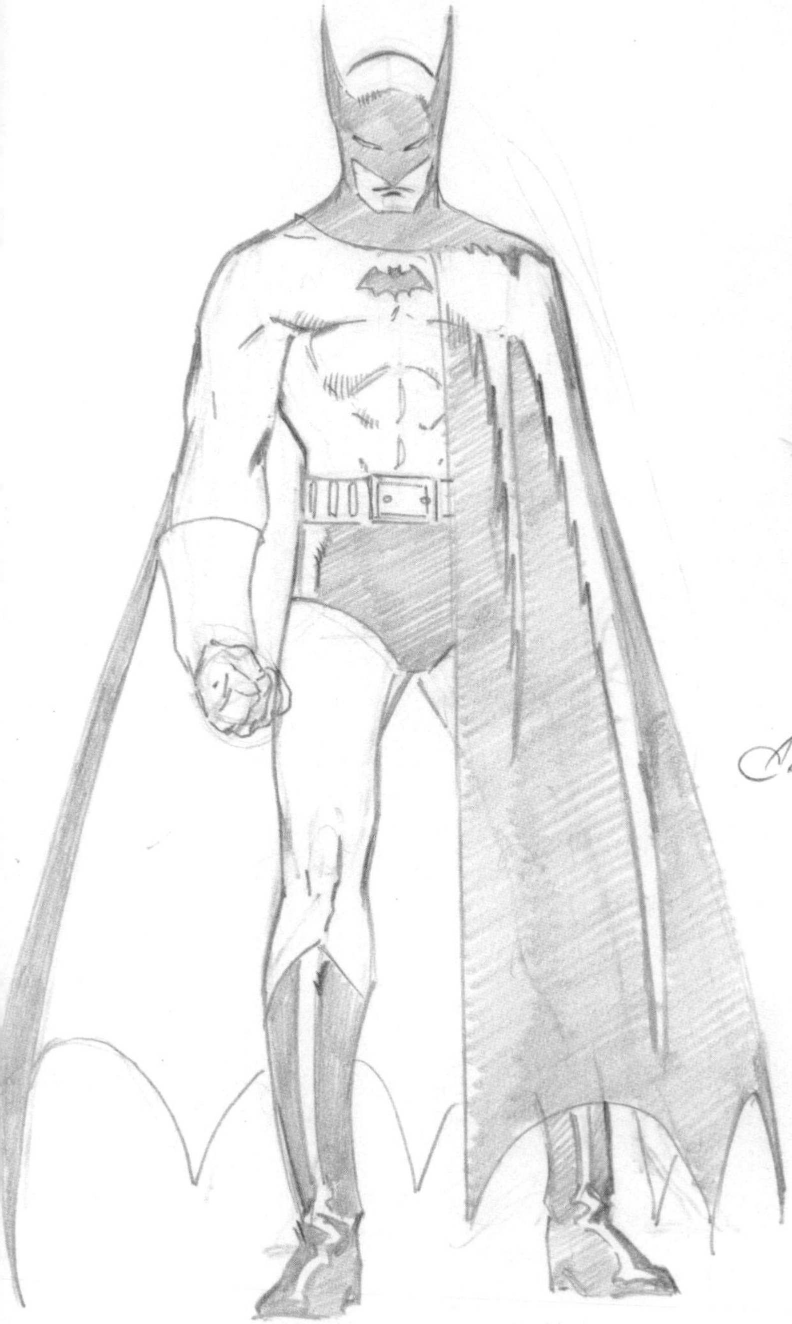

'BOB KANE' BATMAN 1939

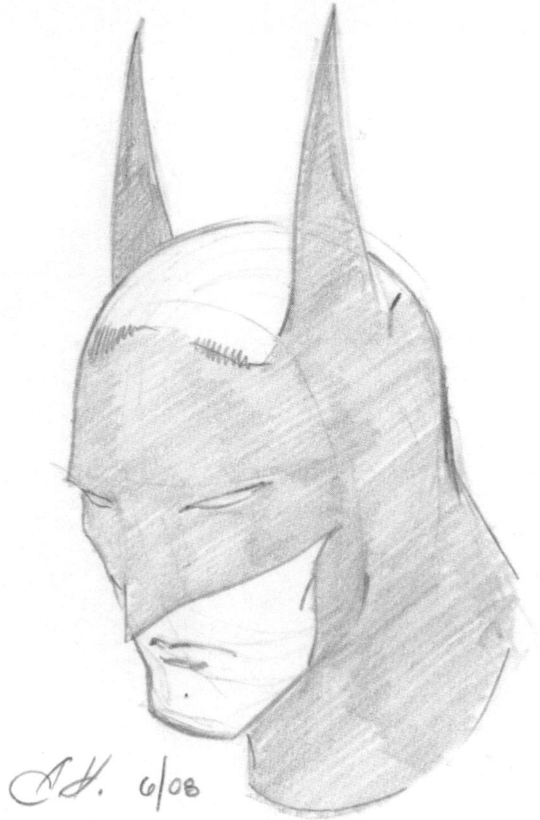
6/08

Featured here are EXCLUSIVE sketches by BATMAN artist ANDY KUBERT.

While developing "Whatever Happened to the Caped Crusader?" writer NEIL GAIMAN and artist ANDY KUBERT discussed showcasing different versions of Batman that would act as tributes to the artists who helped shape the Dark Knight, such as Bob Kane, Dick Sprang, Jim Aparo, Neal Adams and others.

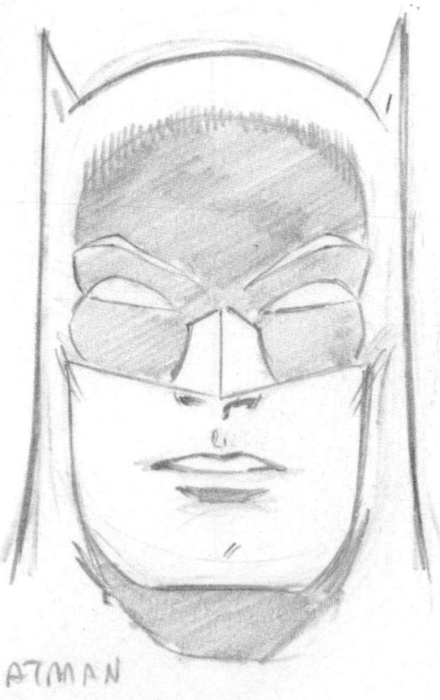

'DICK SPRANG' BATMAN 1950'S

shadow from blonde pg. 20

Shown here is Andy's Kubert's initial rough layout for an interior page...

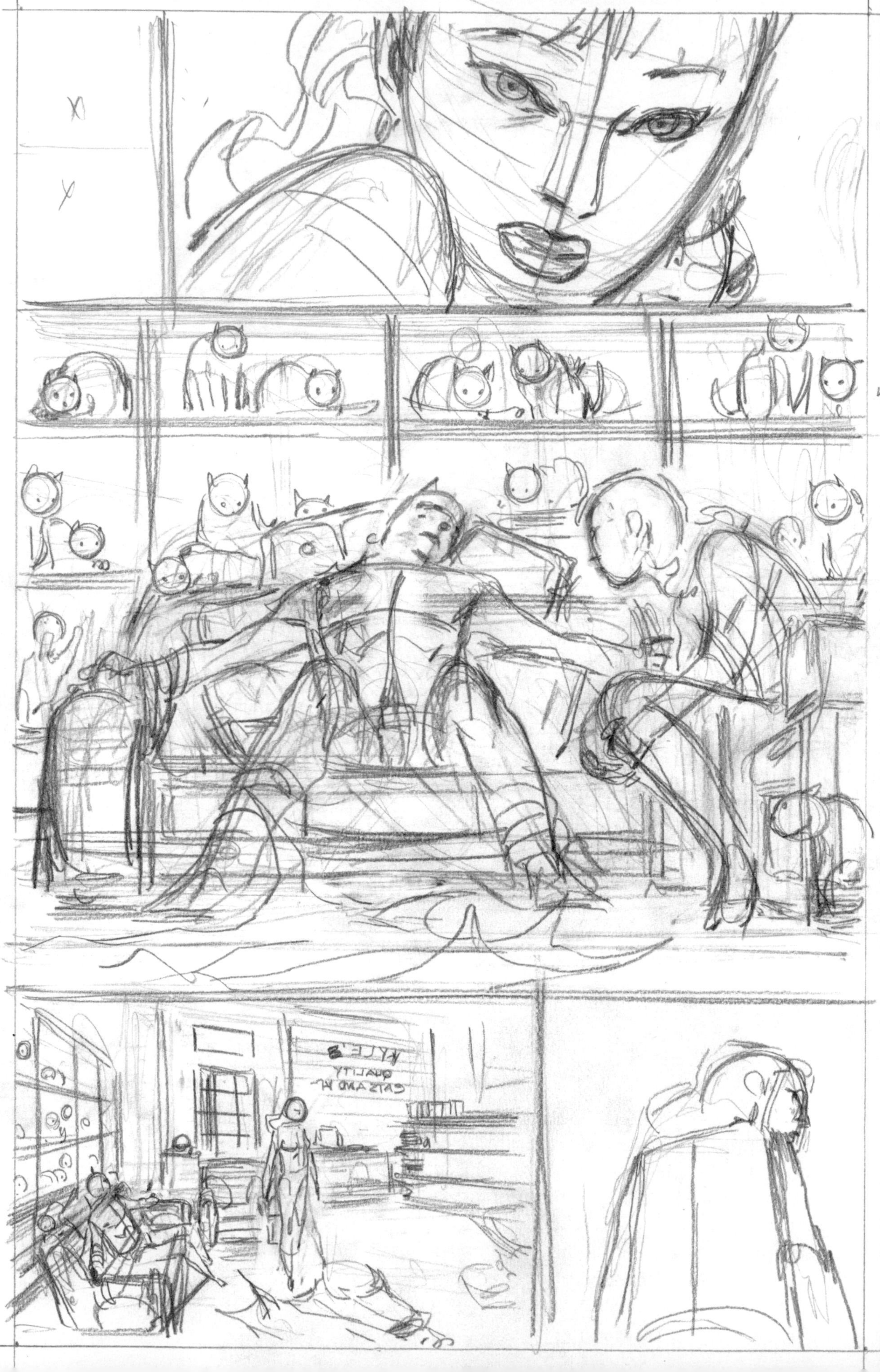

…and the completed, fully rendered pencilled version.

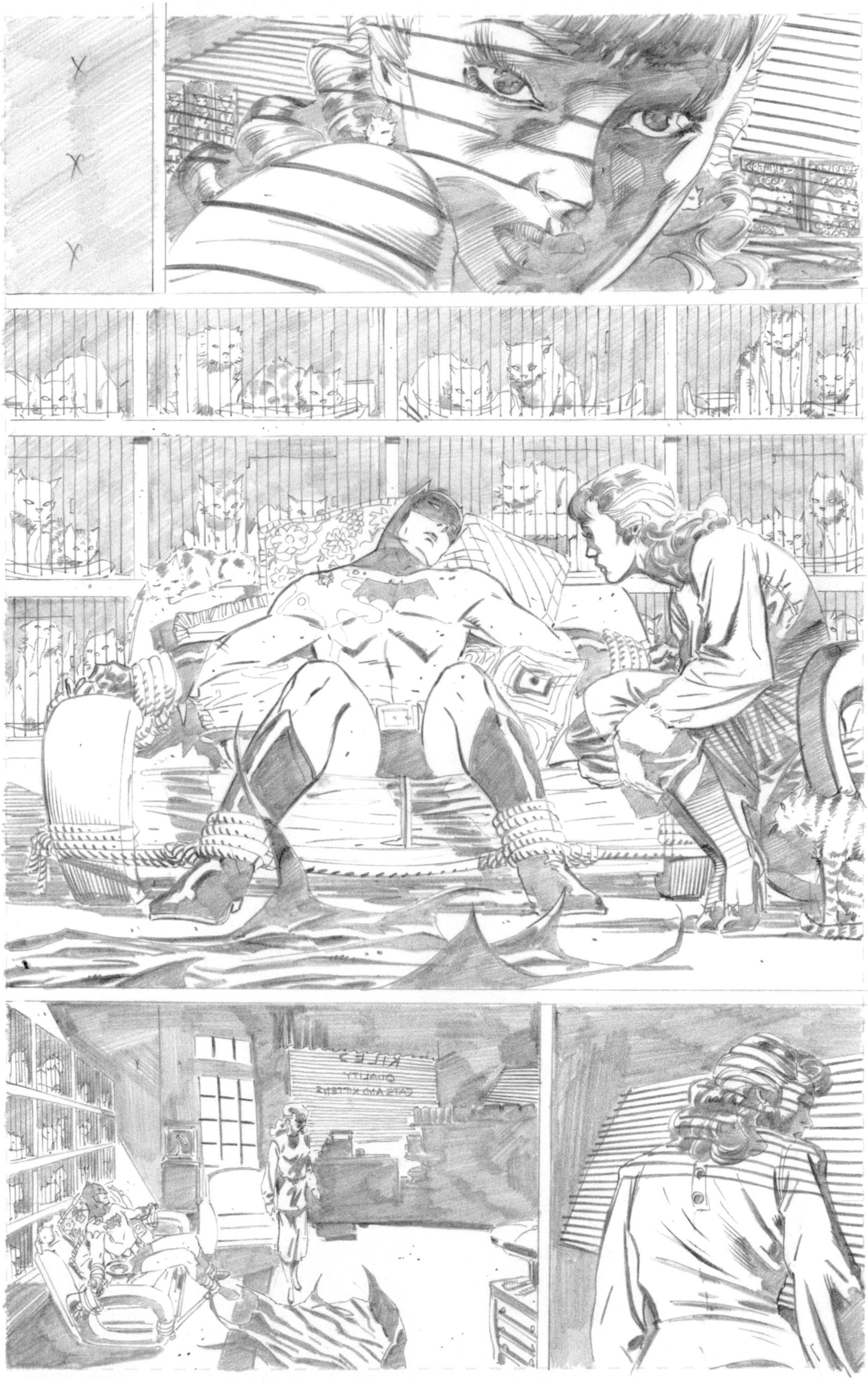

Here's an early concept sketch
for Selina Kyle, a.k.a. CATWOMAN.

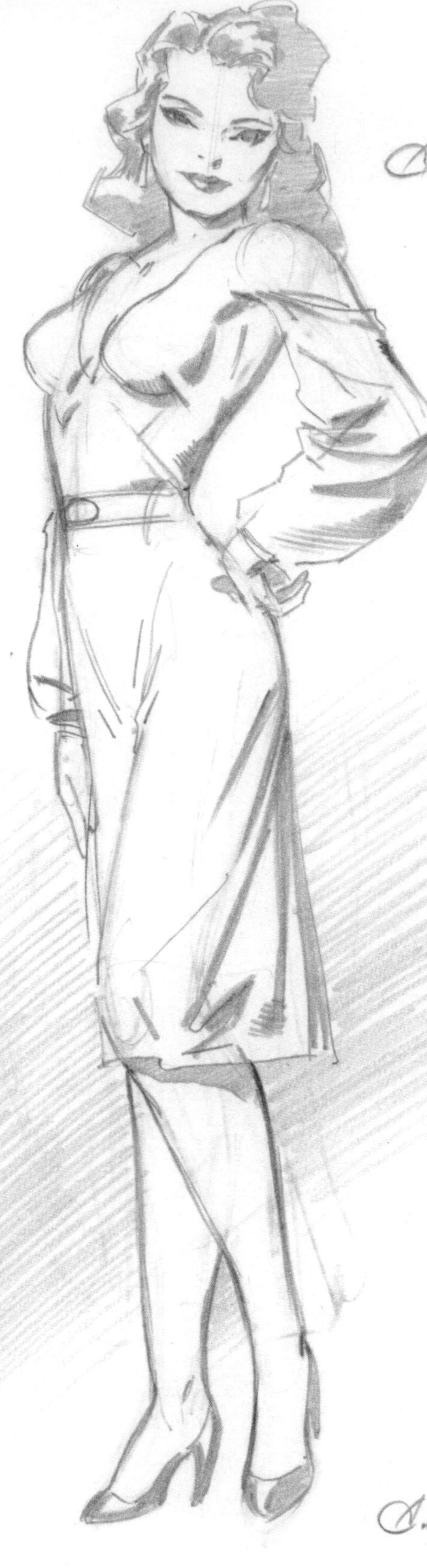

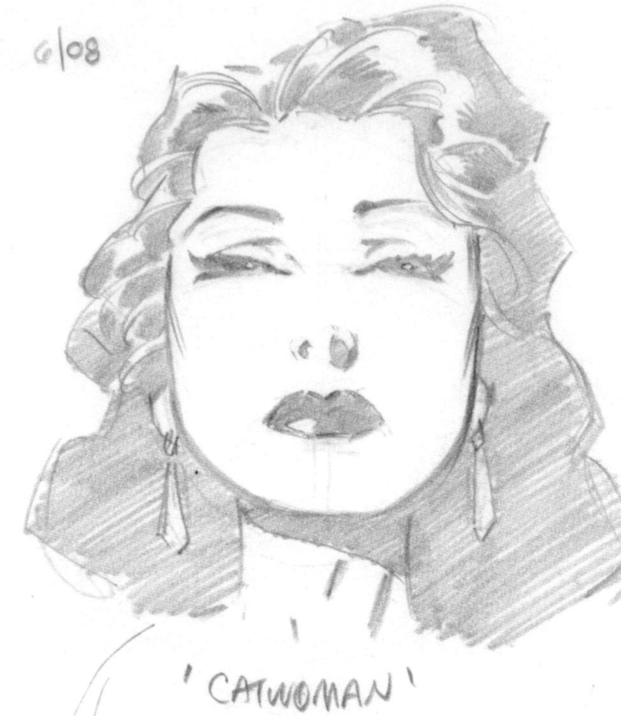
'CATWOMAN'

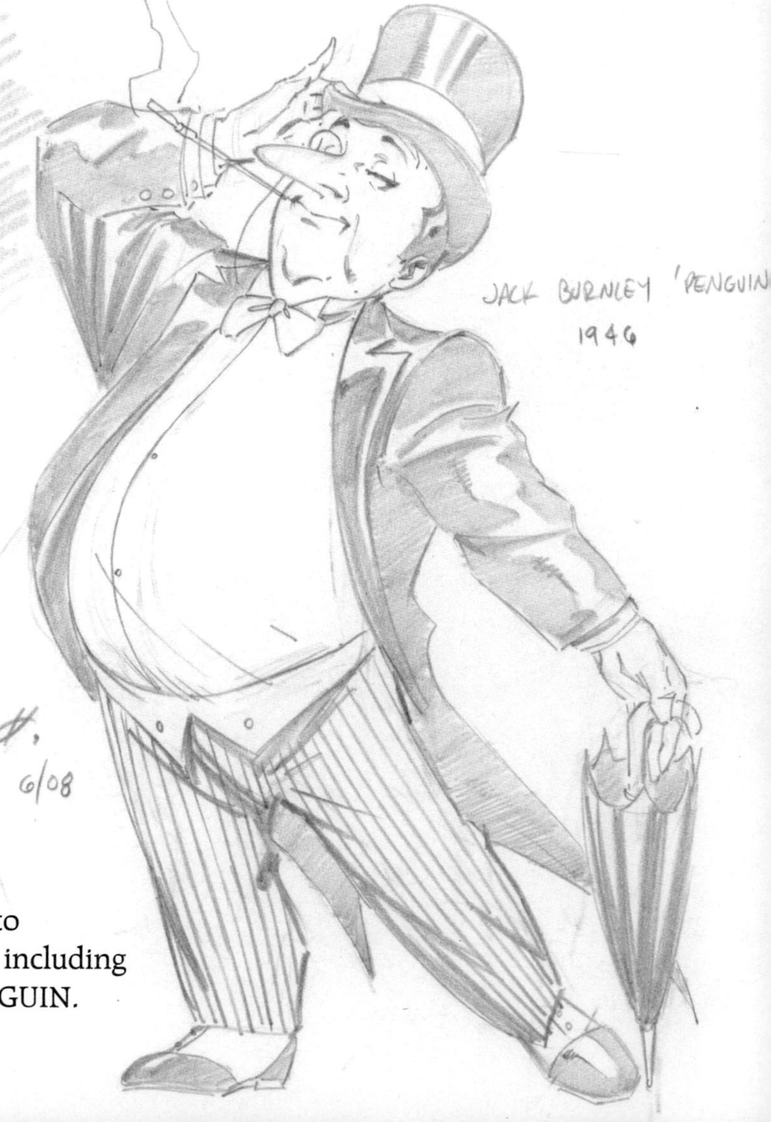
JACK BURNLEY 'PENGUIN'
1946

The "tribute" approach extended to Batman's large cast of characters, including this version of Jack Burnley's PENGUIN.

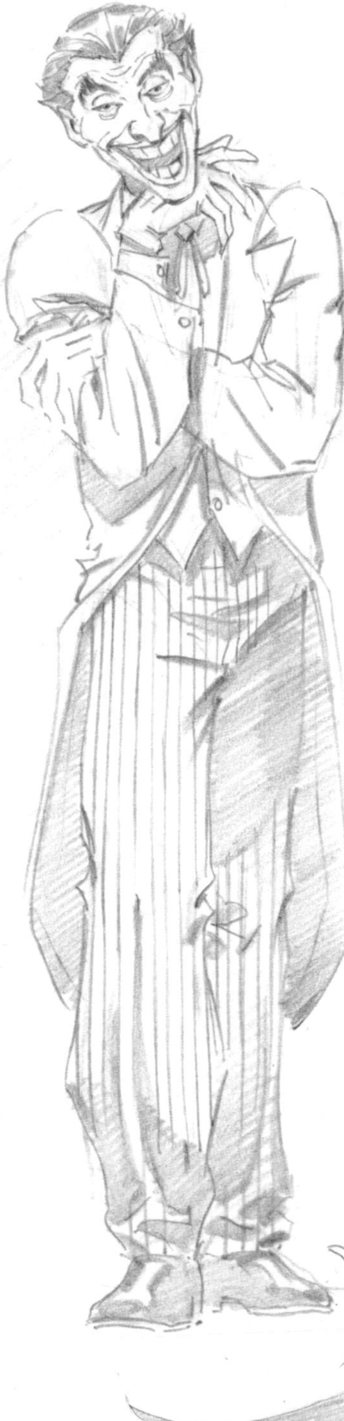

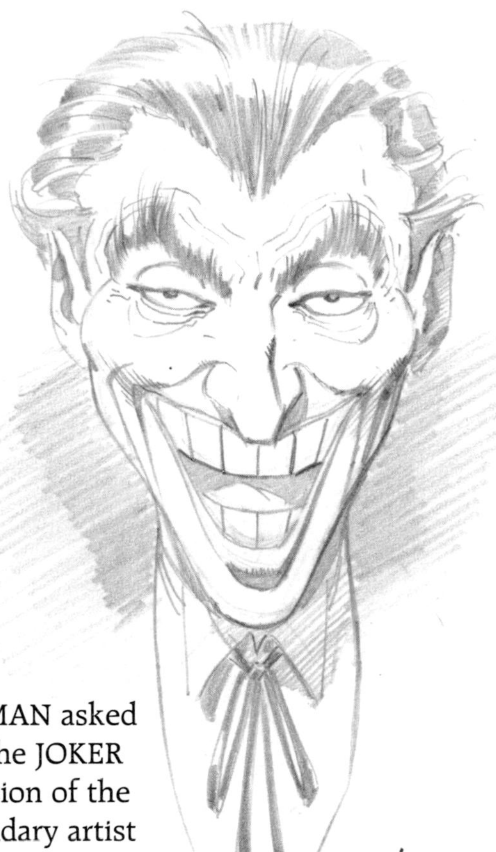

Writer NEIL GAIMAN asked Andy to design the JOKER based on the version of the character by legendary artist Jerry Robinson.

'JOKER' JERRY ROBINSON 1942

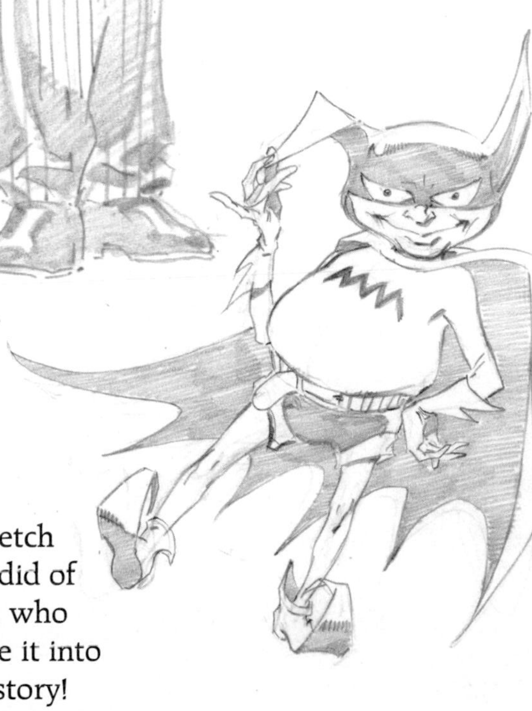

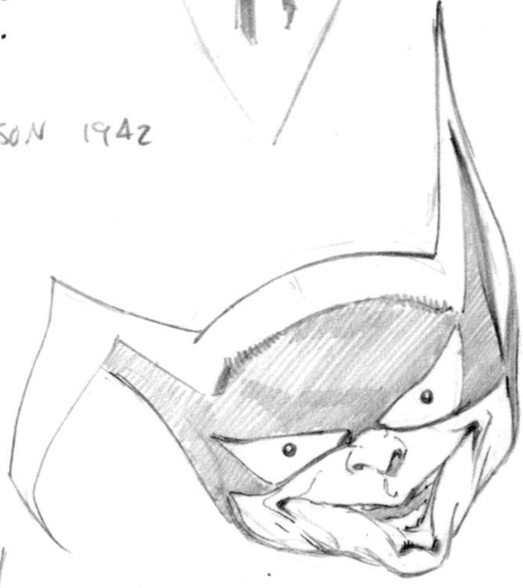
'BATMITE'

Here's a sketch that Andy did of BAT-MITE, who never made it into the actual story!

Shown here is the rough sketch that Andy did for one of the final double-page spreads of the story...

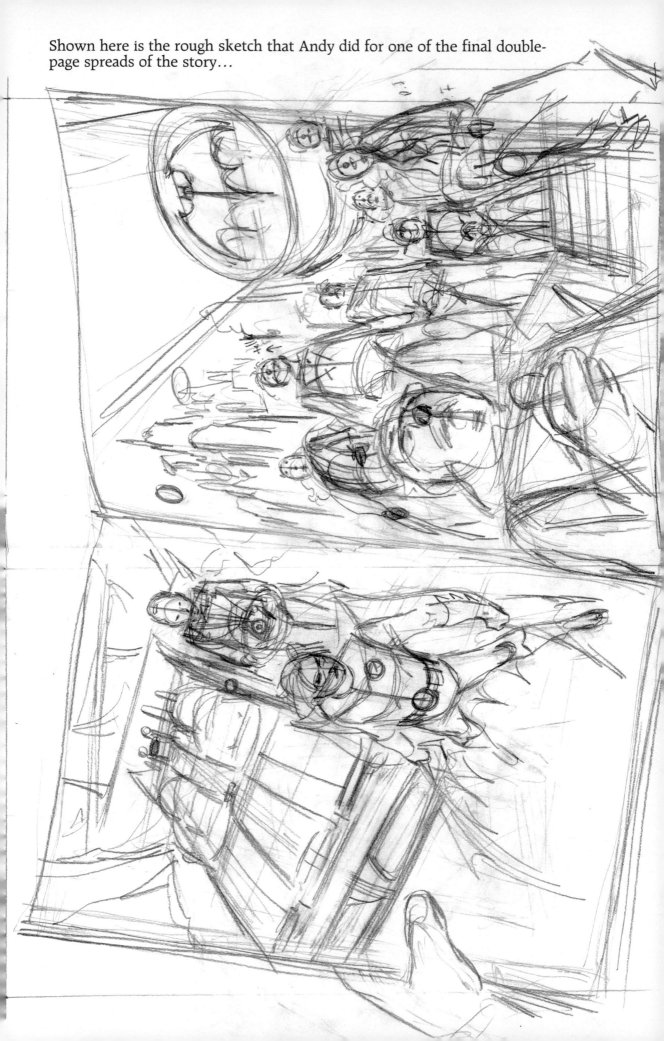

…and the completed, fully rendered pencilled version.

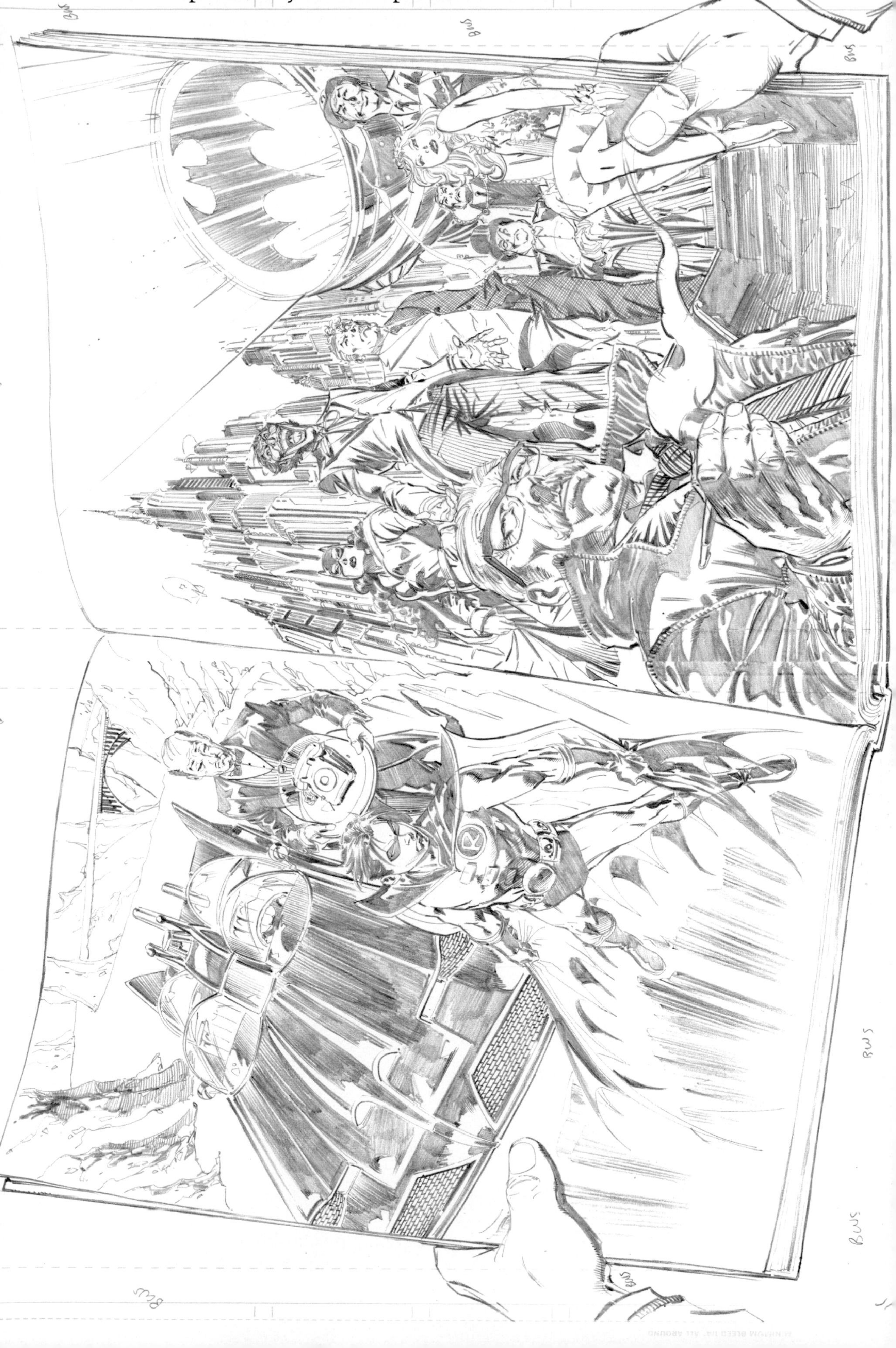

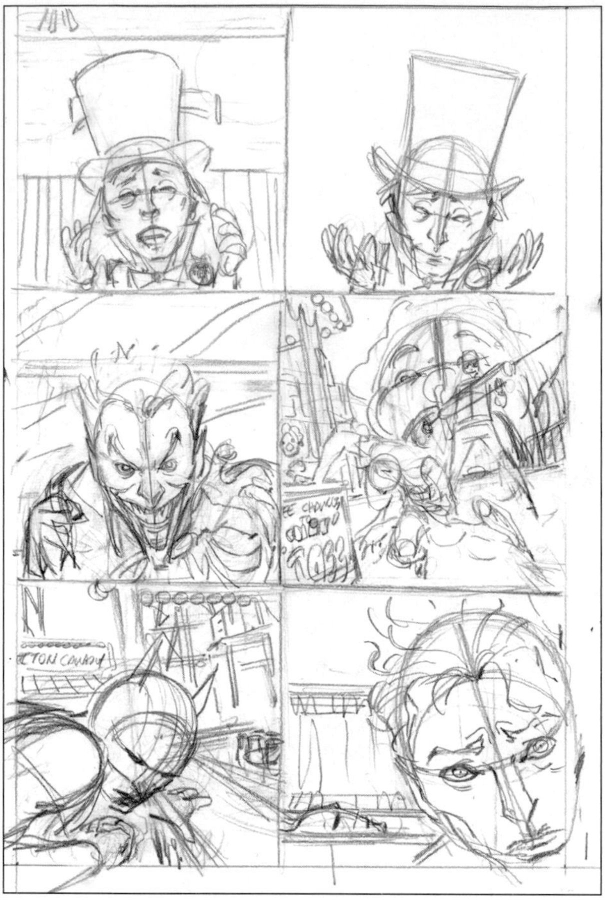

Andy uses a three-step approach to his pages...

First, he works out "rough pencils"...

...then he refines the page to what he calls a "linear breakdown"...

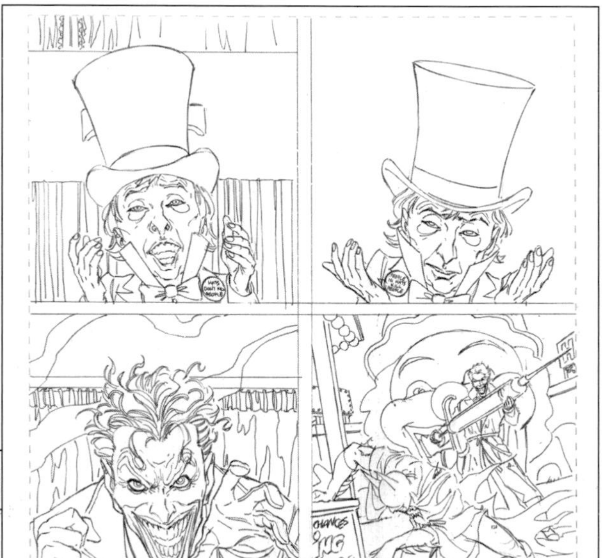
TTON CANDY

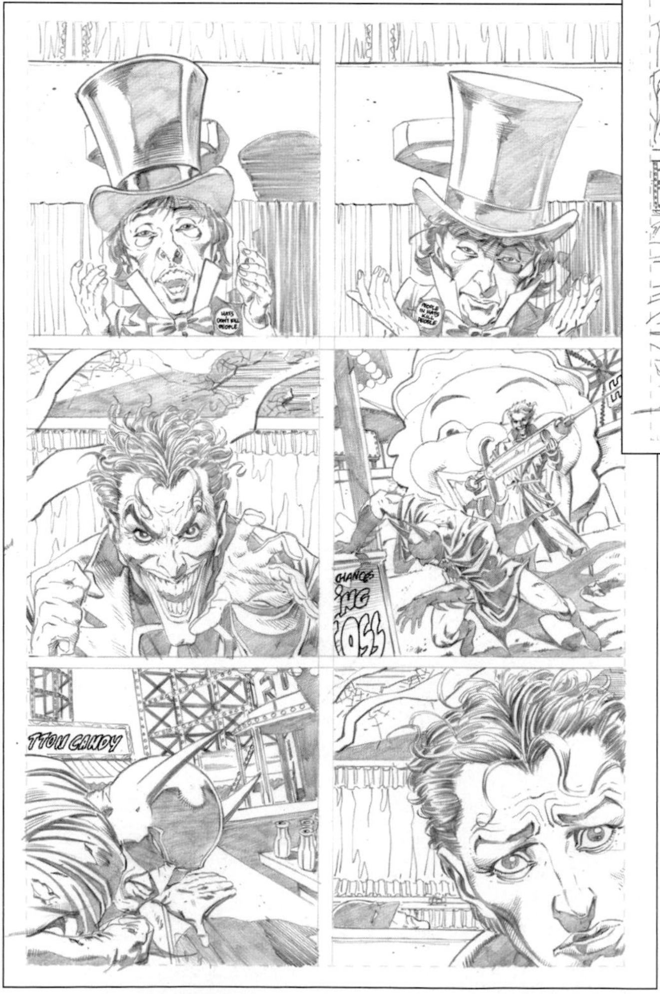
TTON CANDY

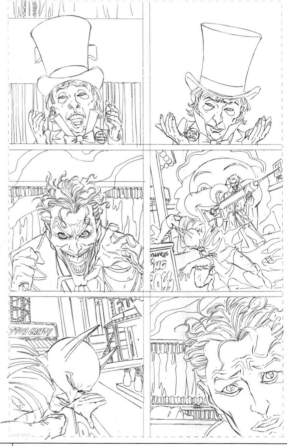

...and then finally he completes the page with "finished pencils".

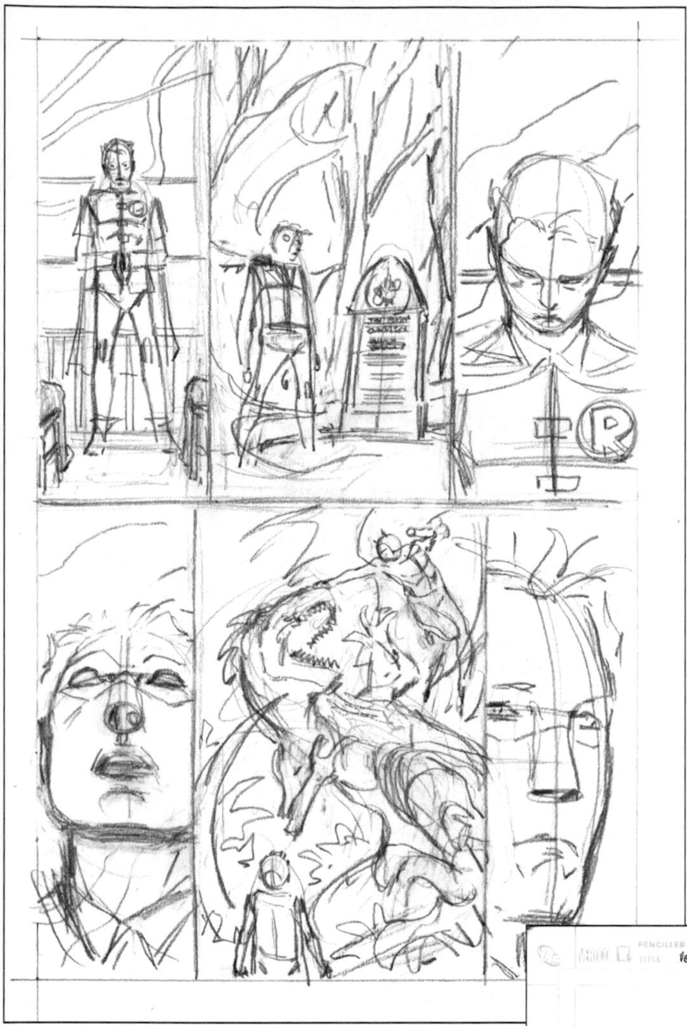

Here are Andy's roughs and finished pencils for Page 4 of Part Two.

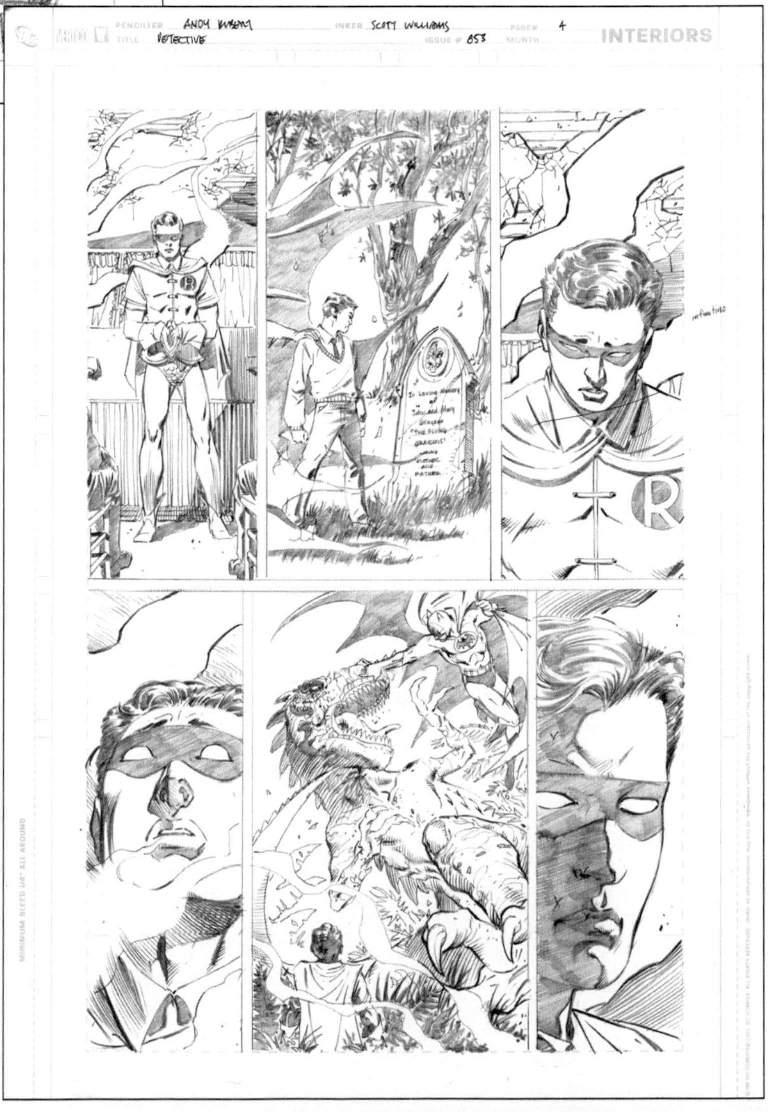
PENCILLER ANDY KUBERT
INKER SCOTT WILLIAMS
PAGE# 4
TITLE DETECTIVE
ISSUE # 853
MONTH
INTERIORS

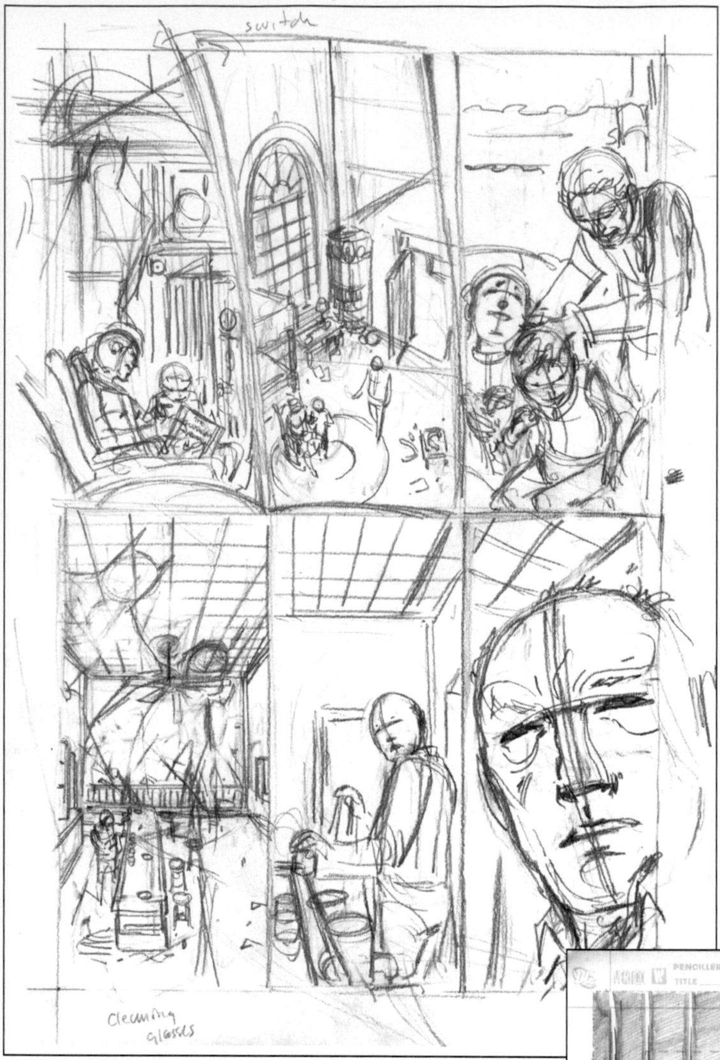
switch
Cleaning glasses

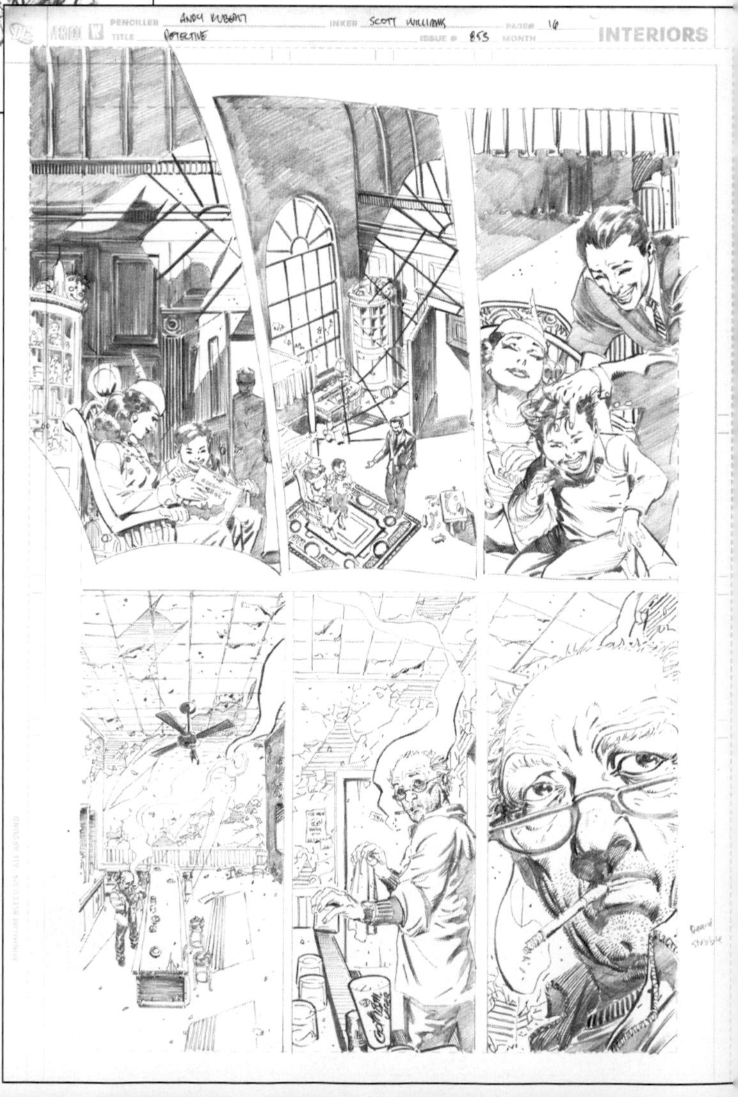
PENCILLER ANDY KUBERT
INKER SCOTT WILLIAMS
PAGE# 16
TITLE DETECTIVE
ISSUE # 853
MONTH
INTERIORS

And finally, the before and after versions , featuring young Bruce Wayne with his parents and an aging Joe Chill.

A BLACK AND WHITE WORLD

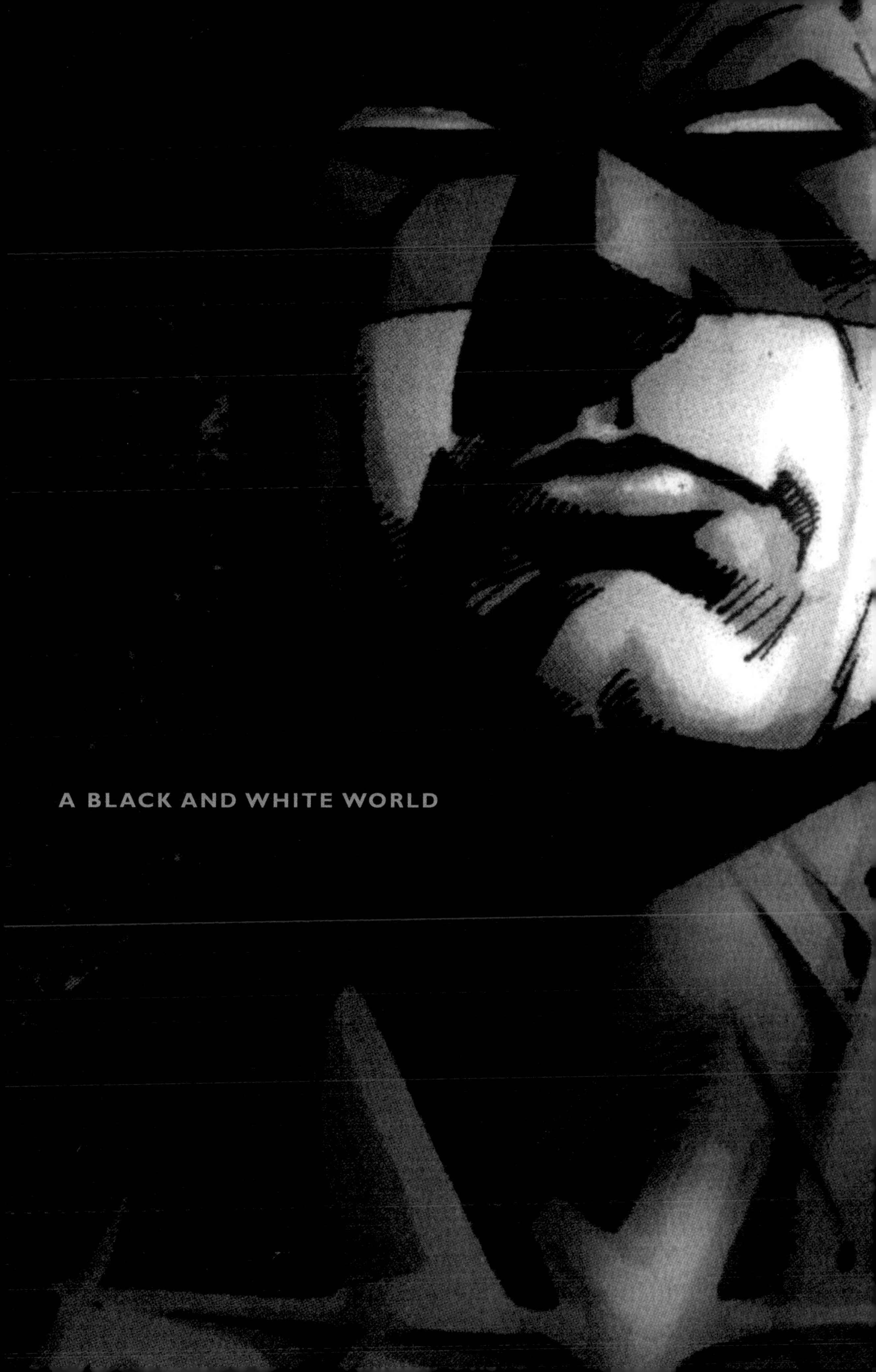

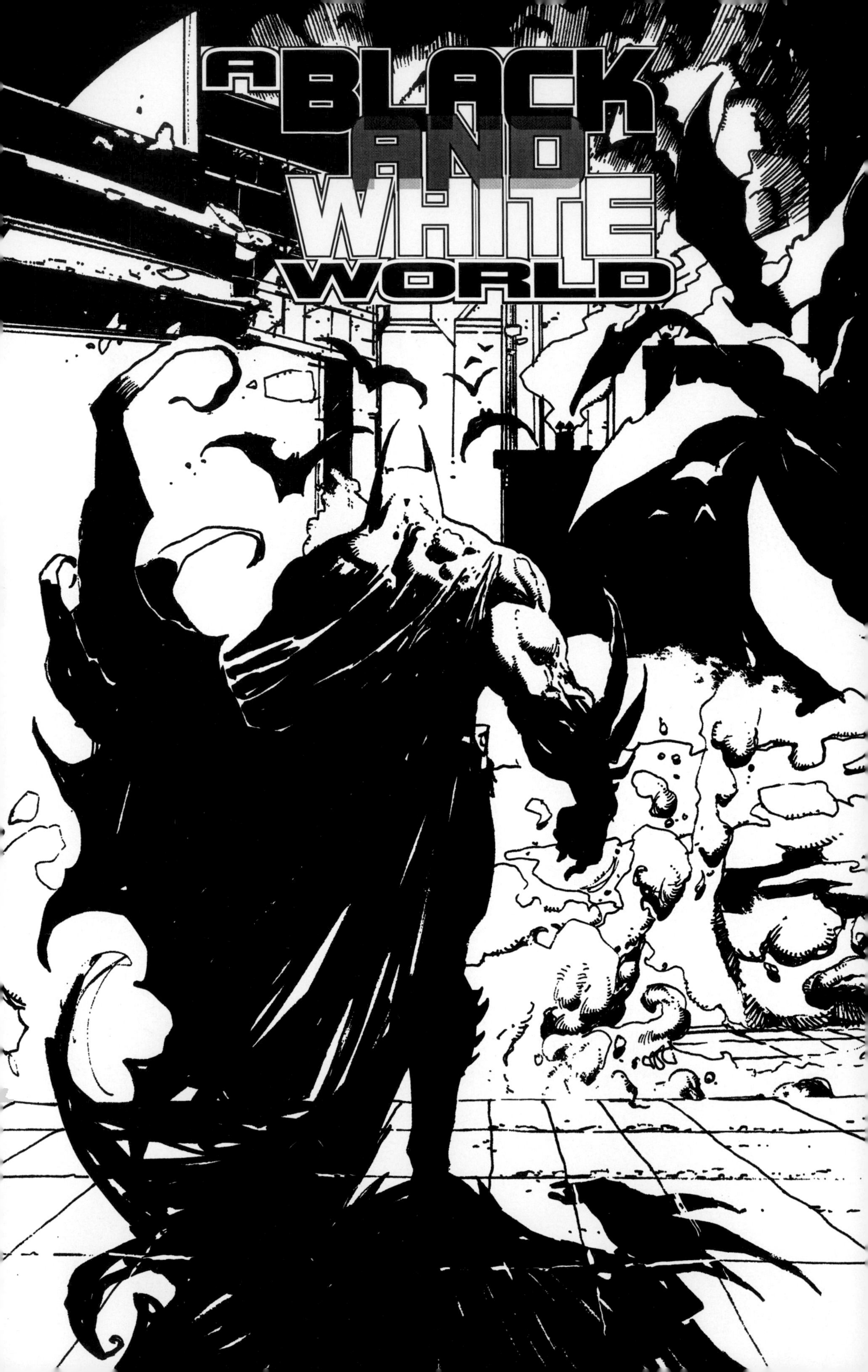
A BLACK AND WHITE WORLD

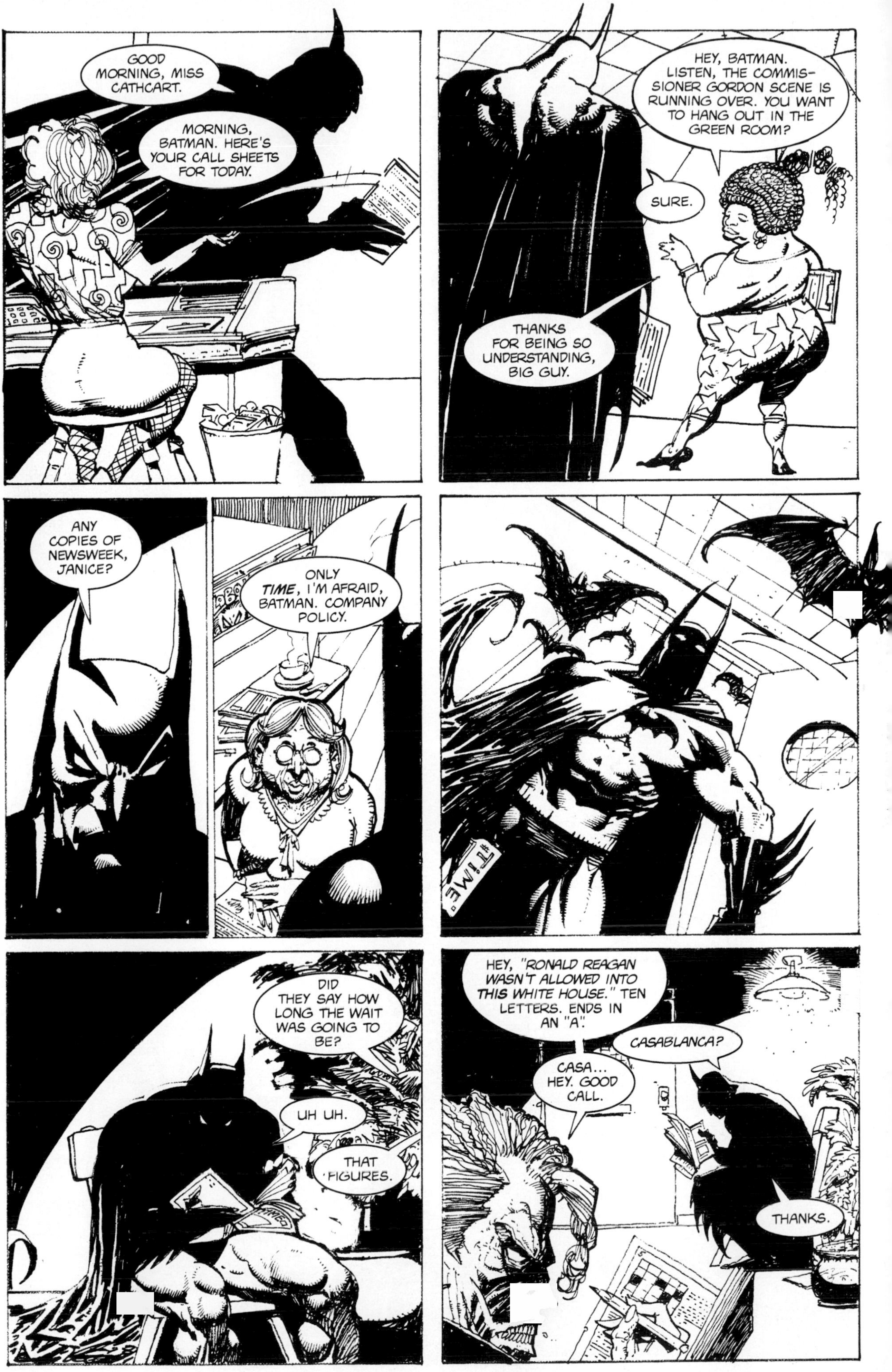
GOOD MORNING, MISS CATHCART.
MORNING, BATMAN. HERE'S YOUR CALL SHEETS FOR TODAY.
HEY, BATMAN. LISTEN, THE COMMISSIONER GORDON SCENE IS RUNNING OVER. YOU WANT TO HANG OUT IN THE GREEN ROOM?
SURE.
THANKS FOR BEING SO UNDERSTANDING, BIG GUY.
ANY COPIES OF NEWSWEEK, JANICE?
ONLY *TIME*, I'M AFRAID, BATMAN. COMPANY POLICY.
TIME
DID THEY SAY HOW LONG THE WAIT WAS GOING TO BE?
UH UH.
THAT FIGURES.
HEY, "*RONALD REAGAN WASN'T ALLOWED INTO THIS WHITE HOUSE.*" TEN LETTERS. ENDS IN AN "A".
CASABLANCA?
CASA... HEY. GOOD CALL.
THANKS.

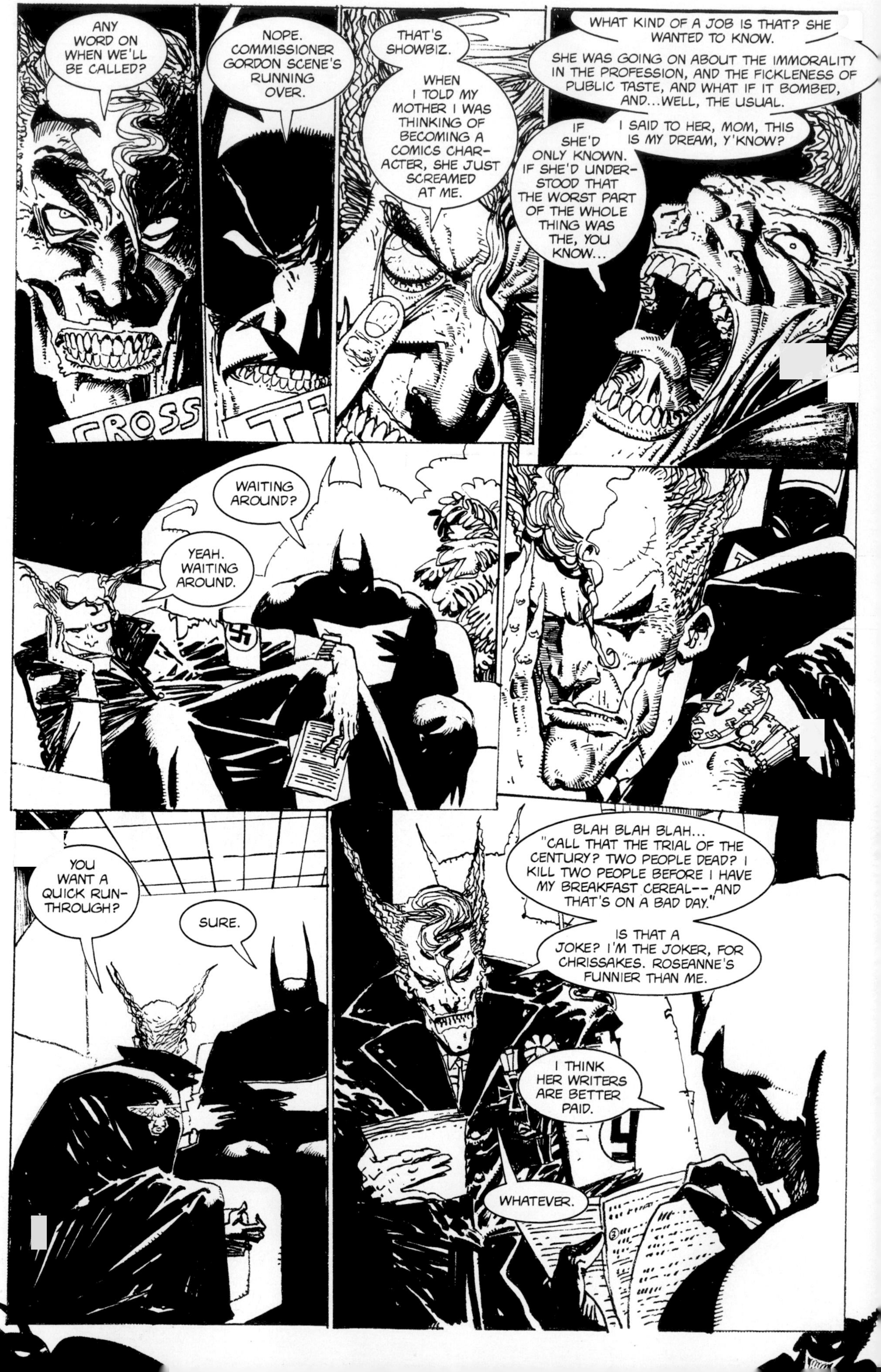

ANY WORD ON WHEN WE'LL BE CALLED?
NOPE. COMMISSIONER GORDON SCENE'S RUNNING OVER.
CROSS
THAT'S SHOWBIZ.
WHEN I TOLD MY MOTHER I WAS THINKING OF BECOMING A COMICS CHARACTER, SHE JUST SCREAMED AT ME.
WHAT KIND OF A JOB IS THAT? SHE WANTED TO KNOW.
SHE WAS GOING ON ABOUT THE IMMORALITY IN THE PROFESSION, AND THE FICKLENESS OF PUBLIC TASTE, AND WHAT IF IT BOMBED, AND...WELL, THE USUAL.
I SAID TO HER, MOM, THIS IS MY DREAM, Y'KNOW?
IF SHE'D ONLY KNOWN. IF SHE'D UNDERSTOOD THAT THE WORST PART OF THE WHOLE THING WAS THE, YOU KNOW...
WAITING AROUND?
YEAH. WAITING AROUND.
YOU WANT A QUICK RUN-THROUGH?
SURE.
BLAH BLAH BLAH... "CALL THAT THE TRIAL OF THE CENTURY? TWO PEOPLE DEAD? I KILL TWO PEOPLE BEFORE I HAVE MY BREAKFAST CEREAL-- AND THAT'S ON A BAD DAY."
IS THAT A JOKE? I'M THE JOKER, FOR CHRISSAKES. ROSEANNE'S FUNNIER THAN ME.
I THINK HER WRITERS ARE BETTER PAID.
WHATEVER.

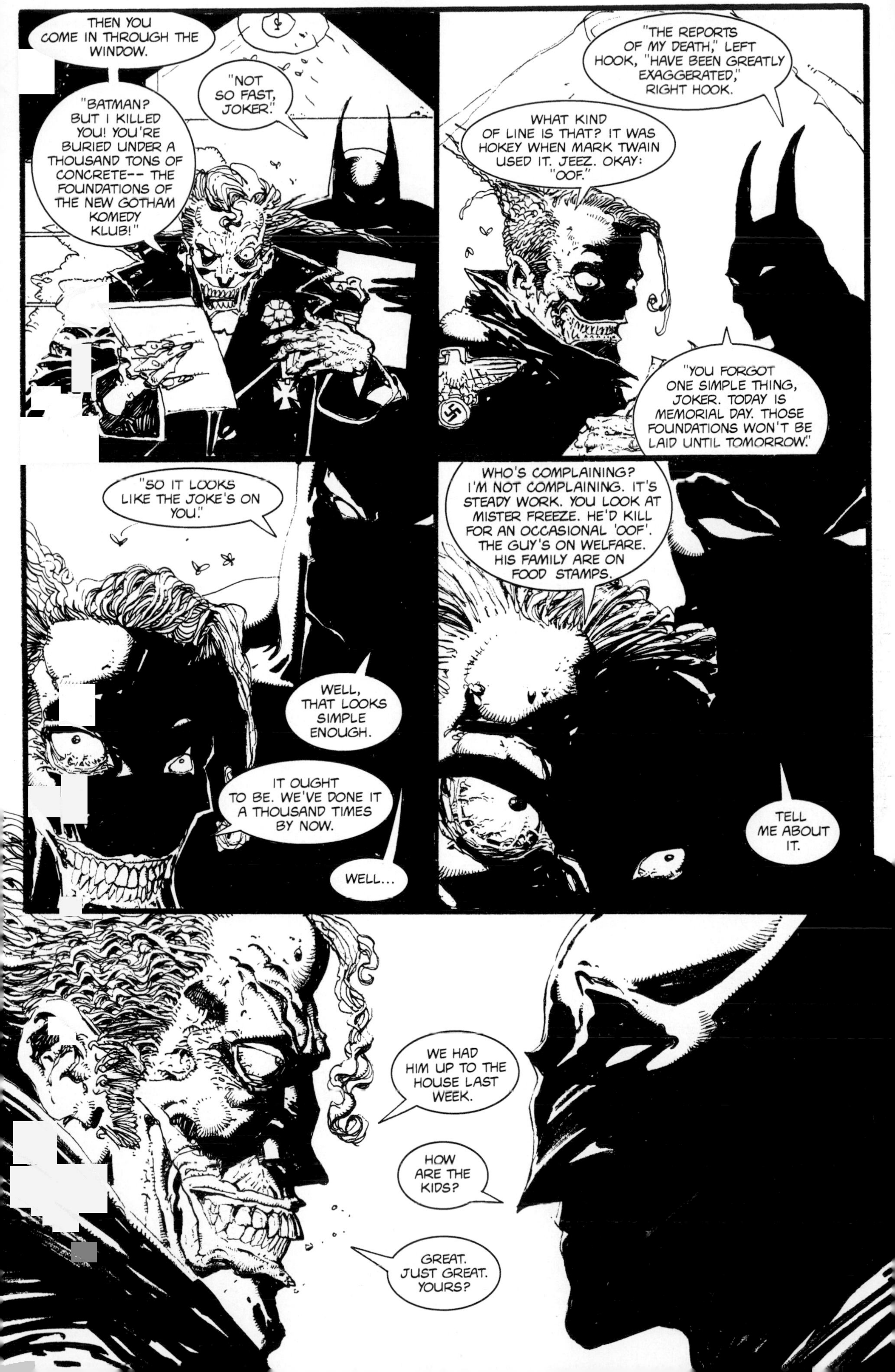
THEN YOU COME IN THROUGH THE WINDOW.
"BATMAN? BUT I KILLED YOU! YOU'RE BURIED UNDER A THOUSAND TONS OF CONCRETE-- THE FOUNDATIONS OF THE NEW GOTHAM KOMEDY KLUB!"
"NOT SO FAST, JOKER."
"THE REPORTS OF MY DEATH," LEFT HOOK, "HAVE BEEN GREATLY EXAGGERATED," RIGHT HOOK.
WHAT KIND OF LINE IS THAT? IT WAS HOKEY WHEN MARK TWAIN USED IT. JEEZ. OKAY: "OOF."
"YOU FORGOT ONE SIMPLE THING, JOKER. TODAY IS MEMORIAL DAY. THOSE FOUNDATIONS WON'T BE LAID UNTIL TOMORROW."
"SO IT LOOKS LIKE THE JOKE'S ON YOU."
WELL, THAT LOOKS SIMPLE ENOUGH.
IT OUGHT TO BE. WE'VE DONE IT A THOUSAND TIMES BY NOW.
WELL...
WHO'S COMPLAINING? I'M NOT COMPLAINING. IT'S STEADY WORK. YOU LOOK AT MISTER FREEZE. HE'D KILL FOR AN OCCASIONAL 'OOF'. THE GUY'S ON WELFARE. HIS FAMILY ARE ON FOOD STAMPS.
TELL ME ABOUT IT.
WE HAD HIM UP TO THE HOUSE LAST WEEK.
HOW ARE THE KIDS?
GREAT. JUST GREAT. YOURS?

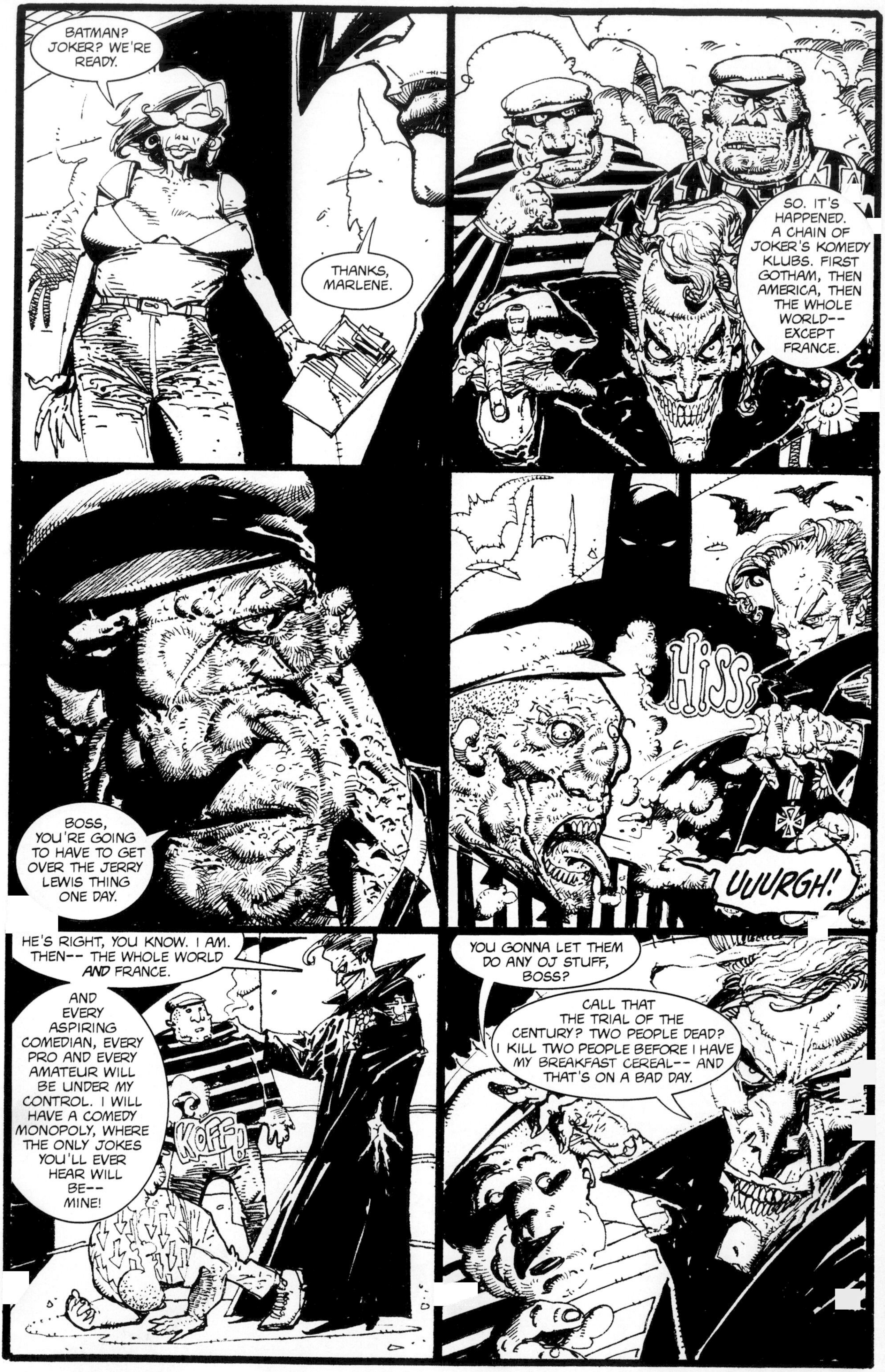
BATMAN? JOKER? WE'RE READY.
THANKS, MARLENE.
SO. IT'S HAPPENED. A CHAIN OF JOKER'S KOMEDY KLUBS. FIRST GOTHAM, THEN AMERICA, THEN THE WHOLE WORLD-- EXCEPT FRANCE.
BOSS, YOU'RE GOING TO HAVE TO GET OVER THE JERRY LEWIS THING ONE DAY.
HISS
UUURGH!
HE'S RIGHT, YOU KNOW. I AM. THEN-- THE WHOLE WORLD AND FRANCE.
AND EVERY ASPIRING COMEDIAN, EVERY PRO AND EVERY AMATEUR WILL BE UNDER MY CONTROL. I WILL HAVE A COMEDY MONOPOLY, WHERE THE ONLY JOKES YOU'LL EVER HEAR WILL BE-- MINE!
KOFF!
YOU GONNA LET THEM DO ANY OJ STUFF, BOSS?
CALL THAT THE TRIAL OF THE CENTURY? TWO PEOPLE DEAD? I KILL TWO PEOPLE BEFORE I HAVE MY BREAKFAST CEREAL-- AND THAT'S ON A BAD DAY.

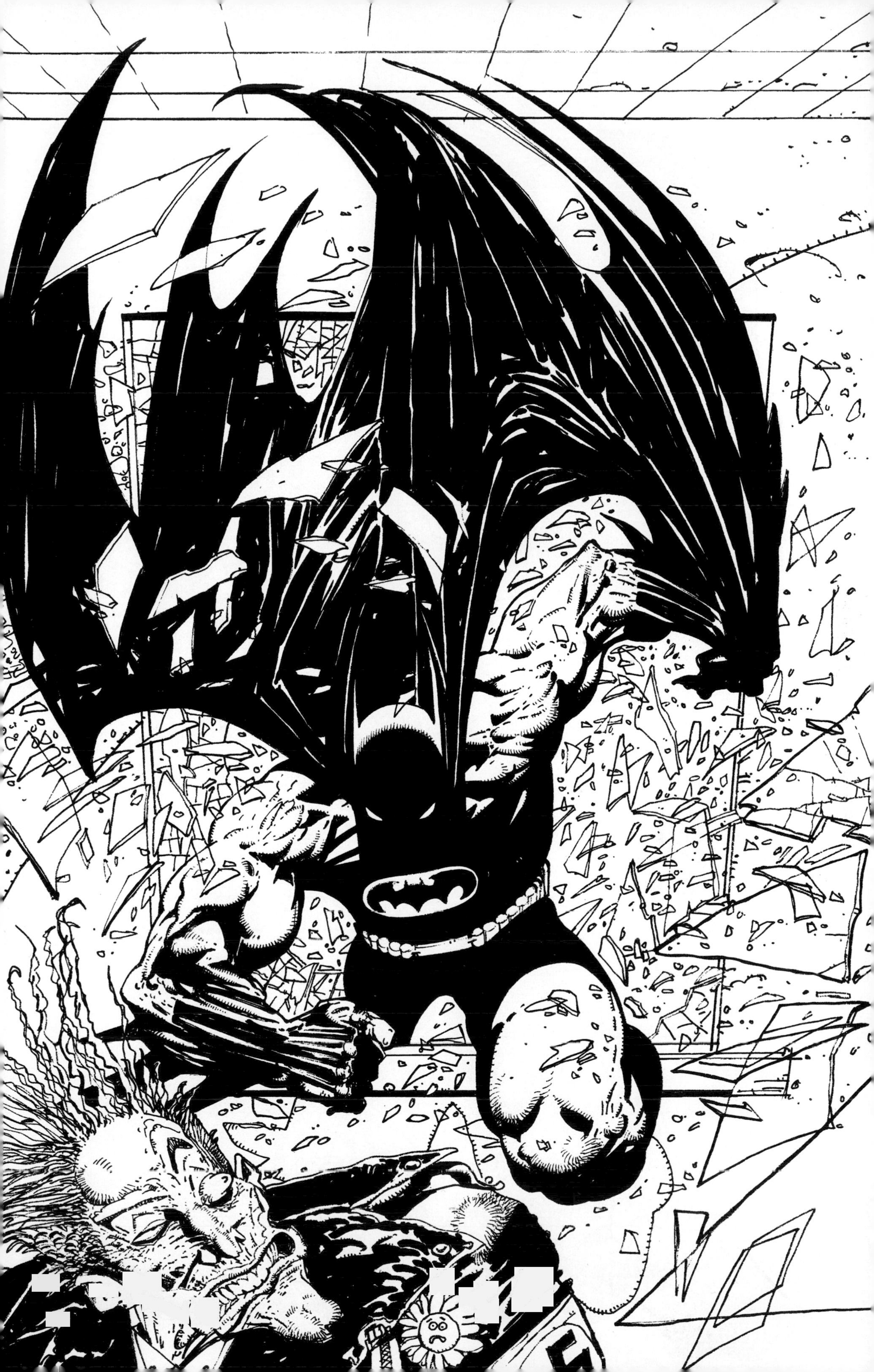

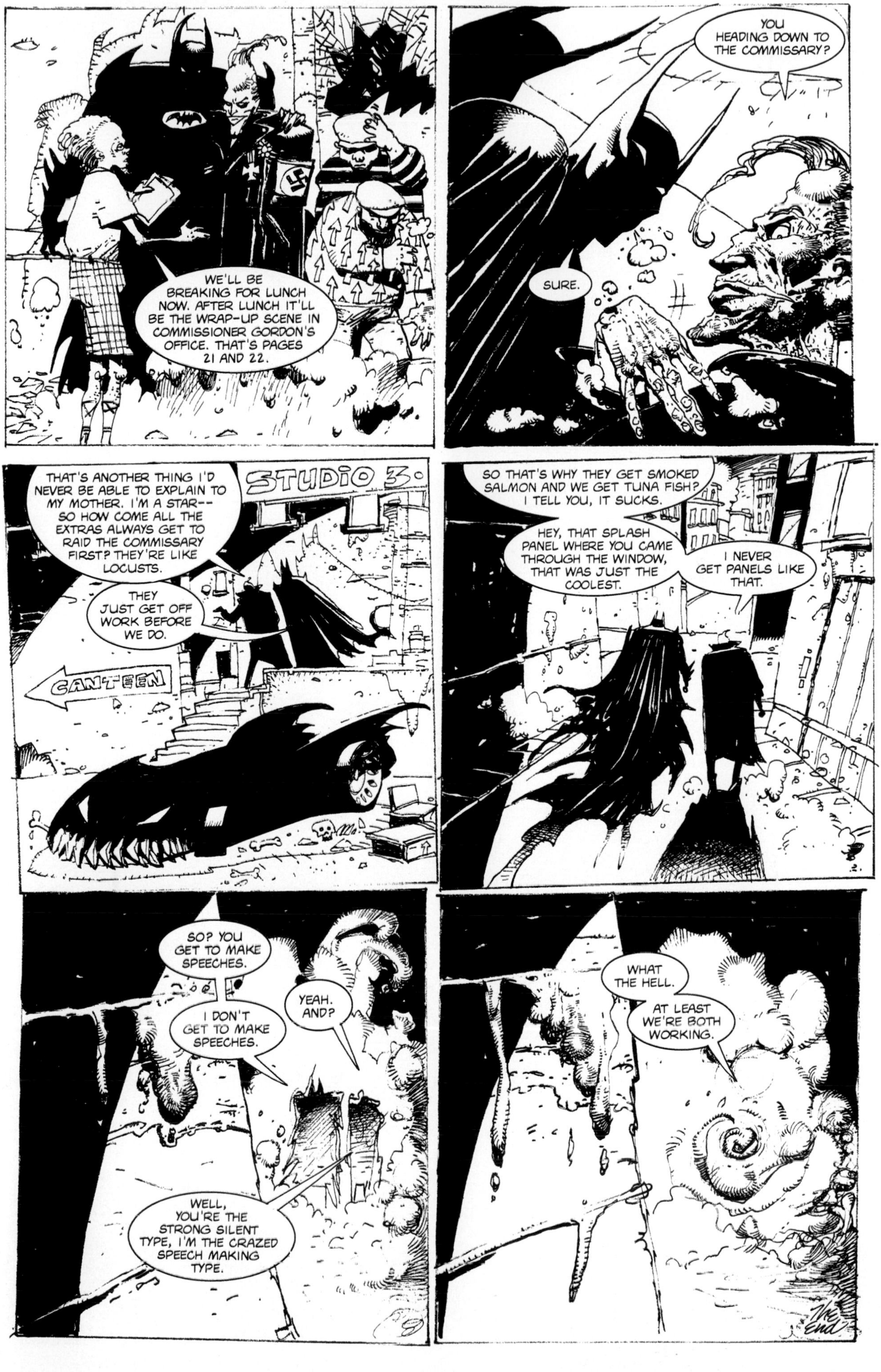
WE'LL BE BREAKING FOR LUNCH NOW. AFTER LUNCH IT'LL BE THE WRAP-UP SCENE IN COMMISSIONER GORDON'S OFFICE. THAT'S PAGES 21 AND 22.
YOU HEADING DOWN TO THE COMMISSARY?
SURE.
STUDIO 3
THAT'S ANOTHER THING I'D NEVER BE ABLE TO EXPLAIN TO MY MOTHER. I'M A STAR-- SO HOW COME ALL THE EXTRAS ALWAYS GET TO RAID THE COMMISSARY FIRST? THEY'RE LIKE LOCUSTS.
THEY JUST GET OFF WORK BEFORE WE DO.
CANTEEN
SO THAT'S WHY THEY GET SMOKED SALMON AND WE GET TUNA FISH? I TELL YOU, IT SUCKS.
HEY, THAT SPLASH PANEL WHERE YOU CAME THROUGH THE WINDOW, THAT WAS JUST THE COOLEST.
I NEVER GET PANELS LIKE THAT.
SO? YOU GET TO MAKE SPEECHES.
I DON'T GET TO MAKE SPEECHES.
YEAH. AND?
WELL, YOU'RE THE STRONG SILENT TYPE, I'M THE CRAZED SPEECH MAKING TYPE.
WHAT THE HELL.
AT LEAST WE'RE BOTH WORKING.
THE END

PAVANE

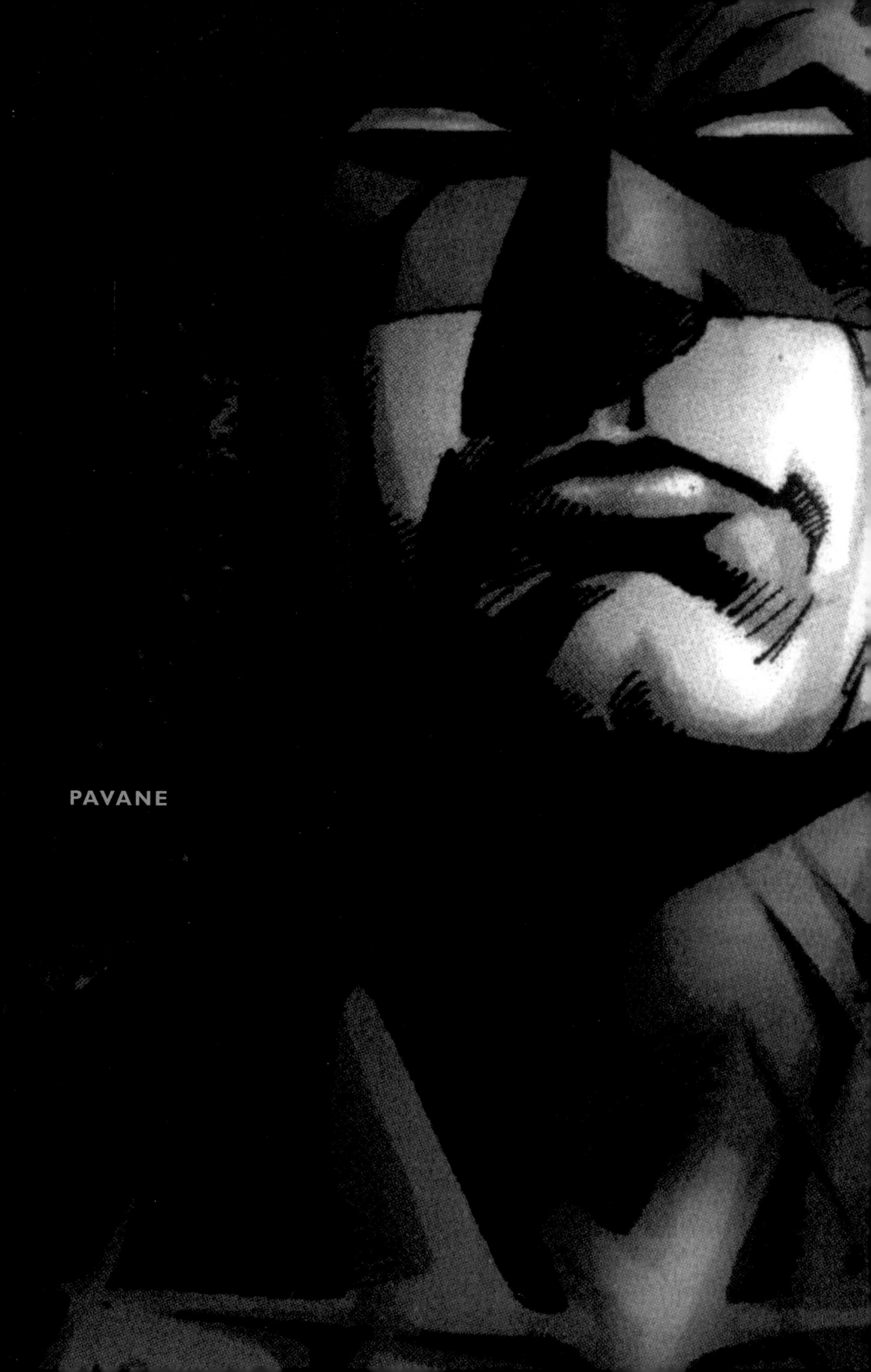

I CAN SEE HER ON THE MONITOR, STROKING A LILY-OF-THE-VALLEY, STARING OUT AT THE HILL. SHE'S ALWAYS ON THE SCREEN: AT NIGHT IT SWITCHES TO INFRA-RED.

YOU CAN TURN DOWN THE SOUND, BUT YOU CAN'T TURN OFF THE PICTURE.

RETURN TO THE FILES. IT'S BEEN THREE DAYS NOW, AND THE MORE MATERIAL COMES IN, THE MORE CONFUSING IT GETS.

I'VE GOT TO TALK TO HER. TAKE THE FBI FILE, THE CIA FILE, GOTHAM POLICE FILE, PRISON SERVICES FILE, PRESS CUTTINGS FILE...

UH, GUARD? PRISONER ISLEY

YESSIR THIS WAY, SIR

DOWN ECHOING, DISINFECTED CORRIDORS. PAST A GROUP OF PRISONERS RETURNING FROM THE FARM.

THEY STARE AT ME HUNGRILY, WHISPER AND JOKE TO EACH OTHER COARSELY IN LOW VOICES.

I STARE STRAIGHT AHEAD, SWALLOW, PRETEND NOT TO NOTICE

DO THEY UPSET YOU?

WHAT? OH. N-NOOO, I CAN UNDERSTAND THAT THEY DON'T GET TO SEE MANY MEN IN HERE. IT DOESN'T BOTHER ME I'M A PROFESSIONAL.

THAT'S GOOD.

WHY?

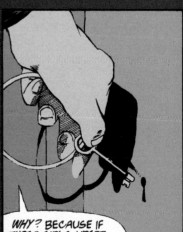

WHY? BECAUSE IF THOSE GIRLS UPSET YOU, THEN POISON IVY mmm, POISON IVY...

1

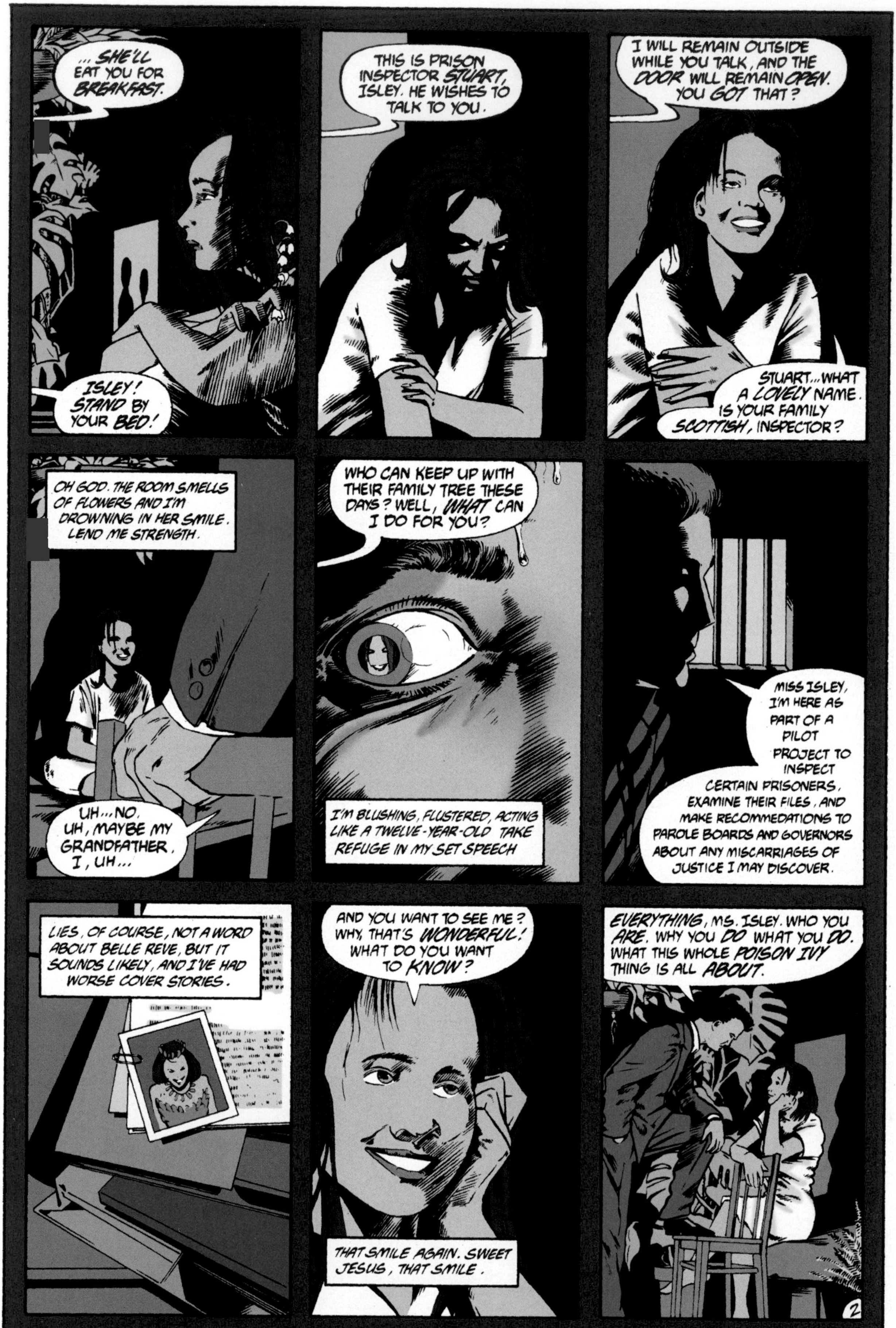
...SHE'LL EAT YOU FOR BREAKFAST.
ISLEY! STAND BY YOUR BED!
THIS IS PRISON INSPECTOR STUART, ISLEY. HE WISHES TO TALK TO YOU.
I WILL REMAIN OUTSIDE WHILE YOU TALK, AND THE DOOR WILL REMAIN OPEN. YOU GOT THAT?
STUART...WHAT A LOVELY NAME. IS YOUR FAMILY SCOTTISH, INSPECTOR?
OH GOD. THE ROOM SMELLS OF FLOWERS AND I'M DROWNING IN HER SMILE. LEND ME STRENGTH.
UH...NO. UH, MAYBE MY GRANDFATHER. I, UH...
WHO CAN KEEP UP WITH THEIR FAMILY TREE THESE DAYS? WELL, WHAT CAN I DO FOR YOU?
I'M BLUSHING, FLUSTERED, ACTING LIKE A TWELVE-YEAR-OLD. TAKE REFUGE IN MY SET SPEECH
MISS ISLEY, I'M HERE AS PART OF A PILOT PROJECT TO INSPECT CERTAIN PRISONERS, EXAMINE THEIR FILES, AND MAKE RECOMMEDATIONS TO PAROLE BOARDS AND GOVERNORS ABOUT ANY MISCARRIAGES OF JUSTICE I MAY DISCOVER.
LIES, OF COURSE, NOT A WORD ABOUT BELLE REVE, BUT IT SOUNDS LIKELY, AND I'VE HAD WORSE COVER STORIES.
AND YOU WANT TO SEE ME? WHY, THAT'S WONDERFUL! WHAT DO YOU WANT TO KNOW?
THAT SMILE AGAIN. SWEET JESUS, THAT SMILE.
EVERYTHING, MS. ISLEY. WHO YOU ARE. WHY YOU DO WHAT YOU DO. WHAT THIS WHOLE POISON IVY THING IS ALL ABOUT.
2

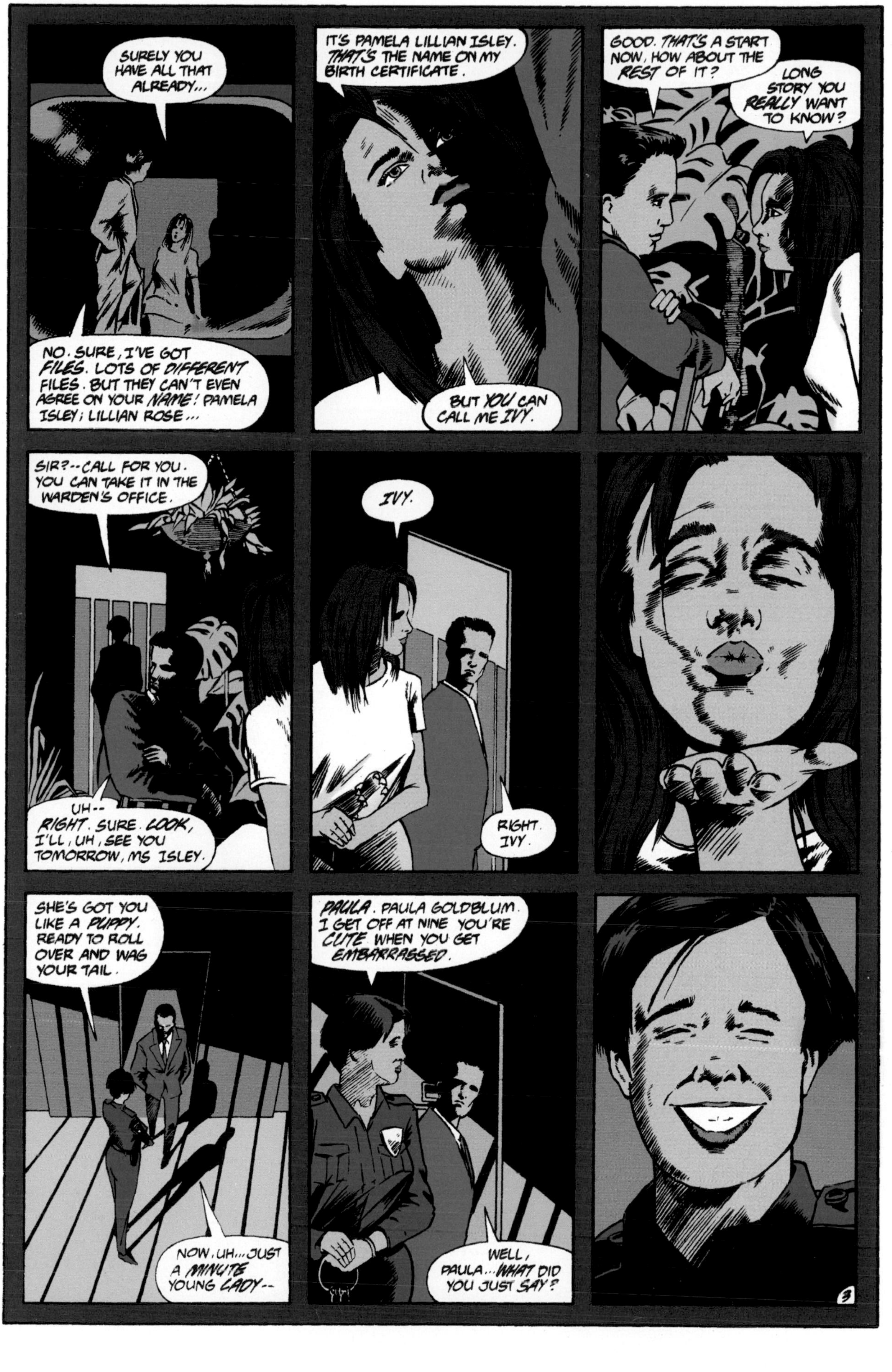
SURELY YOU HAVE ALL THAT ALREADY...
NO. SURE, I'VE GOT FILES. LOTS OF DIFFERENT FILES. BUT THEY CAN'T EVEN AGREE ON YOUR NAME! PAMELA ISLEY; LILLIAN ROSE...
IT'S PAMELA LILLIAN ISLEY. THAT'S THE NAME ON MY BIRTH CERTIFICATE.
BUT YOU CAN CALL ME IVY.
GOOD. THAT'S A START NOW, HOW ABOUT THE REST OF IT?
LONG STORY YOU REALLY WANT TO KNOW?
SIR?--CALL FOR YOU. YOU CAN TAKE IT IN THE WARDEN'S OFFICE.
UH--
RIGHT. SURE. LOOK, I'LL, UH, SEE YOU TOMORROW, MS ISLEY.
IVY.
RIGHT. IVY.
SHE'S GOT YOU LIKE A PUPPY. READY TO ROLL OVER AND WAG YOUR TAIL.
NOW, UH...JUST A MINUTE YOUNG LADY--
PAULA. PAULA GOLDBLUM. I GET OFF AT NINE. YOU'RE CUTE WHEN YOU GET EMBARRASSED.
WELL, PAULA...WHAT DID YOU JUST SAY?
3

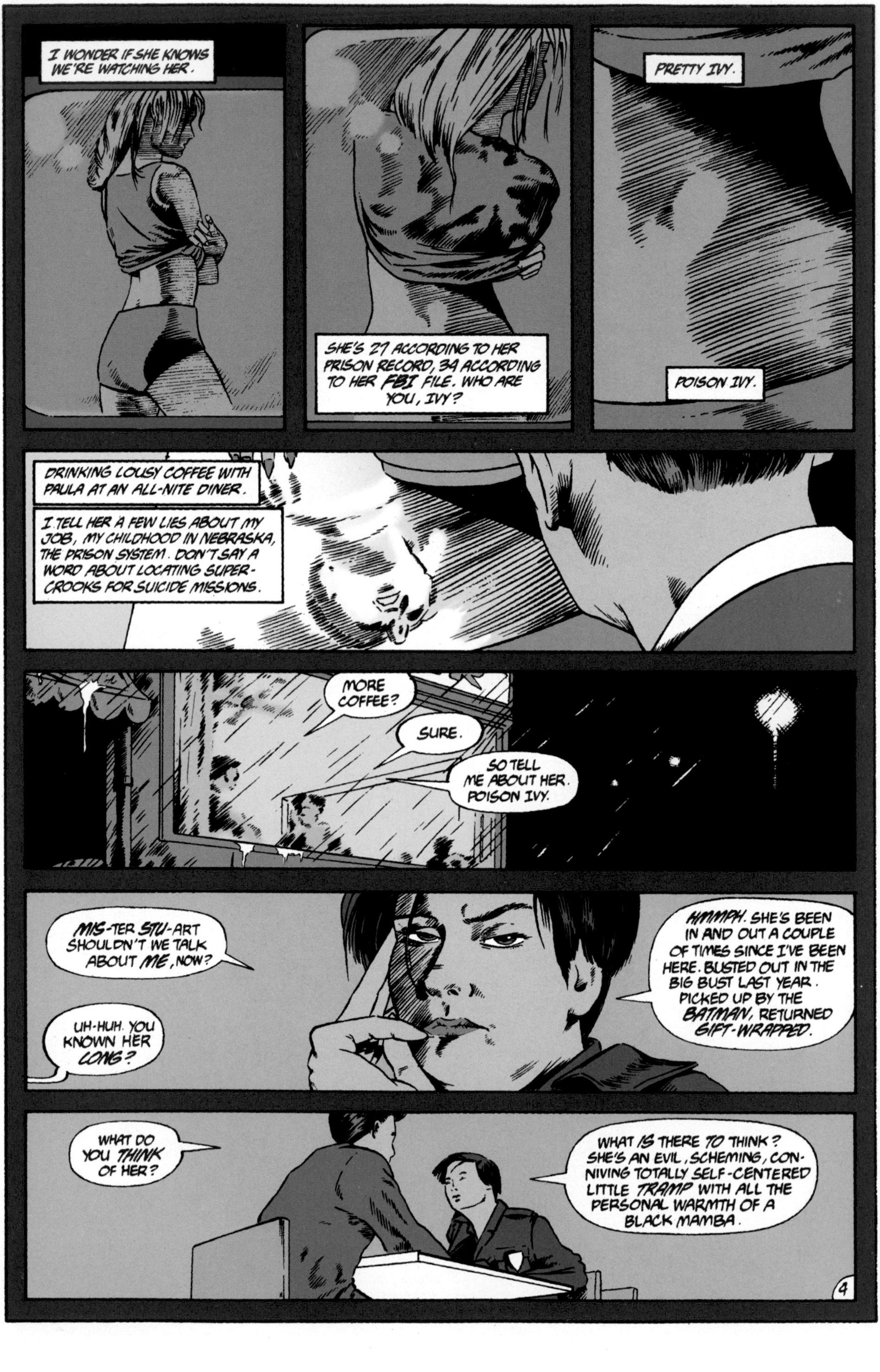
I WONDER IF SHE KNOWS WE'RE WATCHING HER.
SHE'S 27 ACCORDING TO HER PRISON RECORD, 34 ACCORDING TO HER FBI FILE. WHO ARE YOU, IVY?
PRETTY IVY.
POISON IVY.
DRINKING LOUSY COFFEE WITH PAULA AT AN ALL-NITE DINER.
I TELL HER A FEW LIES ABOUT MY JOB, MY CHILDHOOD IN NEBRASKA, THE PRISON SYSTEM. DON'T SAY A WORD ABOUT LOCATING SUPER-CROOKS FOR SUICIDE MISSIONS.
MORE COFFEE?
SURE.
SO TELL ME ABOUT HER. POISON IVY.
MIS-TER STU-ART SHOULDN'T WE TALK ABOUT ME, NOW?
UH-HUH. YOU KNOWN HER LONG?
HMMPH. SHE'S BEEN IN AND OUT A COUPLE OF TIMES SINCE I'VE BEEN HERE. BUSTED OUT IN THE BIG BUST LAST YEAR. PICKED UP BY THE BATMAN, RETURNED GIFT-WRAPPED.
WHAT DO YOU THINK OF HER?
WHAT IS THERE TO THINK? SHE'S AN EVIL, SCHEMING, CONNIVING TOTALLY SELF-CENTERED LITTLE TRAMP WITH ALL THE PERSONAL WARMTH OF A BLACK MAMBA.
4

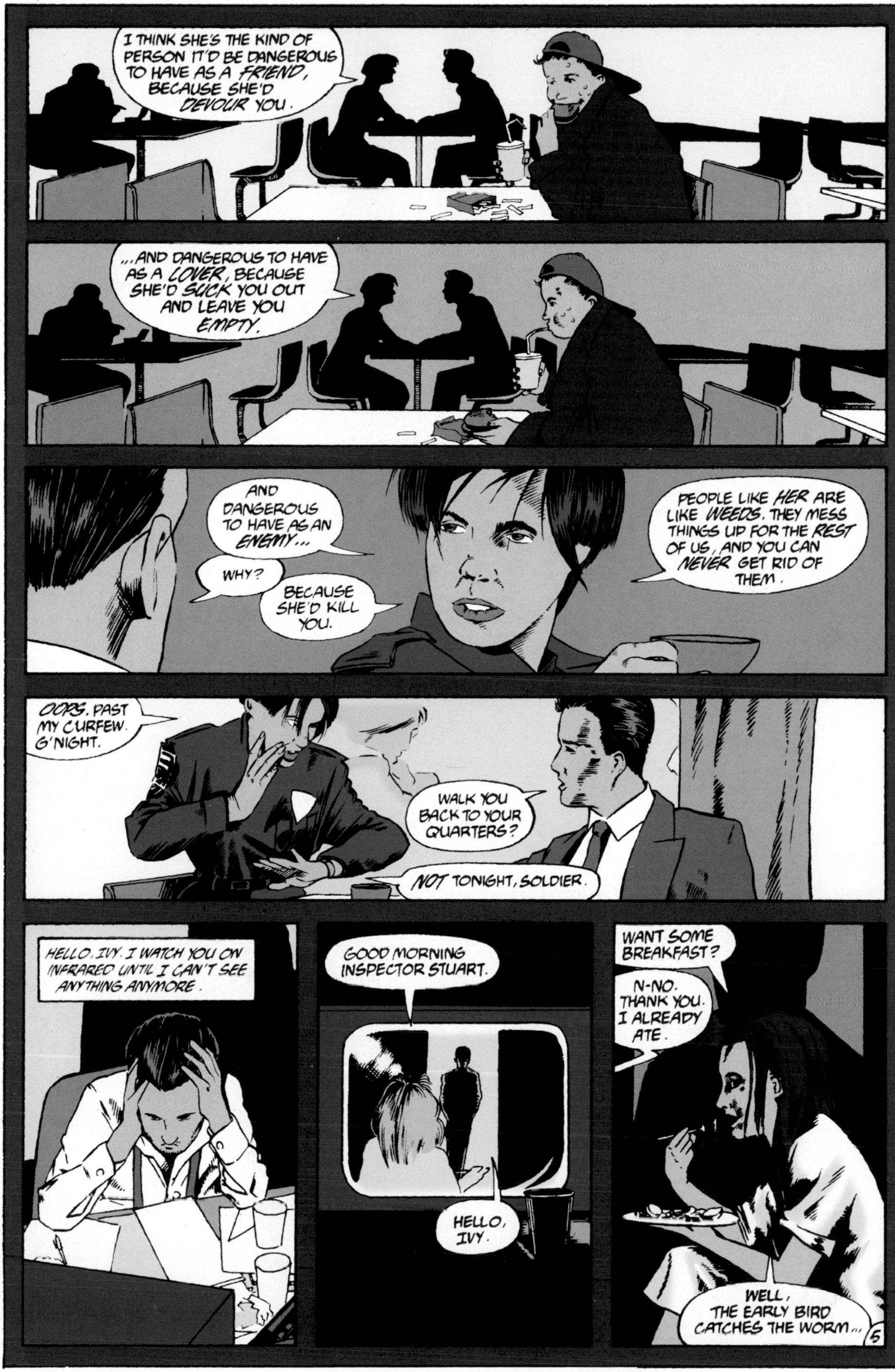
I THINK SHE'S THE KIND OF PERSON IT'D BE DANGEROUS TO HAVE AS A FRIEND, BECAUSE SHE'D DEVOUR YOU.
...AND DANGEROUS TO HAVE AS A LOVER, BECAUSE SHE'D SUCK YOU OUT AND LEAVE YOU EMPTY.
AND DANGEROUS TO HAVE AS AN ENEMY...
WHY?
BECAUSE SHE'D KILL YOU.
PEOPLE LIKE HER ARE LIKE WEEDS. THEY MESS THINGS UP FOR THE REST OF US, AND YOU CAN NEVER GET RID OF THEM.
OOPS. PAST MY CURFEW. G'NIGHT.
WALK YOU BACK TO YOUR QUARTERS?
NOT TONIGHT, SOLDIER.
HELLO, IVY. I WATCH YOU ON INFRARED UNTIL I CAN'T SEE ANYTHING ANYMORE.
GOOD MORNING INSPECTOR STUART.
HELLO, IVY.
WANT SOME BREAKFAST?
N-NO. THANK YOU. I ALREADY ATE.
WELL, THE EARLY BIRD CATCHES THE WORM...

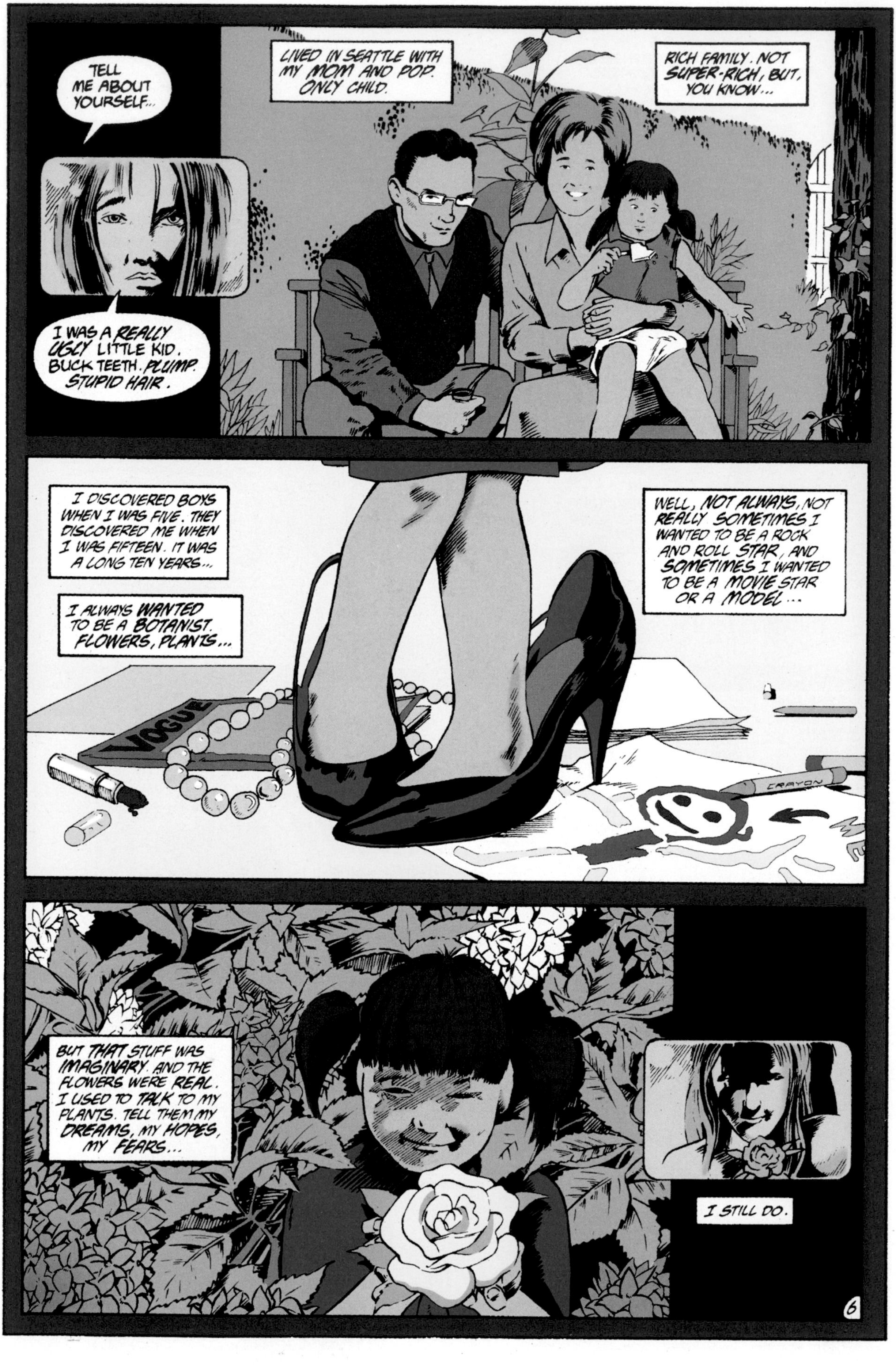
TELL ME ABOUT YOURSELF...
I WAS A REALLY UGLY LITTLE KID. BUCK TEETH. PLUMP. STUPID HAIR.
LIVED IN SEATTLE WITH MY MOM AND POP. ONLY CHILD.
RICH FAMILY. NOT SUPER-RICH, BUT, YOU KNOW...
I DISCOVERED BOYS WHEN I WAS FIVE. THEY DISCOVERED ME WHEN I WAS FIFTEEN. IT WAS A LONG TEN YEARS...
I ALWAYS WANTED TO BE A BOTANIST. FLOWERS, PLANTS...
WELL, NOT ALWAYS, NOT REALLY. SOMETIMES I WANTED TO BE A ROCK AND ROLL STAR, AND SOMETIMES I WANTED TO BE A MOVIE STAR OR A MODEL...
VOGUE
CRAYON
ME
BUT THAT STUFF WAS IMAGINARY. AND THE FLOWERS WERE REAL. I USED TO TALK TO MY PLANTS. TELL THEM MY DREAMS, MY HOPES, MY FEARS...
I STILL DO.
6

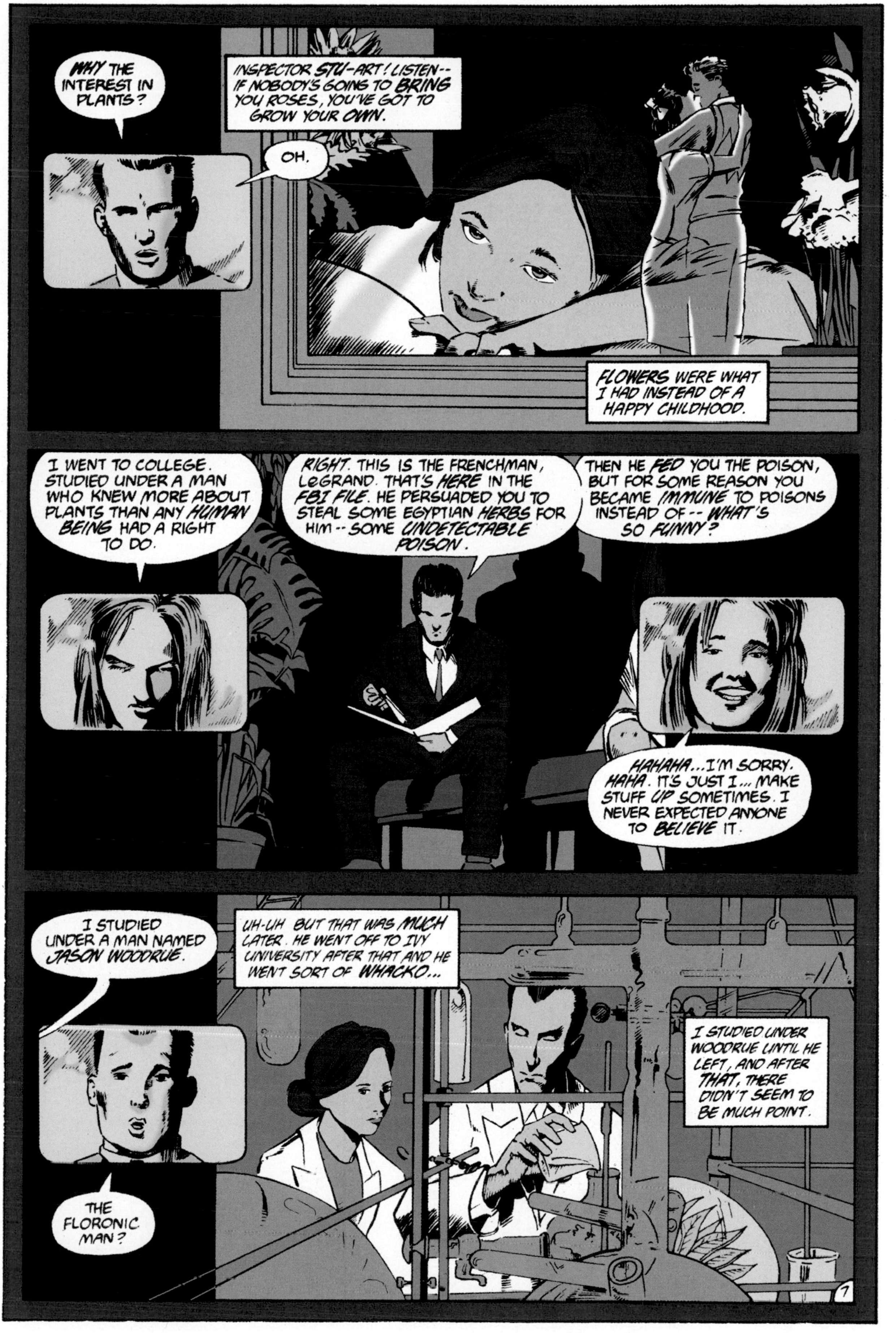

WHY THE INTEREST IN PLANTS?
INSPECTOR STU-ART! LISTEN-- IF NOBODY'S GOING TO BRING YOU ROSES, YOU'VE GOT TO GROW YOUR OWN.
OH.
FLOWERS WERE WHAT I HAD INSTEAD OF A HAPPY CHILDHOOD.
I WENT TO COLLEGE. STUDIED UNDER A MAN WHO KNEW MORE ABOUT PLANTS THAN ANY HUMAN BEING HAD A RIGHT TO DO.
RIGHT. THIS IS THE FRENCHMAN, LeGRAND. THAT'S HERE IN THE FBI FILE. HE PERSUADED YOU TO STEAL SOME EGYPTIAN HERBS FOR HIM -- SOME UNDETECTABLE POISON.
THEN HE FED YOU THE POISON, BUT FOR SOME REASON YOU BECAME IMMUNE TO POISONS INSTEAD OF -- WHAT'S SO FUNNY?
HAHAHA... I'M SORRY. HAHA. IT'S JUST I... MAKE STUFF UP SOMETIMES. I NEVER EXPECTED ANYONE TO BELIEVE IT.
I STUDIED UNDER A MAN NAMED JASON WOODRUE.
UH-UH BUT THAT WAS MUCH LATER. HE WENT OFF TO IVY UNIVERSITY AFTER THAT AND HE WENT SORT OF WHACKO...
I STUDIED UNDER WOODRUE UNTIL HE LEFT, AND AFTER THAT, THERE DIDN'T SEEM TO BE MUCH POINT.
THE FLORONIC MAN?
7

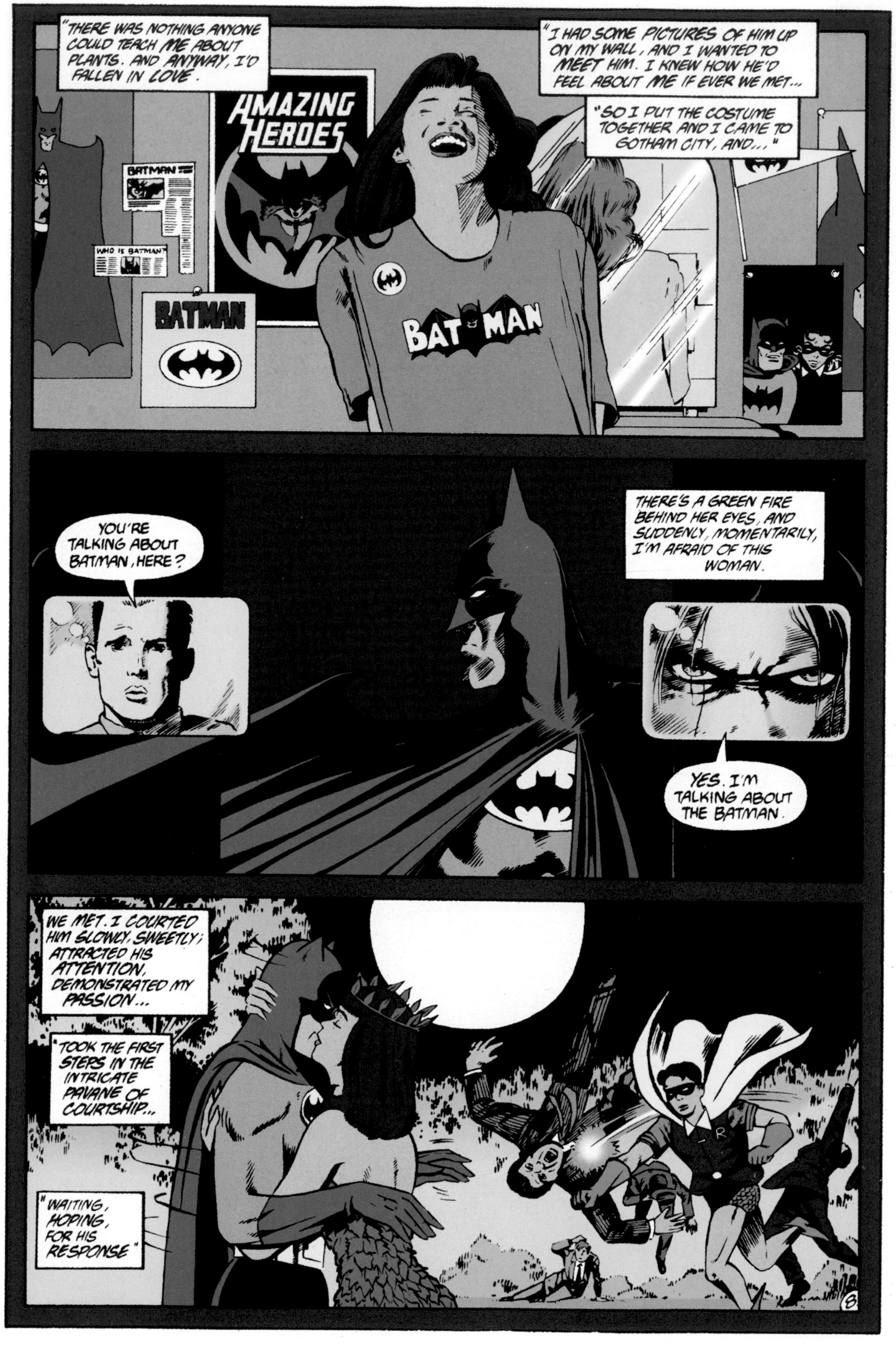
"THERE WAS NOTHING ANYONE COULD TEACH ME ABOUT PLANTS. AND ANYWAY, I'D FALLEN IN LOVE.
"I HAD SOME PICTURES OF HIM UP ON MY WALL, AND I WANTED TO MEET HIM. I KNEW HOW HE'D FEEL ABOUT ME IF EVER WE MET...
"SO I PUT THE COSTUME TOGETHER AND I CAME TO GOTHAM CITY, AND..."
AMAZING HEROES
BATMAN
WHO IS BATMAN?
BATMAN
BATMAN
YOU'RE TALKING ABOUT BATMAN, HERE?
THERE'S A GREEN FIRE BEHIND HER EYES, AND SUDDENLY, MOMENTARILY, I'M AFRAID OF THIS WOMAN.
YES. I'M TALKING ABOUT THE BATMAN.
WE MET. I COURTED HIM SLOWLY, SWEETLY; ATTRACTED HIS ATTENTION, DEMONSTRATED MY PASSION...
"TOOK THE FIRST STEPS IN THE INTRICATE PAVANE OF COURTSHIP...
"WAITING, HOPING, FOR HIS RESPONSE"
R
8

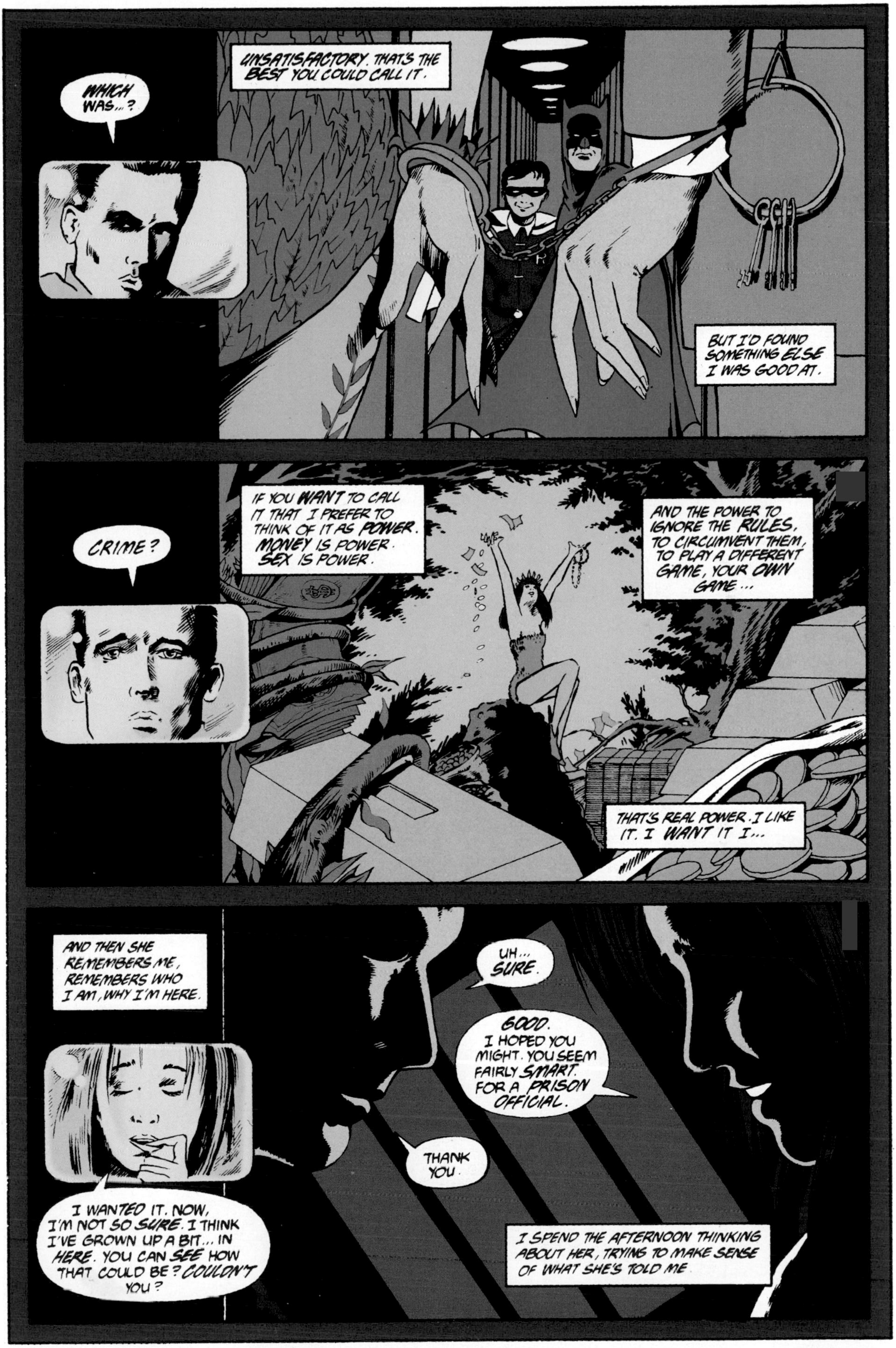
UNSATISFACTORY. THAT'S THE BEST YOU COULD CALL IT.
WHICH WAS...?
BUT I'D FOUND SOMETHING ELSE I WAS GOOD AT.
CRIME?
IF YOU WANT TO CALL IT THAT. I PREFER TO THINK OF IT AS POWER. MONEY IS POWER. SEX IS POWER.
AND THE POWER TO IGNORE THE RULES, TO CIRCUMVENT THEM, TO PLAY A DIFFERENT GAME, YOUR OWN GAME...
THAT'S REAL POWER. I LIKE IT. I WANT IT. I...
AND THEN SHE REMEMBERS ME, REMEMBERS WHO I AM, WHY I'M HERE.
I WANTED IT. NOW, I'M NOT SO SURE. I THINK I'VE GROWN UP A BIT... IN HERE. YOU CAN SEE HOW THAT COULD BE? COULDN'T YOU?
UH... SURE.
GOOD. I HOPED YOU MIGHT. YOU SEEM FAIRLY SMART. FOR A PRISON OFFICIAL.
THANK YOU.
I SPEND THE AFTERNOON THINKING ABOUT HER, TRYING TO MAKE SENSE OF WHAT SHE'S TOLD ME.

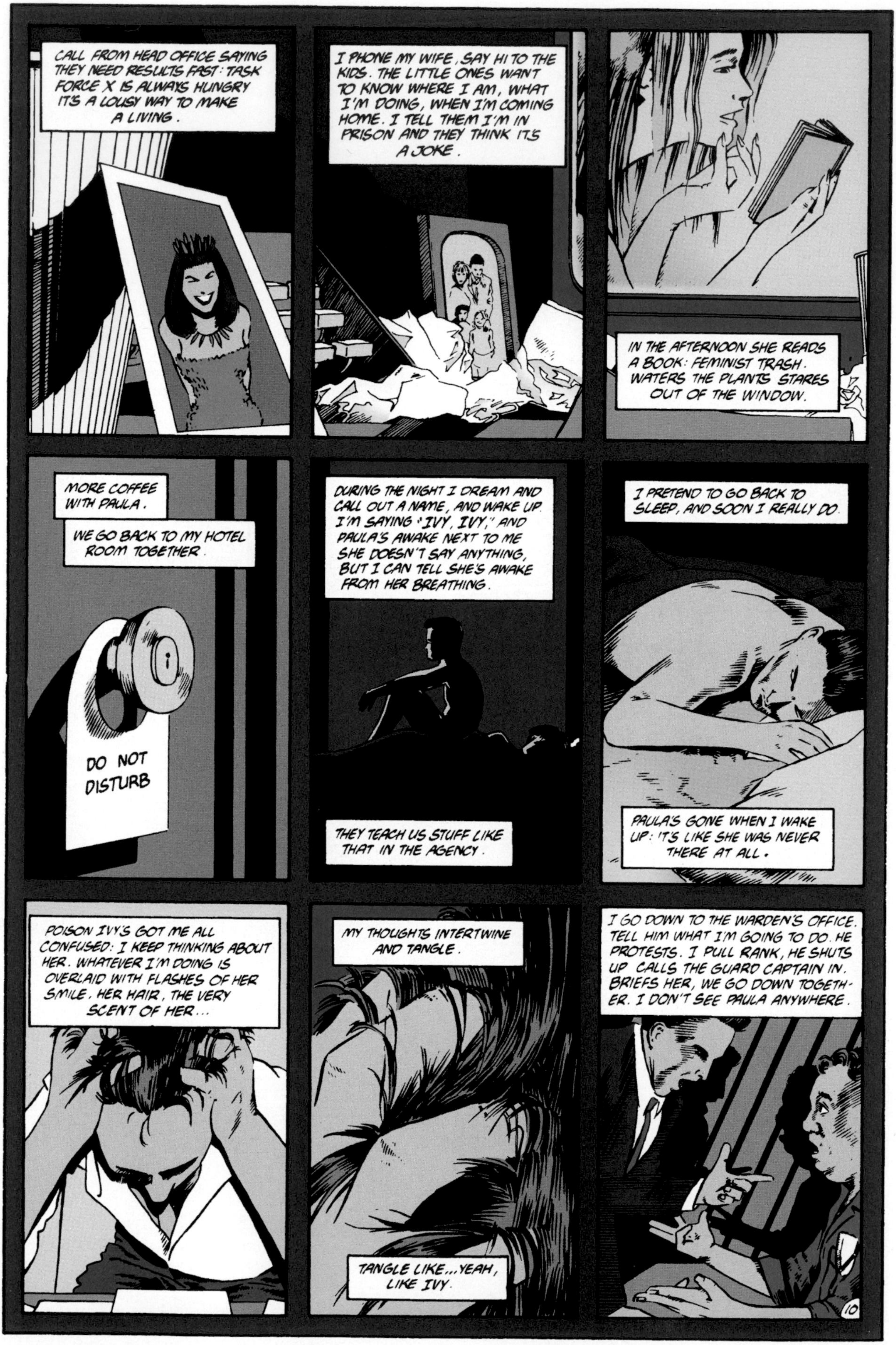
CALL FROM HEAD OFFICE SAYING THEY NEED RESULTS FAST: TASK FORCE X IS ALWAYS HUNGRY IT'S A LOUSY WAY TO MAKE A LIVING.
I PHONE MY WIFE, SAY HI TO THE KIDS. THE LITTLE ONES WANT TO KNOW WHERE I AM, WHAT I'M DOING, WHEN I'M COMING HOME. I TELL THEM I'M IN PRISON AND THEY THINK IT'S A JOKE.
IN THE AFTERNOON SHE READS A BOOK: FEMINIST TRASH. WATERS THE PLANTS STARES OUT OF THE WINDOW.
MORE COFFEE WITH PAULA.
WE GO BACK TO MY HOTEL ROOM TOGETHER.
DO NOT DISTURB
DURING THE NIGHT I DREAM AND CALL OUT A NAME, AND WAKE UP I'M SAYING "IVY, IVY," AND PAULA'S AWAKE NEXT TO ME SHE DOESN'T SAY ANYTHING, BUT I CAN TELL SHE'S AWAKE FROM HER BREATHING.
THEY TEACH US STUFF LIKE THAT IN THE AGENCY.
I PRETEND TO GO BACK TO SLEEP, AND SOON I REALLY DO.
PAULA'S GONE WHEN I WAKE UP: IT'S LIKE SHE WAS NEVER THERE AT ALL.
POISON IVY'S GOT ME ALL CONFUSED: I KEEP THINKING ABOUT HER. WHATEVER I'M DOING IS OVERLAID WITH FLASHES OF HER SMILE. HER HAIR, THE VERY SCENT OF HER...
MY THOUGHTS INTERTWINE AND TANGLE.
TANGLE LIKE...YEAH, LIKE IVY.
I GO DOWN TO THE WARDEN'S OFFICE. TELL HIM WHAT I'M GOING TO DO. HE PROTESTS. I PULL RANK, HE SHUTS UP CALLS THE GUARD CAPTAIN IN. BRIEFS HER, WE GO DOWN TOGETHER. I DON'T SEE PAULA ANYWHERE.
10

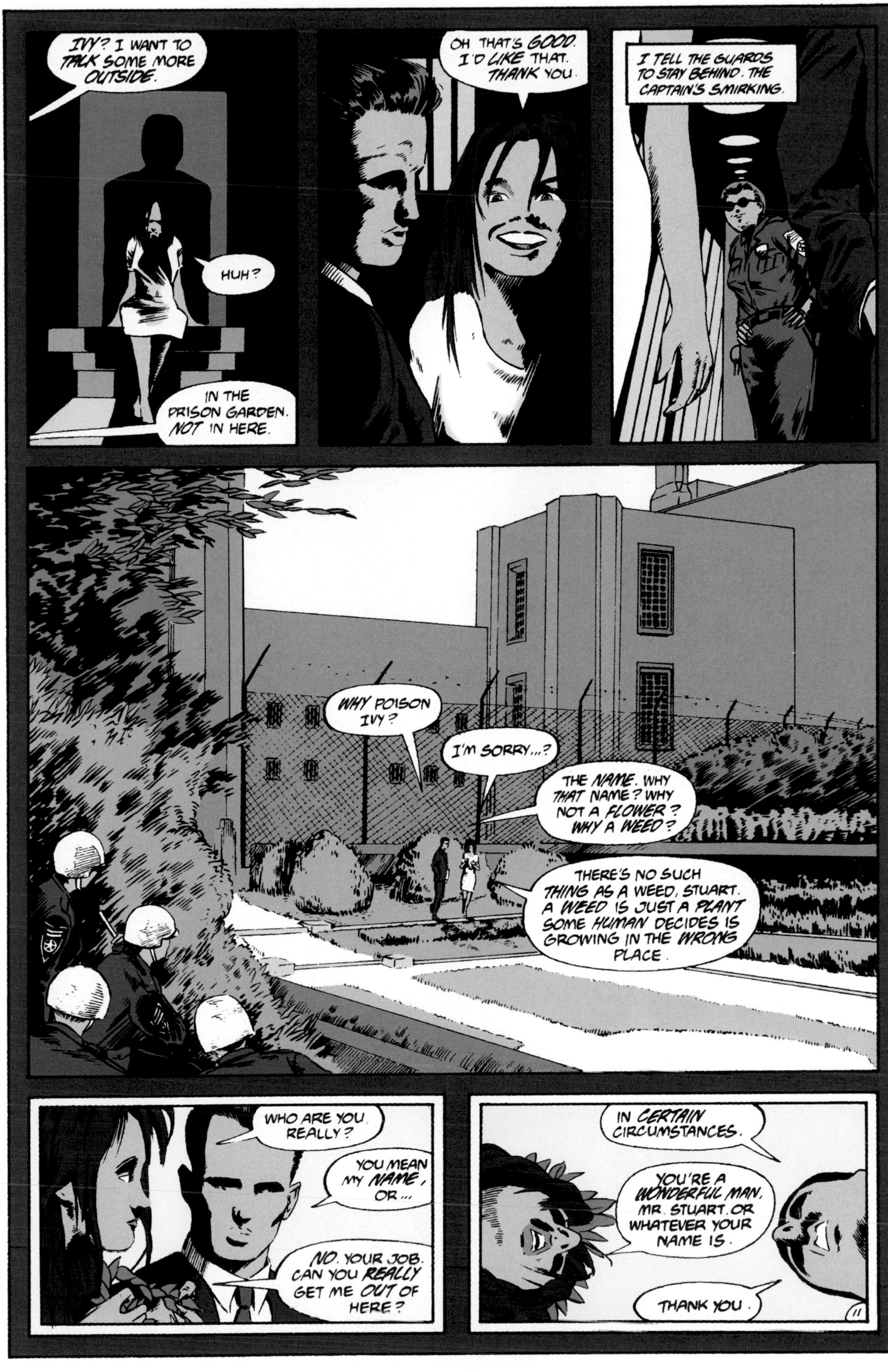
IVY? I WANT TO TALK SOME MORE OUTSIDE.
HUH?
IN THE PRISON GARDEN. NOT IN HERE.
OH THAT'S GOOD. I'D LIKE THAT. THANK YOU.
I TELL THE GUARDS TO STAY BEHIND. THE CAPTAIN'S SMIRKING.
WHY POISON IVY?
I'M SORRY...?
THE NAME. WHY THAT NAME? WHY NOT A FLOWER? WHY A WEED?
THERE'S NO SUCH THING AS A WEED, STUART. A WEED IS JUST A PLANT SOME HUMAN DECIDES IS GROWING IN THE WRONG PLACE.
WHO ARE YOU, REALLY?
YOU MEAN MY NAME, OR...
NO. YOUR JOB. CAN YOU REALLY GET ME OUT OF HERE?
IN CERTAIN CIRCUMSTANCES.
YOU'RE A WONDERFUL MAN, MR. STUART. OR WHATEVER YOUR NAME IS.
THANK YOU.
11

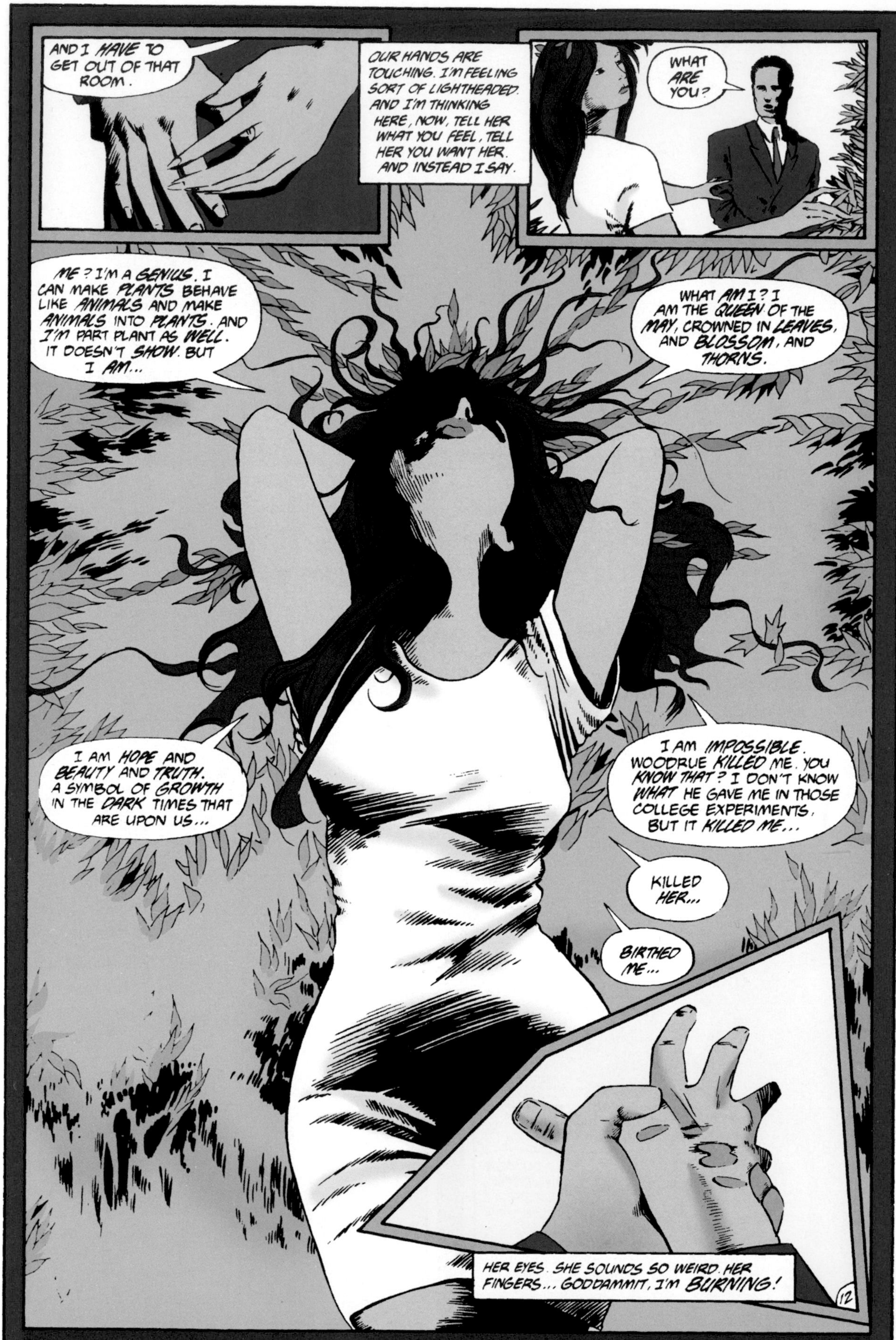
AND I HAVE TO GET OUT OF THAT ROOM.
OUR HANDS ARE TOUCHING. I'M FEELING SORT OF LIGHTHEADED. AND I'M THINKING HERE, NOW, TELL HER WHAT YOU FEEL, TELL HER YOU WANT HER. AND INSTEAD I SAY.
WHAT ARE YOU?
ME? I'M A GENIUS. I CAN MAKE PLANTS BEHAVE LIKE ANIMALS AND MAKE ANIMALS INTO PLANTS. AND I'M PART PLANT AS WELL. IT DOESN'T SHOW. BUT I AM...
WHAT AM I? I AM THE QUEEN OF THE MAY, CROWNED IN LEAVES, AND BLOSSOM, AND THORNS.
I AM HOPE AND BEAUTY AND TRUTH. A SYMBOL OF GROWTH IN THE DARK TIMES THAT ARE UPON US...
I AM IMPOSSIBLE. WOODRUE KILLED ME. YOU KNOW THAT? I DON'T KNOW WHAT HE GAVE ME IN THOSE COLLEGE EXPERIMENTS, BUT IT KILLED ME...
KILLED HER...
BIRTHED ME...
HER EYES. SHE SOUNDS SO WEIRD. HER FINGERS... GODDAMMIT, I'M BURNING!
12

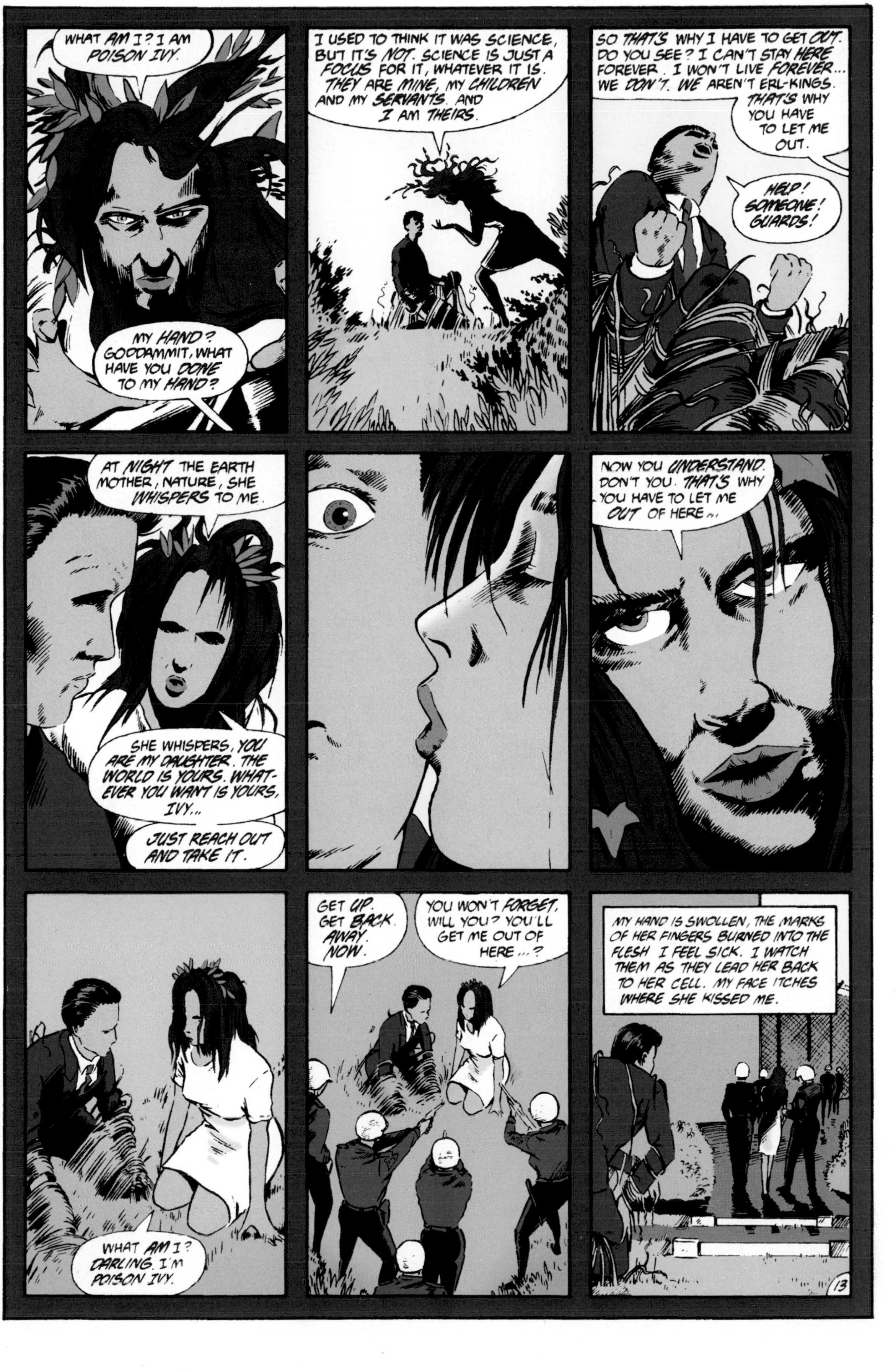
WHAT AM I? I AM POISON IVY.
MY HAND? GODDAMMIT, WHAT HAVE YOU DONE TO MY HAND?
I USED TO THINK IT WAS SCIENCE, BUT IT'S NOT. SCIENCE IS JUST A FOCUS FOR IT, WHATEVER IT IS. THEY ARE MINE, MY CHILDREN AND MY SERVANTS. AND I AM THEIRS.
SO THAT'S WHY I HAVE TO GET OUT. DO YOU SEE? I CAN'T STAY HERE FOREVER. I WON'T LIVE FOREVER... WE DON'T. WE AREN'T ERL-KINGS.
THAT'S WHY YOU HAVE TO LET ME OUT.
HELP! SOMEONE! GUARDS!
AT NIGHT THE EARTH MOTHER, NATURE, SHE WHISPERS TO ME.
SHE WHISPERS, YOU ARE MY DAUGHTER. THE WORLD IS YOURS. WHATEVER YOU WANT IS YOURS, IVY...
JUST REACH OUT AND TAKE IT.
NOW YOU UNDERSTAND. DON'T YOU. THAT'S WHY YOU HAVE TO LET ME OUT OF HERE...
WHAT AM I? DARLING. I'M POISON IVY.
GET UP. GET BACK. AWAY. NOW.
YOU WON'T FORGET, WILL YOU? YOU'LL GET ME OUT OF HERE...?
MY HAND IS SWOLLEN, THE MARKS OF HER FINGERS BURNED INTO THE FLESH. I FEEL SICK. I WATCH THEM AS THEY LEAD HER BACK TO HER CELL. MY FACE ITCHES WHERE SHE KISSED ME.
13

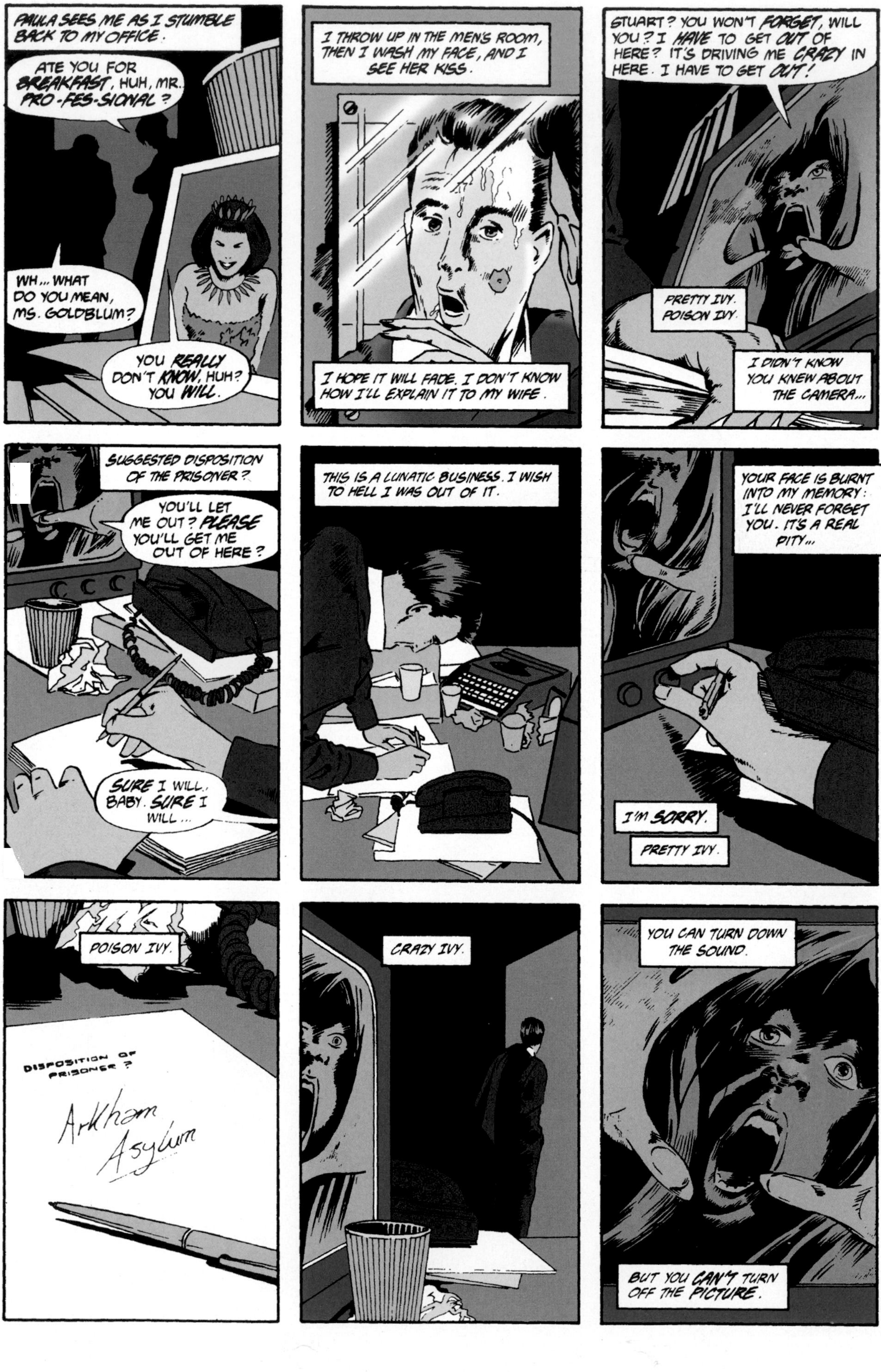
PAULA SEES ME AS I STUMBLE BACK TO MY OFFICE.
ATE YOU FOR BREAKFAST, HUH, MR. PRO-FES-SIONAL?
WH... WHAT DO YOU MEAN, MS. GOLDBLUM?
YOU REALLY DON'T KNOW, HUH? YOU WILL.
I THROW UP IN THE MEN'S ROOM, THEN I WASH MY FACE, AND I SEE HER KISS.
I HOPE IT WILL FADE. I DON'T KNOW HOW I'LL EXPLAIN IT TO MY WIFE.
STUART? YOU WON'T FORGET, WILL YOU? I HAVE TO GET OUT OF HERE? IT'S DRIVING ME CRAZY IN HERE. I HAVE TO GET OUT!
PRETTY IVY. POISON IVY.
I DIDN'T KNOW YOU KNEW ABOUT THE CAMERA...
SUGGESTED DISPOSITION OF THE PRISONER?
YOU'LL LET ME OUT? PLEASE YOU'LL GET ME OUT OF HERE?
SURE I WILL, BABY. SURE I WILL...
THIS IS A LUNATIC BUSINESS. I WISH TO HELL I WAS OUT OF IT.
YOUR FACE IS BURNT INTO MY MEMORY: I'LL NEVER FORGET YOU. IT'S A REAL PITY...
I'M SORRY.
PRETTY IVY.
POISON IVY.
DISPOSITION OF PRISONER?
Arkham Asylum
CRAZY IVY.
YOU CAN TURN DOWN THE SOUND.
BUT YOU CAN'T TURN OFF THE PICTURE.

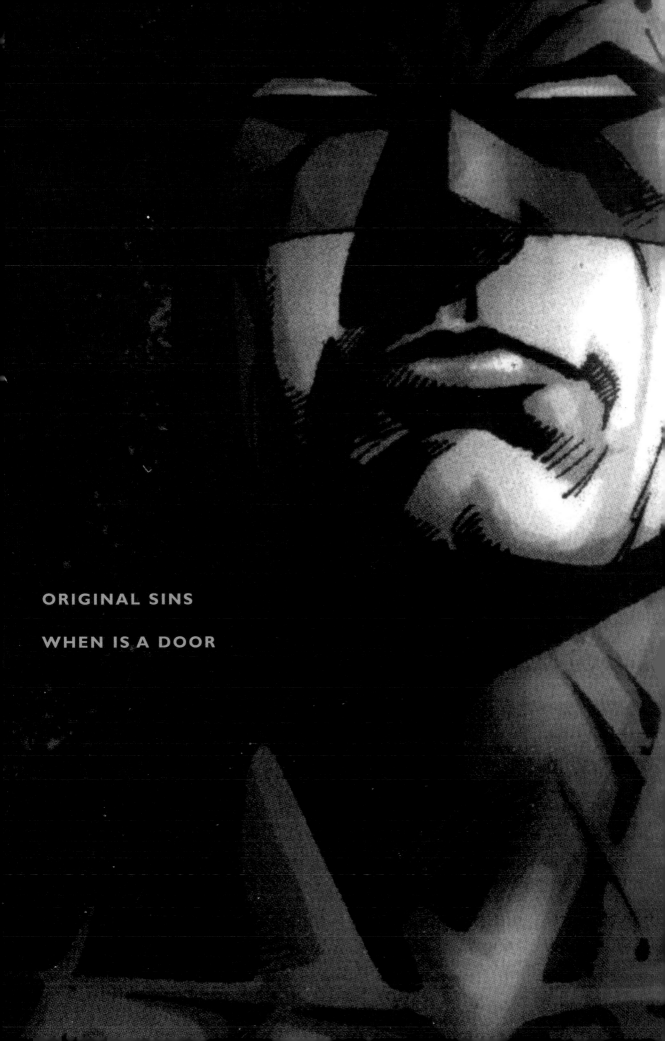

ORIGINAL SINS

WHEN IS A DOOR

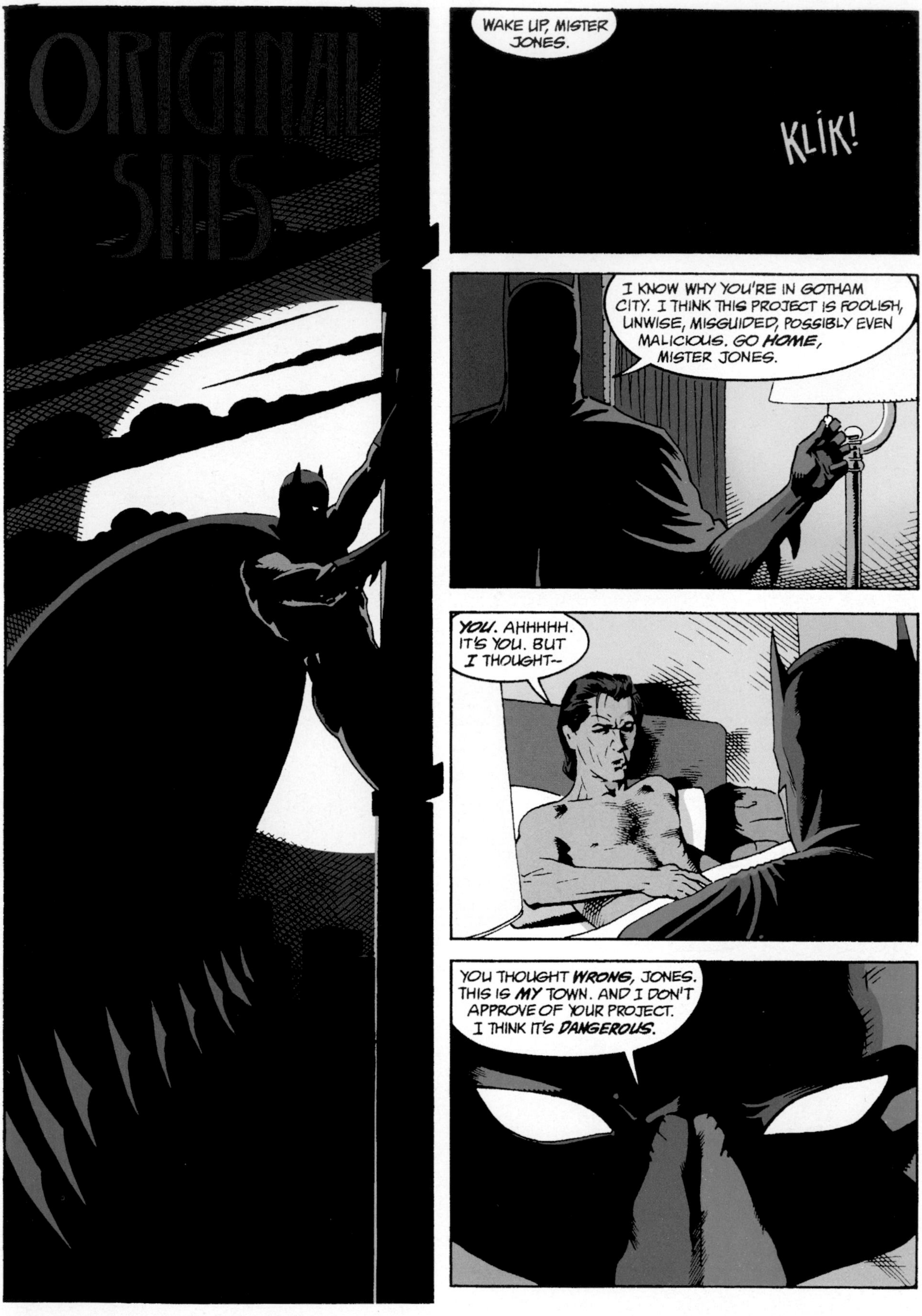
ORIGINAL SINS
WAKE UP, MISTER JONES.
KLIK!
I KNOW WHY YOU'RE IN GOTHAM CITY. I THINK THIS PROJECT IS FOOLISH, UNWISE, MISGUIDED, POSSIBLY EVEN MALICIOUS. GO HOME, MISTER JONES.
YOU. AHHHHH. IT'S YOU. BUT I THOUGHT--
YOU THOUGHT WRONG, JONES. THIS IS MY TOWN. AND I DON'T APPROVE OF YOUR PROJECT. I THINK IT'S DANGEROUS.

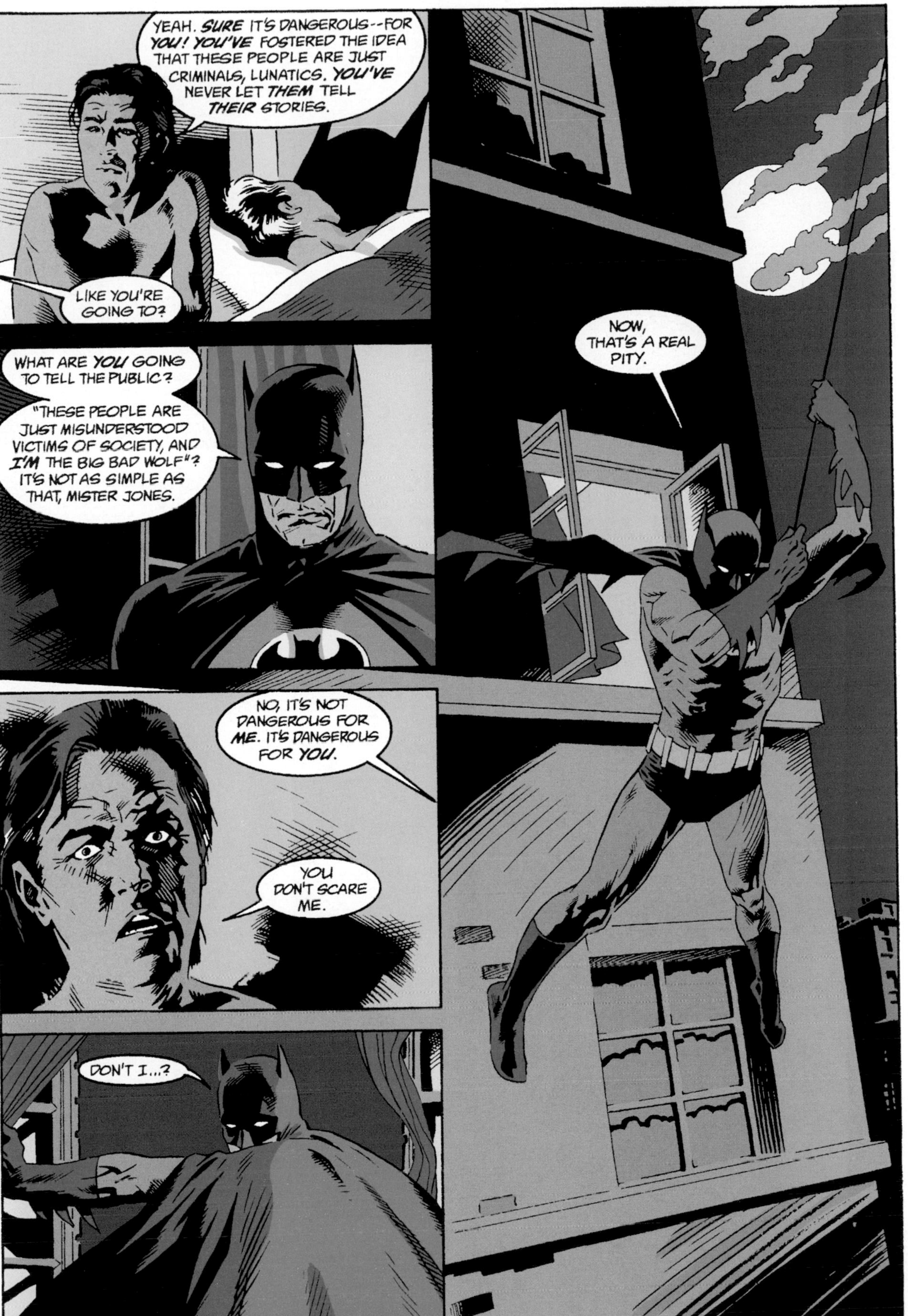
YEAH. SURE IT'S DANGEROUS--FOR YOU! YOU'VE FOSTERED THE IDEA THAT THESE PEOPLE ARE JUST CRIMINALS, LUNATICS. YOU'VE NEVER LET THEM TELL THEIR STORIES.
LIKE YOU'RE GOING TO?
WHAT ARE YOU GOING TO TELL THE PUBLIC?
"THESE PEOPLE ARE JUST MISUNDERSTOOD VICTIMS OF SOCIETY, AND I'M THE BIG BAD WOLF"? IT'S NOT AS SIMPLE AS THAT, MISTER JONES.
NO, IT'S NOT DANGEROUS FOR ME. IT'S DANGEROUS FOR YOU.
YOU DON'T SCARE ME.
DON'T I...?
NOW, THAT'S A REAL PITY.

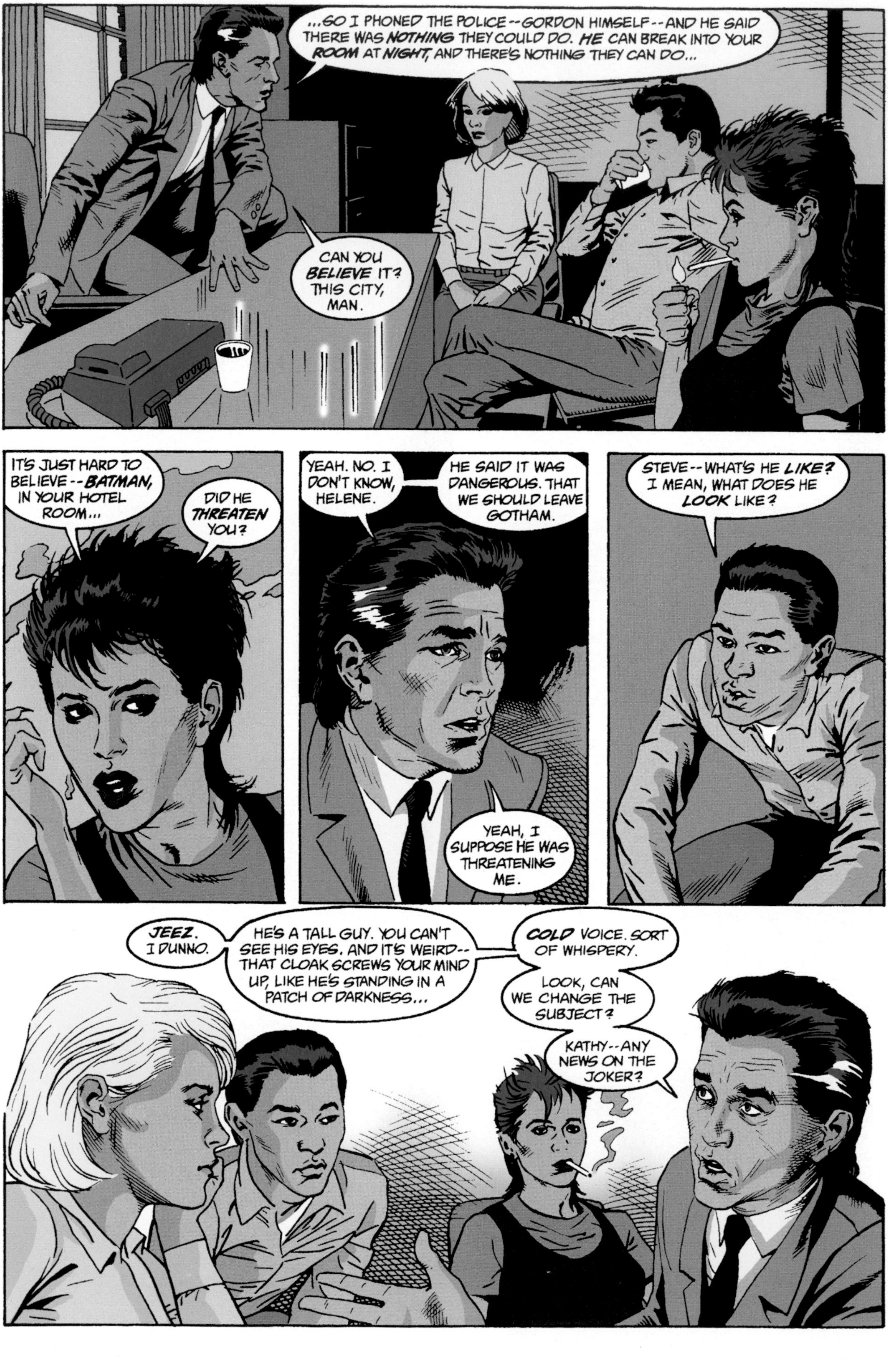
...SO I PHONED THE POLICE--GORDON HIMSELF--AND HE SAID THERE WAS NOTHING THEY COULD DO. HE CAN BREAK INTO YOUR ROOM AT NIGHT, AND THERE'S NOTHING THEY CAN DO...
CAN YOU BELIEVE IT? THIS CITY, MAN.
IT'S JUST HARD TO BELIEVE--BATMAN, IN YOUR HOTEL ROOM...
DID HE THREATEN YOU?
YEAH. NO. I DON'T KNOW, HELENE.
HE SAID IT WAS DANGEROUS. THAT WE SHOULD LEAVE GOTHAM.
YEAH, I SUPPOSE HE WAS THREATENING ME.
STEVE--WHAT'S HE LIKE? I MEAN, WHAT DOES HE LOOK LIKE?
JEEZ. I DUNNO.
HE'S A TALL GUY. YOU CAN'T SEE HIS EYES. AND IT'S WEIRD--THAT CLOAK SCREWS YOUR MIND UP, LIKE HE'S STANDING IN A PATCH OF DARKNESS...
COLD VOICE. SORT OF WHISPERY.
LOOK, CAN WE CHANGE THE SUBJECT?
KATHY--ANY NEWS ON THE JOKER?

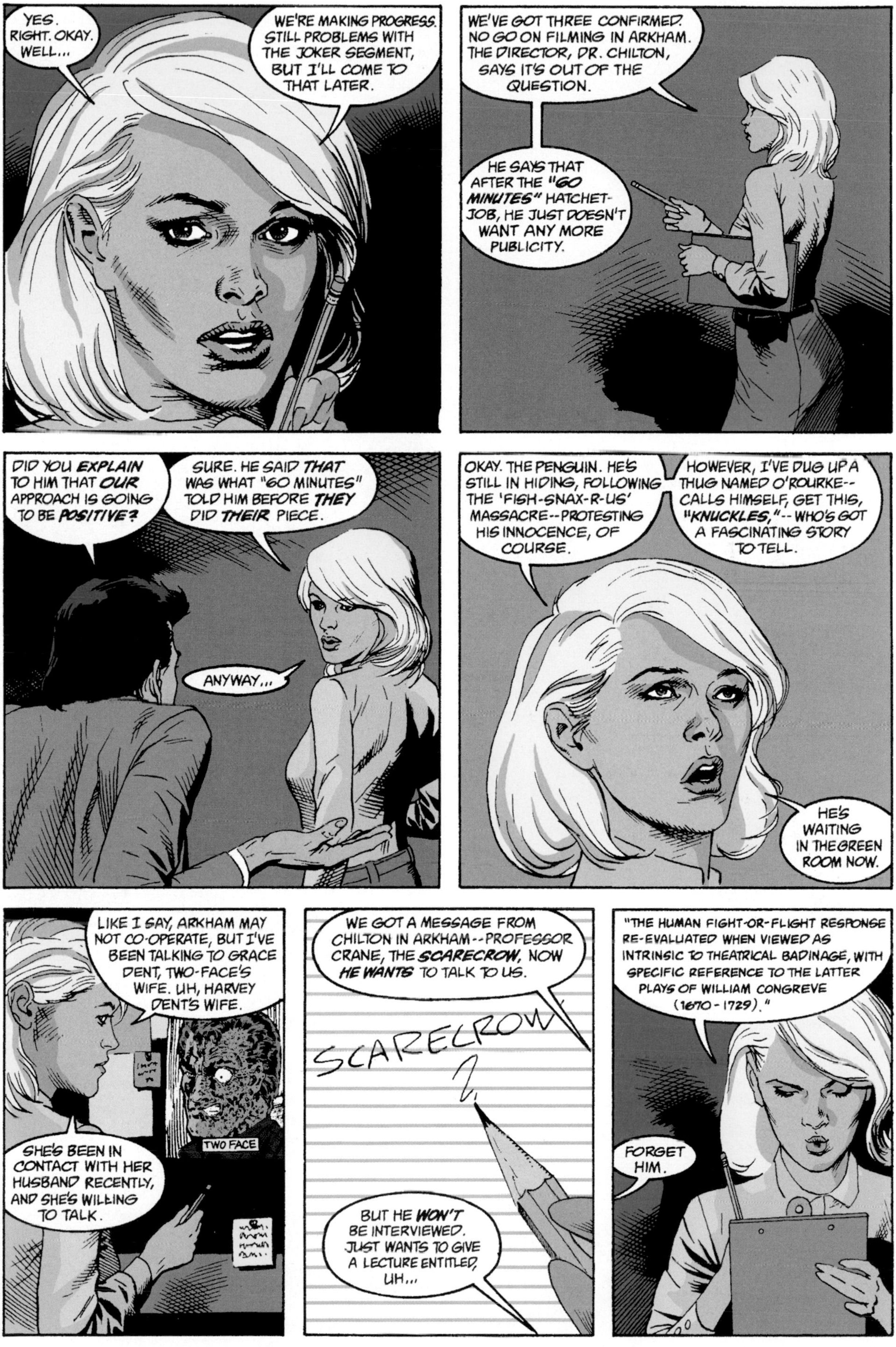

YES. RIGHT. OKAY. WELL...
WE'RE MAKING PROGRESS. STILL PROBLEMS WITH THE JOKER SEGMENT, BUT I'LL COME TO THAT LATER.
WE'VE GOT THREE CONFIRMED. NO GO ON FILMING IN ARKHAM. THE DIRECTOR, DR. CHILTON, SAYS IT'S OUT OF THE QUESTION.
HE SAYS THAT AFTER THE "60 MINUTES" HATCHET-JOB, HE JUST DOESN'T WANT ANY MORE PUBLICITY.
DID YOU EXPLAIN TO HIM THAT OUR APPROACH IS GOING TO BE POSITIVE?
SURE. HE SAID THAT WAS WHAT "60 MINUTES" TOLD HIM BEFORE THEY DID THEIR PIECE.
ANYWAY...
OKAY. THE PENGUIN. HE'S STILL IN HIDING, FOLLOWING THE 'FISH-SNAX-R-US' MASSACRE--PROTESTING HIS INNOCENCE, OF COURSE.
HOWEVER, I'VE DUG UP A THUG NAMED O'ROURKE--CALLS HIMSELF, GET THIS, "KNUCKLES,"--WHO'S GOT A FASCINATING STORY TO TELL.
HE'S WAITING IN THE GREEN ROOM NOW.
LIKE I SAY, ARKHAM MAY NOT CO-OPERATE, BUT I'VE BEEN TALKING TO GRACE DENT, TWO-FACE'S WIFE. UH, HARVEY DENT'S WIFE.
TWO FACE
SHE'S BEEN IN CONTACT WITH HER HUSBAND RECENTLY, AND SHE'S WILLING TO TALK.
WE GOT A MESSAGE FROM CHILTON IN ARKHAM--PROFESSOR CRANE, THE SCARECROW, NOW HE WANTS TO TALK TO US.
SCARECROW ?
BUT HE WON'T BE INTERVIEWED. JUST WANTS TO GIVE A LECTURE ENTITLED, UH...
"THE HUMAN FIGHT-OR-FLIGHT RESPONSE RE-EVALUATED WHEN VIEWED AS INTRINSIC TO THEATRICAL BADINAGE, WITH SPECIFIC REFERENCE TO THE LATTER PLAYS OF WILLIAM CONGREVE (1670 - 1729)."
FORGET HIM.

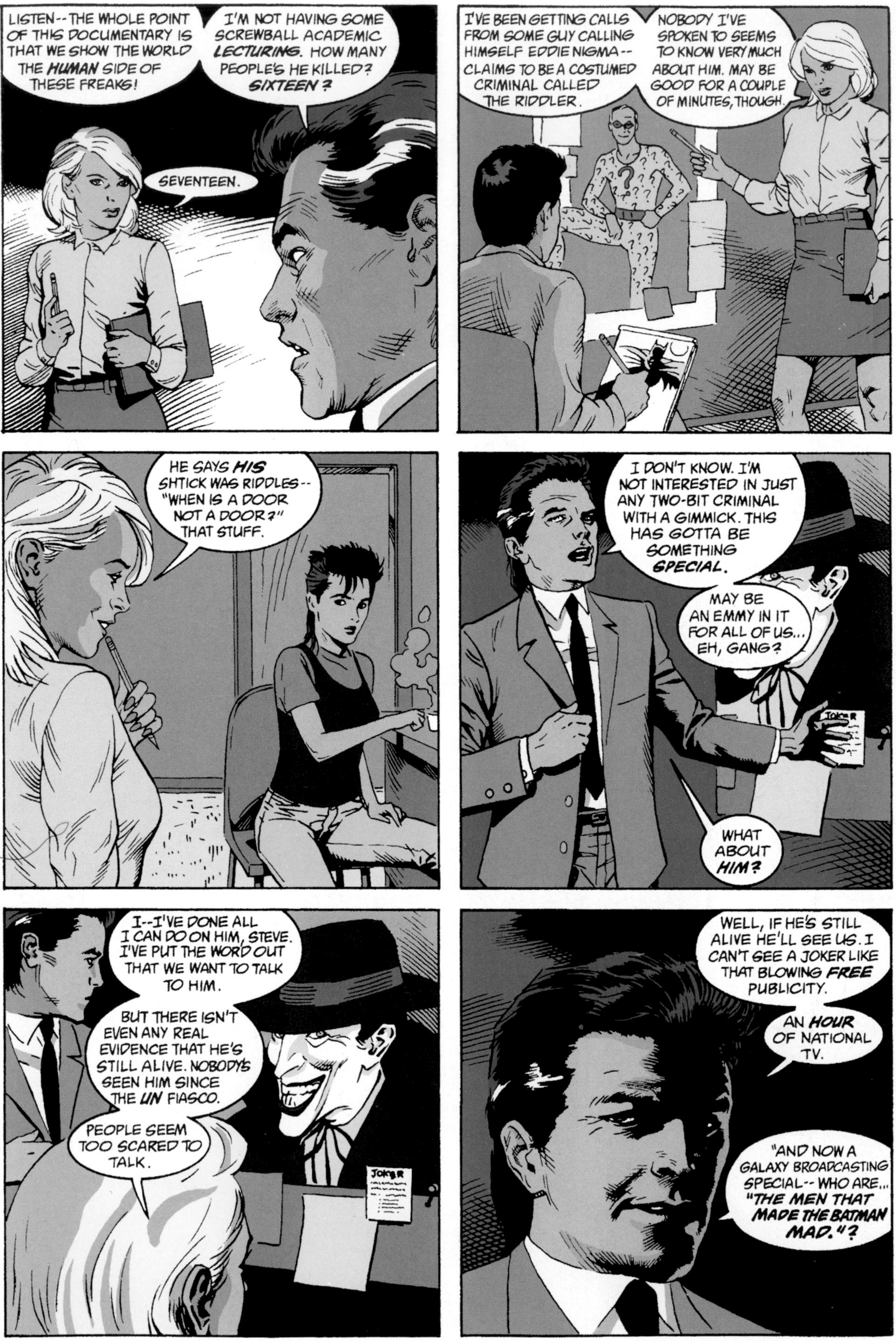

LISTEN-- THE WHOLE POINT OF THIS DOCUMENTARY IS THAT WE SHOW THE WORLD THE HUMAN SIDE OF THESE FREAKS!
I'M NOT HAVING SOME SCREWBALL ACADEMIC LECTURING. HOW MANY PEOPLE'S HE KILLED? SIXTEEN?
SEVENTEEN.
I'VE BEEN GETTING CALLS FROM SOME GUY CALLING HIMSELF EDDIE NIGMA-- CLAIMS TO BE A COSTUMED CRIMINAL CALLED THE RIDDLER.
NOBODY I'VE SPOKEN TO SEEMS TO KNOW VERY MUCH ABOUT HIM. MAY BE GOOD FOR A COUPLE OF MINUTES, THOUGH.
HE SAYS HIS SHTICK WAS RIDDLES-- "WHEN IS A DOOR NOT A DOOR?" THAT STUFF.
I DON'T KNOW. I'M NOT INTERESTED IN JUST ANY TWO-BIT CRIMINAL WITH A GIMMICK. THIS HAS GOTTA BE SOMETHING SPECIAL.
MAY BE AN EMMY IN IT FOR ALL OF US... EH, GANG?
JOKER
WHAT ABOUT HIM?
I--I'VE DONE ALL I CAN DO ON HIM, STEVE. I'VE PUT THE WORD OUT THAT WE WANT TO TALK TO HIM.
BUT THERE ISN'T EVEN ANY REAL EVIDENCE THAT HE'S STILL ALIVE. NOBODY'S SEEN HIM SINCE THE UN FIASCO.
PEOPLE SEEM TOO SCARED TO TALK.
JOKER
WELL, IF HE'S STILL ALIVE HE'LL SEE US. I CAN'T SEE A JOKER LIKE THAT BLOWING FREE PUBLICITY.
AN HOUR OF NATIONAL TV.
"AND NOW A GALAXY BROADCASTING SPECIAL-- WHO ARE... "THE MEN THAT MADE THE BATMAN MAD."?

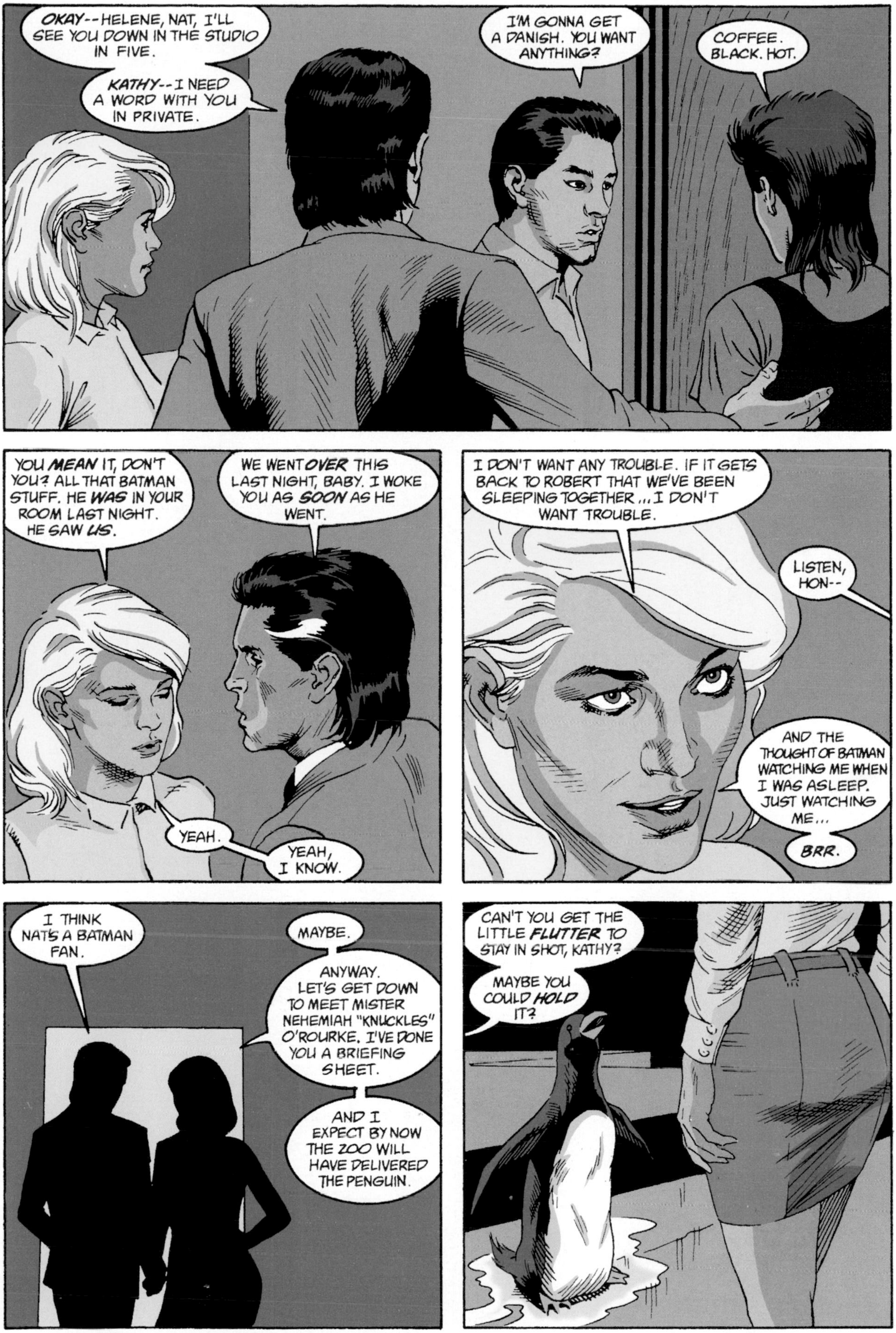
OKAY--HELENE, NAT, I'LL SEE YOU DOWN IN THE STUDIO IN FIVE.
KATHY--I NEED A WORD WITH YOU IN PRIVATE.
I'M GONNA GET A DANISH. YOU WANT ANYTHING?
COFFEE. BLACK. HOT.
YOU MEAN IT, DON'T YOU? ALL THAT BATMAN STUFF. HE WAS IN YOUR ROOM LAST NIGHT. HE SAW US.
WE WENT OVER THIS LAST NIGHT, BABY. I WOKE YOU AS SOON AS HE WENT.
YEAH.
YEAH, I KNOW.
I DON'T WANT ANY TROUBLE. IF IT GETS BACK TO ROBERT THAT WE'VE BEEN SLEEPING TOGETHER ... I DON'T WANT TROUBLE.
LISTEN, HON--
AND THE THOUGHT OF BATMAN WATCHING ME WHEN I WAS ASLEEP. JUST WATCHING ME...
BRR.
I THINK NAT'S A BATMAN FAN.
MAYBE.
ANYWAY. LET'S GET DOWN TO MEET MISTER NEHEMIAH "KNUCKLES" O'ROURKE. I'VE DONE YOU A BRIEFING SHEET.
AND I EXPECT BY NOW THE ZOO WILL HAVE DELIVERED THE PENGUIN.
CAN'T YOU GET THE LITTLE FLUTTER TO STAY IN SHOT, KATHY?
MAYBE YOU COULD HOLD IT?

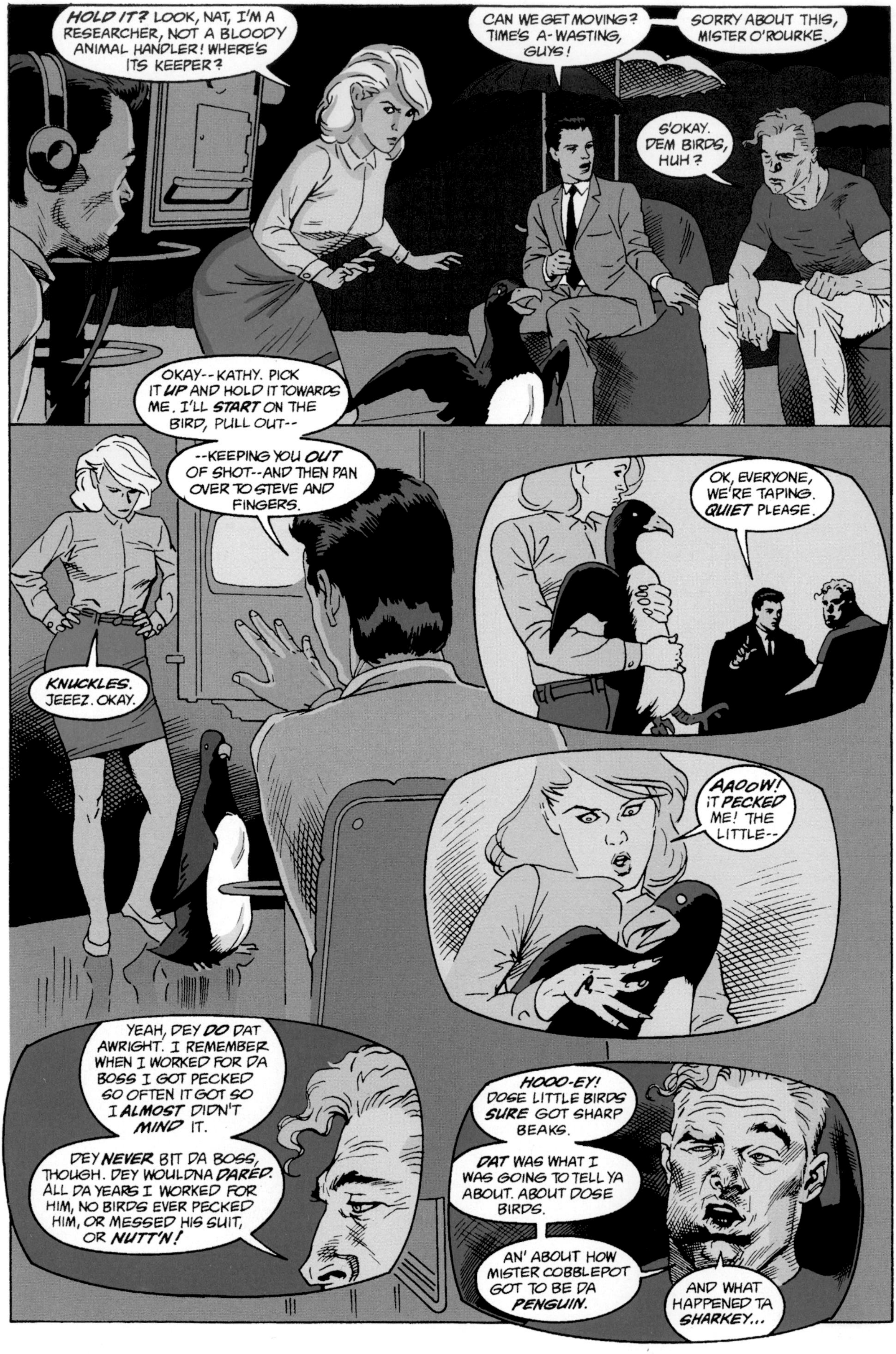
HOLD IT? LOOK, NAT, I'M A RESEARCHER, NOT A BLOODY ANIMAL HANDLER! WHERE'S ITS KEEPER?
CAN WE GET MOVING? TIME'S A-WASTING, GUYS!
SORRY ABOUT THIS, MISTER O'ROURKE.
S'OKAY. DEM BIRDS, HUH?
OKAY--KATHY. PICK IT UP AND HOLD IT TOWARDS ME. I'LL START ON THE BIRD, PULL OUT--
--KEEPING YOU OUT OF SHOT--AND THEN PAN OVER TO STEVE AND FINGERS.
KNUCKLES. JEEEZ. OKAY.
OK, EVERYONE, WE'RE TAPING. QUIET PLEASE.
AAOOW! IT PECKED ME! THE LITTLE--
YEAH, DEY DO DAT AWRIGHT. I REMEMBER WHEN I WORKED FOR DA BOSS I GOT PECKED SO OFTEN IT GOT SO I ALMOST DIDN'T MIND IT.
DEY NEVER BIT DA BOSS, THOUGH. DEY WOULDNA DARED. ALL DA YEARS I WORKED FOR HIM, NO BIRDS EVER PECKED HIM, OR MESSED HIS SUIT, OR NUTT'N!
HOOO-EY! DOSE LITTLE BIRDS SURE GOT SHARP BEAKS.
DAT WAS WHAT I WAS GOING TO TELL YA ABOUT. ABOUT DOSE BIRDS.
AN' ABOUT HOW MISTER COBBLEPOT GOT TO BE DA PENGUIN.
AND WHAT HAPPENED TA SHARKEY...

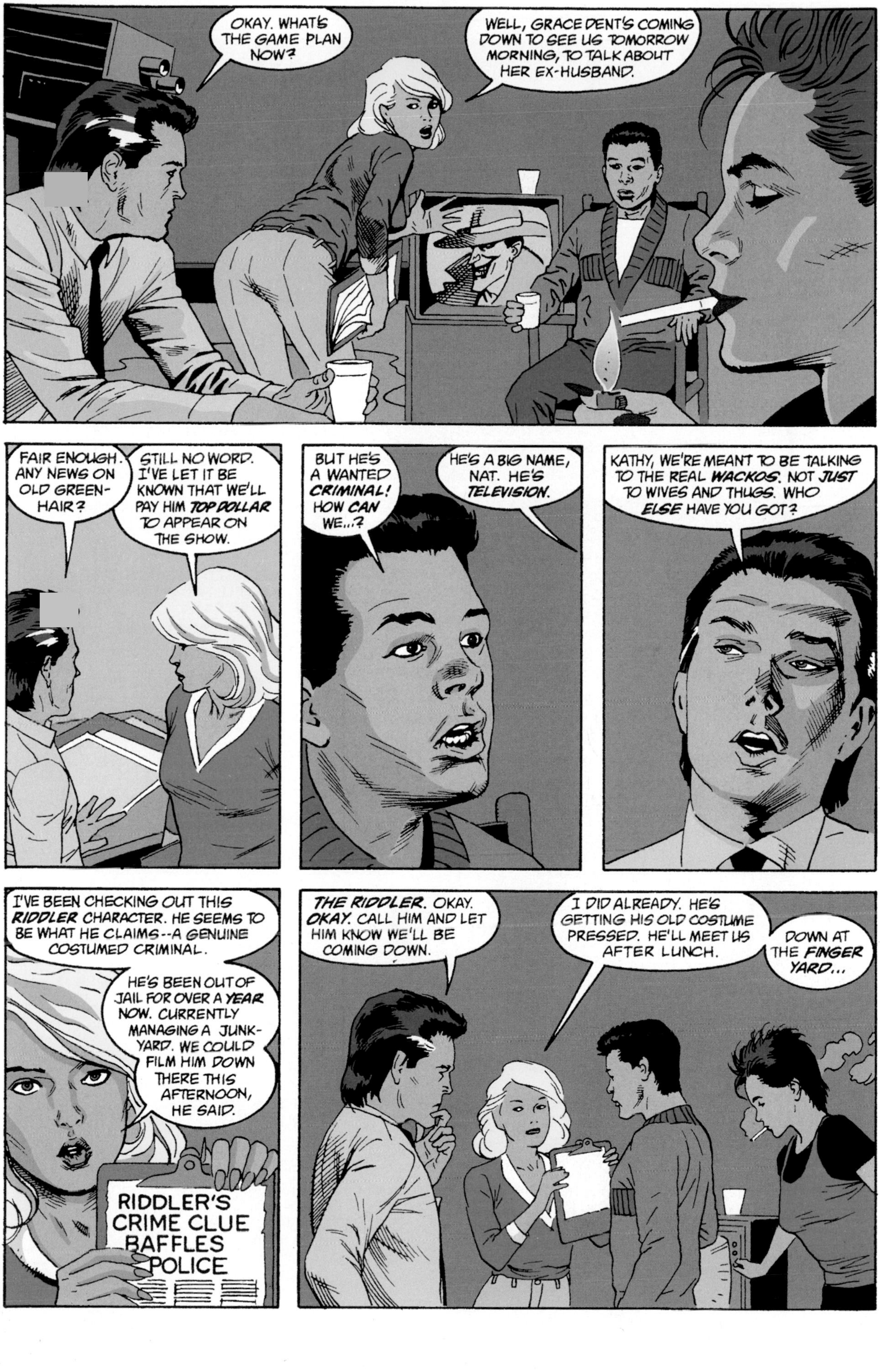
OKAY. WHAT'S THE GAME PLAN NOW?
WELL, GRACE DENT'S COMING DOWN TO SEE US TOMORROW MORNING, TO TALK ABOUT HER EX-HUSBAND.
FAIR ENOUGH. ANY NEWS ON OLD GREEN-HAIR?
STILL NO WORD. I'VE LET IT BE KNOWN THAT WE'LL PAY HIM TOP DOLLAR TO APPEAR ON THE SHOW.
BUT HE'S A WANTED CRIMINAL! HOW CAN WE...?
HE'S A BIG NAME, NAT. HE'S TELEVISION.
KATHY, WE'RE MEANT TO BE TALKING TO THE REAL WACKOS. NOT JUST TO WIVES AND THUGS. WHO ELSE HAVE YOU GOT?
I'VE BEEN CHECKING OUT THIS RIDDLER CHARACTER. HE SEEMS TO BE WHAT HE CLAIMS--A GENUINE COSTUMED CRIMINAL.
HE'S BEEN OUT OF JAIL FOR OVER A YEAR NOW. CURRENTLY MANAGING A JUNK-YARD. WE COULD FILM HIM DOWN THERE THIS AFTERNOON, HE SAID.
RIDDLER'S CRIME CLUE BAFFLES POLICE
THE RIDDLER. OKAY. OKAY. CALL HIM AND LET HIM KNOW WE'LL BE COMING DOWN.
I DID ALREADY. HE'S GETTING HIS OLD COSTUME PRESSED. HE'LL MEET US AFTER LUNCH.
DOWN AT THE FINGER YARD...

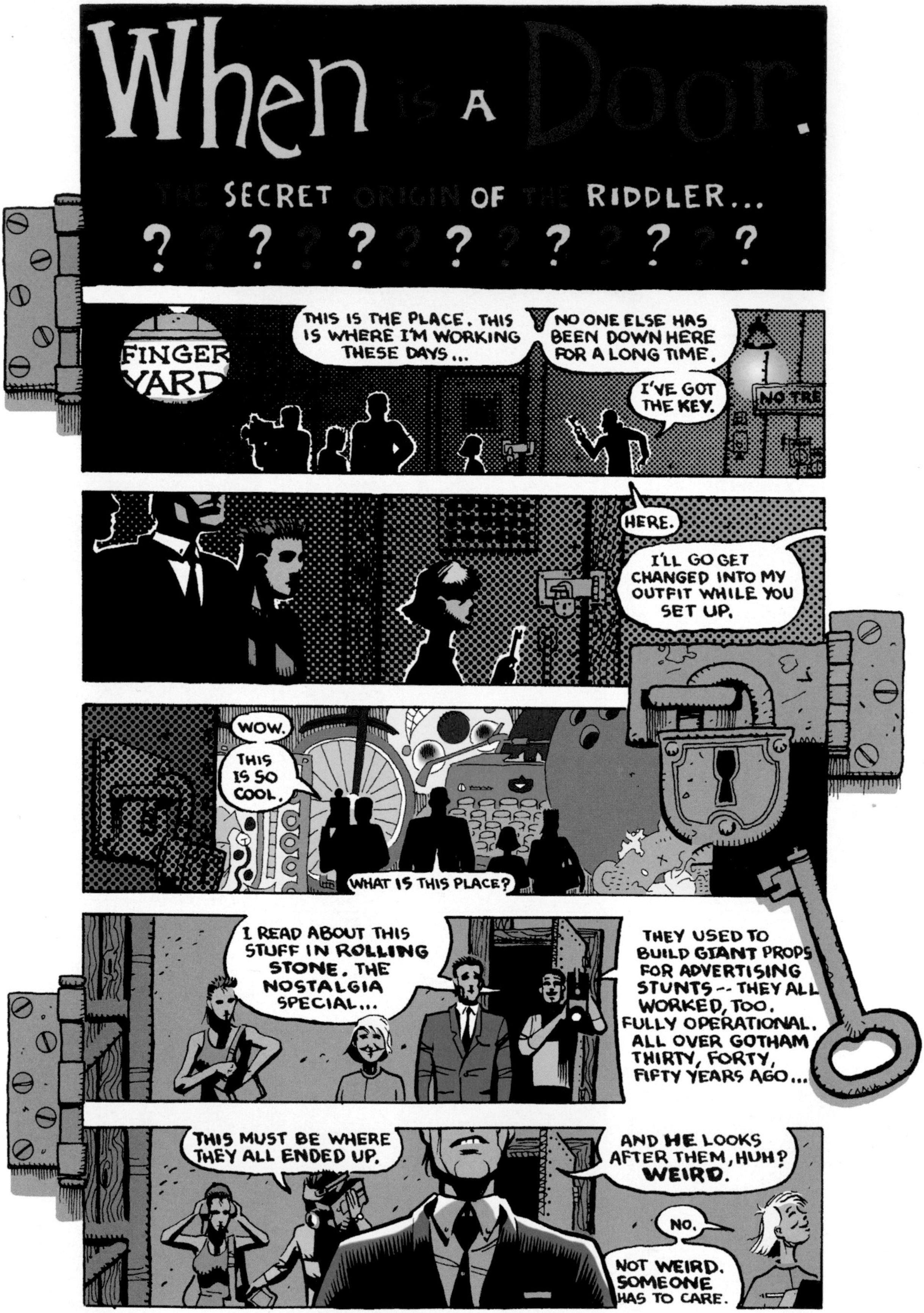
When is a Door.
THE SECRET ORIGIN OF THE RIDDLER...
? ? ? ? ? ? ? ? ? ? ? ? ?
FINGER YARD
THIS IS THE PLACE. THIS IS WHERE I'M WORKING THESE DAYS...
NO ONE ELSE HAS BEEN DOWN HERE FOR A LONG TIME.
I'VE GOT THE KEY.
HERE.
I'LL GO GET CHANGED INTO MY OUTFIT WHILE YOU SET UP.
WOW.
THIS IS SO COOL.
WHAT IS THIS PLACE?
I READ ABOUT THIS STUFF IN ROLLING STONE. THE NOSTALGIA SPECIAL...
THEY USED TO BUILD GIANT PROPS FOR ADVERTISING STUNTS -- THEY ALL WORKED, TOO. FULLY OPERATIONAL. ALL OVER GOTHAM THIRTY, FORTY, FIFTY YEARS AGO...
THIS MUST BE WHERE THEY ALL ENDED UP.
AND HE LOOKS AFTER THEM, HUH? WEIRD.
NO.
NOT WEIRD. SOMEONE HAS TO CARE.

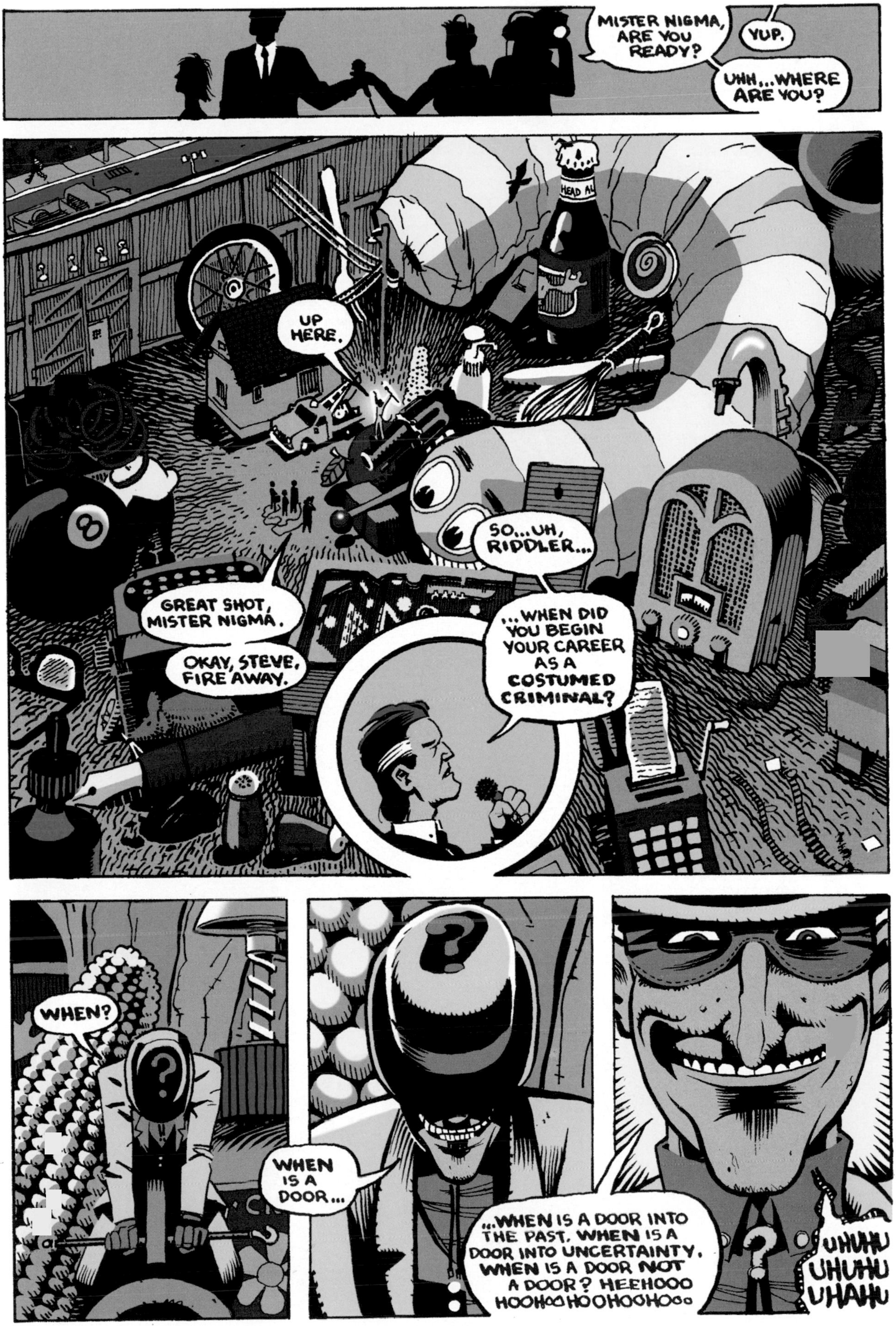
MISTER NIGMA, ARE YOU READY?
YUP.
UHH,...WHERE ARE YOU?
UP HERE.
GREAT SHOT, MISTER NIGMA.
OKAY, STEVE, FIRE AWAY.
SO...UH, RIDDLER...
...WHEN DID YOU BEGIN YOUR CAREER AS A COSTUMED CRIMINAL?
WHEN?
WHEN IS A DOOR...
...WHEN IS A DOOR INTO THE PAST. WHEN IS A DOOR INTO UNCERTAINTY. WHEN IS A DOOR NOT A DOOR? HEEHOOO HOOHOOHOOHOOHOOoo
UHUHU UHUHU UHAHU

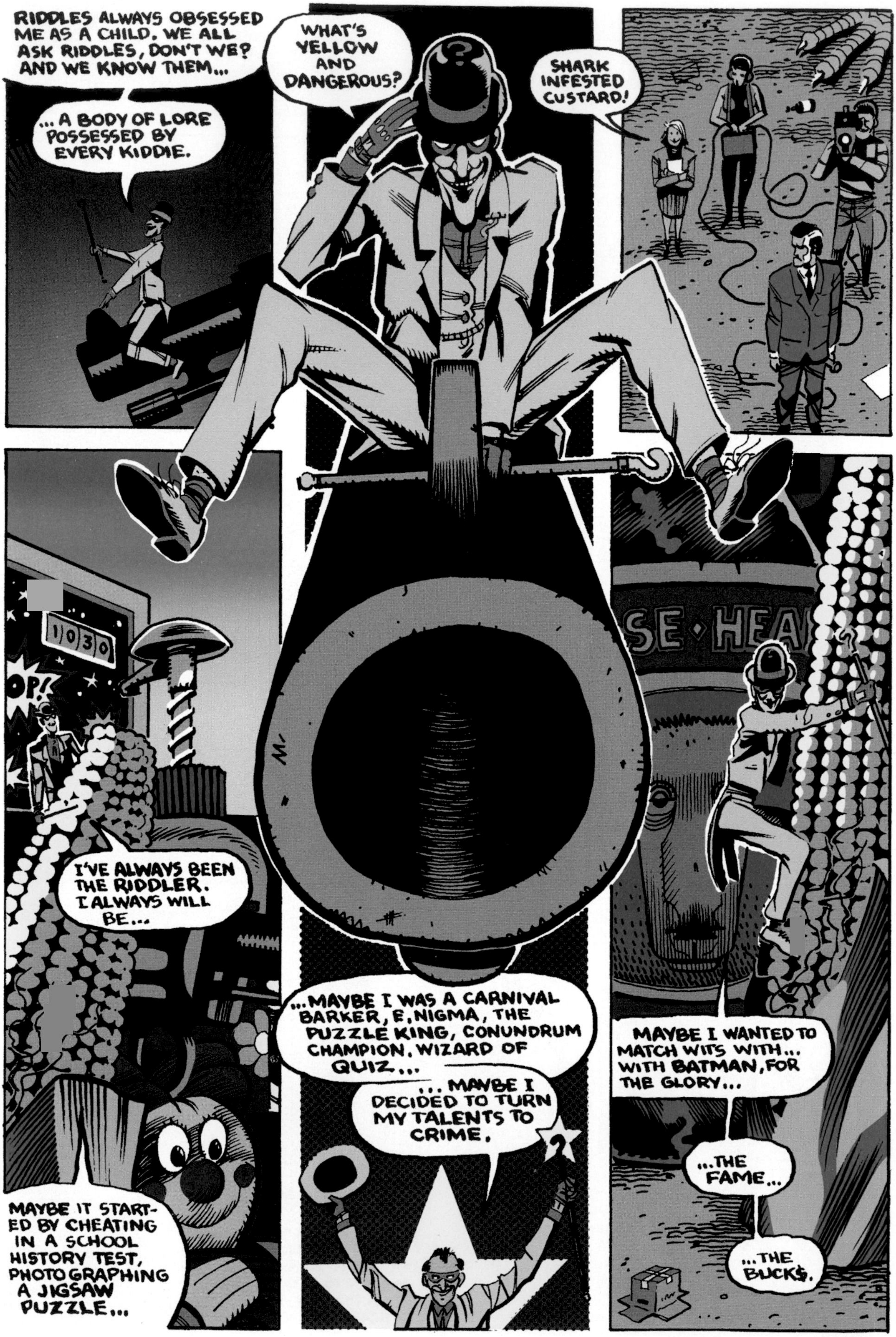
RIDDLES ALWAYS OBSESSED ME AS A CHILD. WE ALL ASK RIDDLES, DON'T WE? AND WE KNOW THEM...
...A BODY OF LORE POSSESSED BY EVERY KIDDIE.
WHAT'S YELLOW AND DANGEROUS?
SHARK INFESTED CUSTARD!
1030
OP!
SE·HEA
I'VE ALWAYS BEEN THE RIDDLER. I ALWAYS WILL BE...
MAYBE IT STARTED BY CHEATING IN A SCHOOL HISTORY TEST, PHOTOGRAPHING A JIGSAW PUZZLE...
...MAYBE I WAS A CARNIVAL BARKER, E. NIGMA, THE PUZZLE KING, CONUNDRUM CHAMPION, WIZARD OF QUIZ...
...MAYBE I DECIDED TO TURN MY TALENTS TO CRIME.
MAYBE I WANTED TO MATCH WITS WITH... WITH BATMAN, FOR THE GLORY...
...THE FAME...
...THE BUCK$.

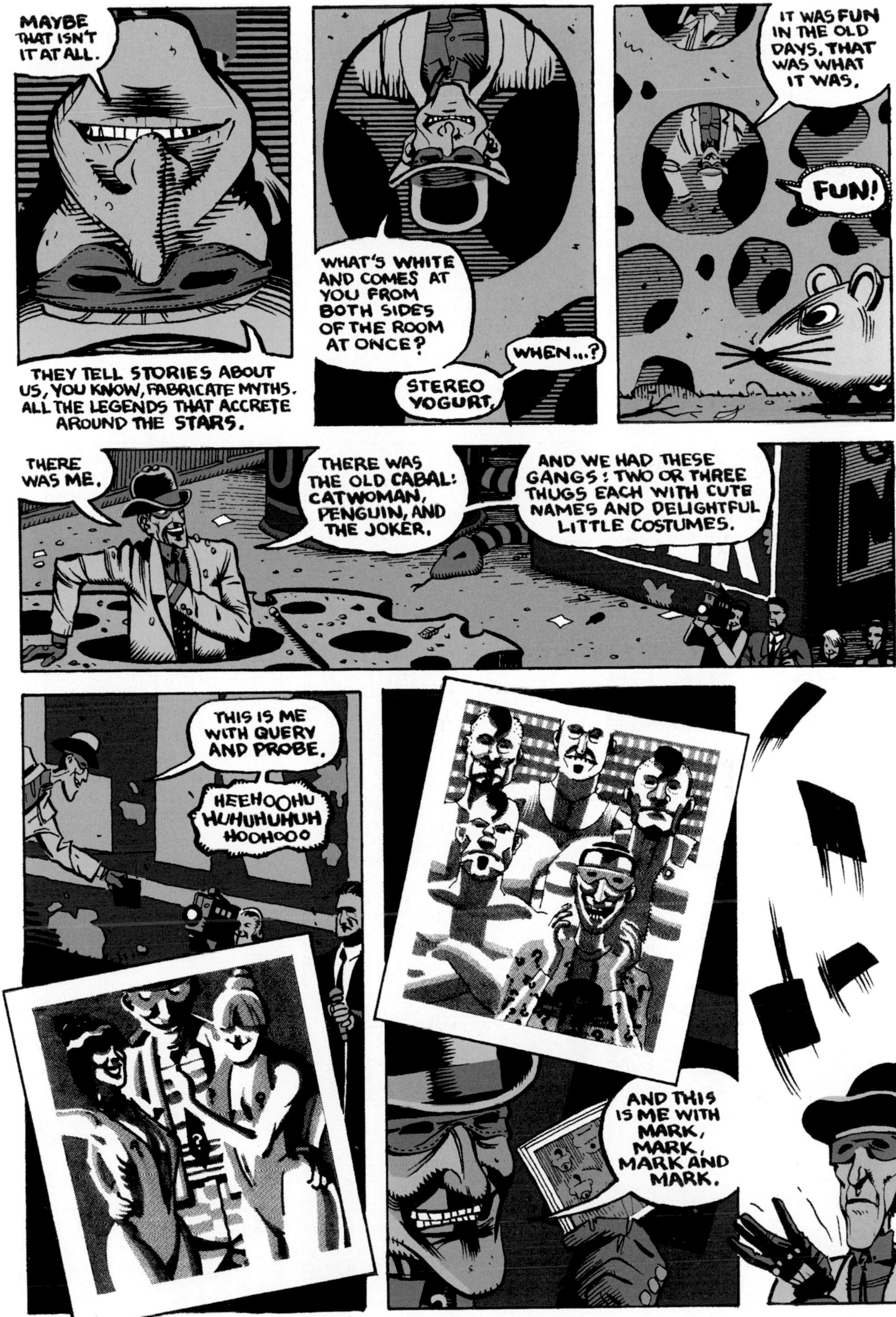
MAYBE THAT ISN'T IT AT ALL.
THEY TELL STORIES ABOUT US, YOU KNOW, FABRICATE MYTHS. ALL THE LEGENDS THAT ACCRETE AROUND THE STARS.
WHAT'S WHITE AND COMES AT YOU FROM BOTH SIDES OF THE ROOM AT ONCE?
WHEN...?
STEREO YOGURT.
IT WAS FUN IN THE OLD DAYS. THAT WAS WHAT IT WAS.
FUN!
THERE WAS ME.
THERE WAS THE OLD CABAL: CATWOMAN, PENGUIN, AND THE JOKER.
AND WE HAD THESE GANGS: TWO OR THREE THUGS EACH WITH CUTE NAMES AND DELIGHTFUL LITTLE COSTUMES.
THIS IS ME WITH QUERY AND PROBE.
HEEHOOHU HUHUHUHUH HOOHOOO
AND THIS IS ME WITH MARK, MARK, MARK AND MARK.

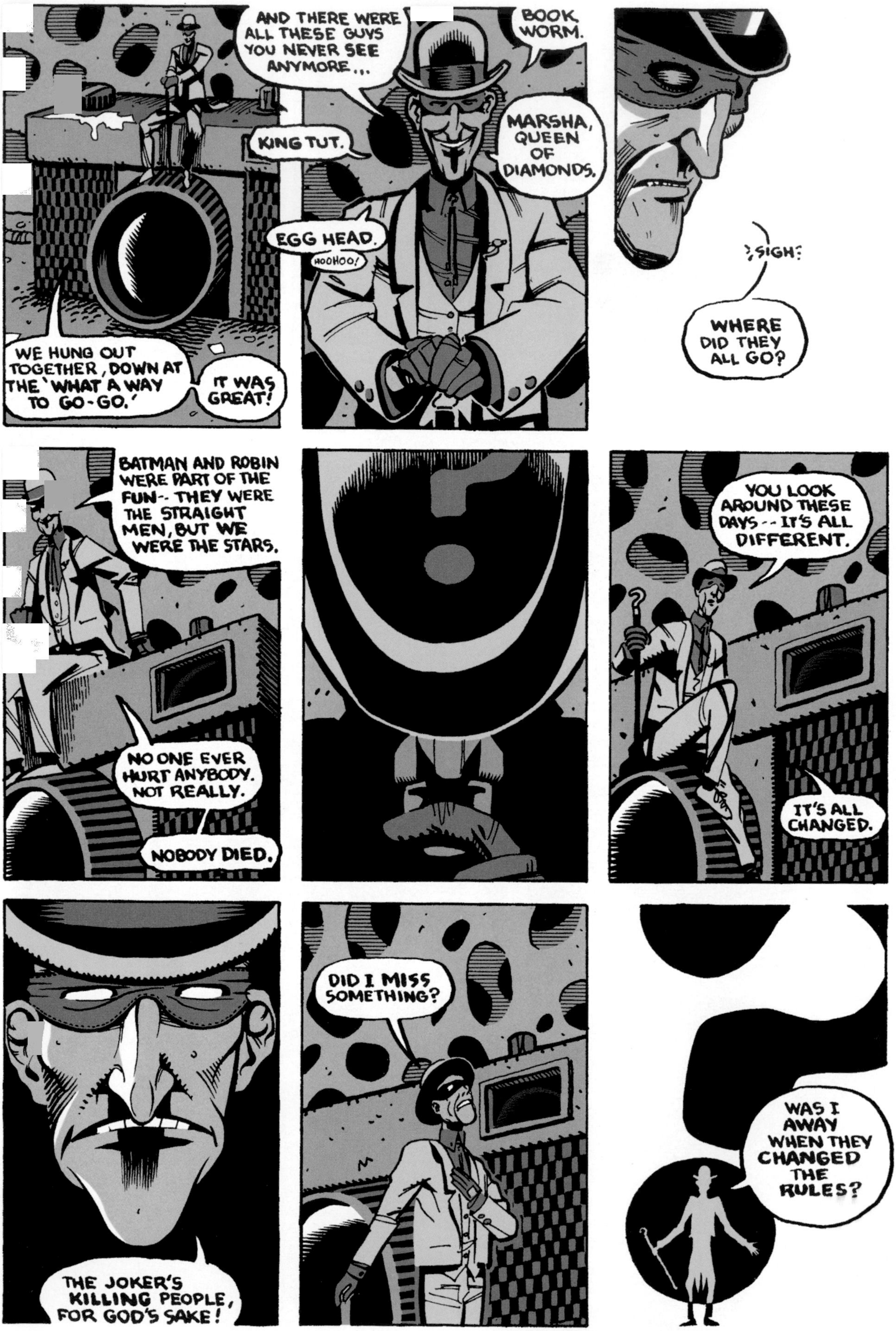
AND THERE WERE ALL THESE GUYS YOU NEVER SEE ANYMORE...
BOOK WORM.
KING TUT.
MARSHA, QUEEN OF DIAMONDS.
EGG HEAD.
HOOHOO!
WE HUNG OUT TOGETHER, DOWN AT THE 'WHAT A WAY TO GO-GO.'
IT WAS GREAT!
SIGH
WHERE DID THEY ALL GO?
BATMAN AND ROBIN WERE PART OF THE FUN-- THEY WERE THE STRAIGHT MEN, BUT WE WERE THE STARS.
NO ONE EVER HURT ANYBODY. NOT REALLY.
NOBODY DIED.
YOU LOOK AROUND THESE DAYS -- IT'S ALL DIFFERENT.
IT'S ALL CHANGED.
THE JOKER'S KILLING PEOPLE, FOR GOD'S SAKE!
DID I MISS SOMETHING?
WAS I AWAY WHEN THEY CHANGED THE RULES?

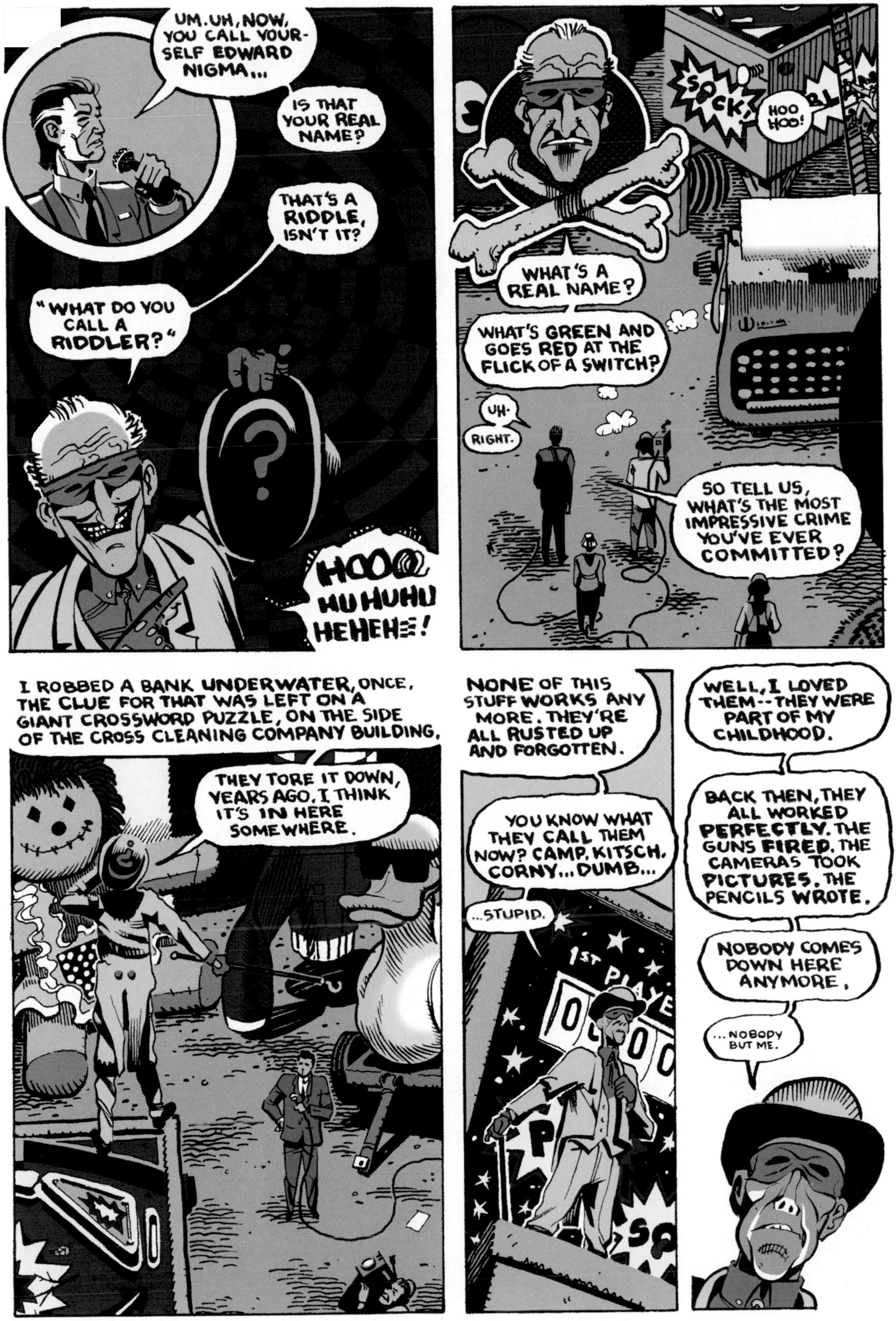
UM.UH, NOW, YOU CALL YOURSELF EDWARD NIGMA...
IS THAT YOUR REAL NAME?
THAT'S A RIDDLE, ISN'T IT?
"WHAT DO YOU CALL A RIDDLER?"
HOOO HUHUHU HEHEHE!
WHAT'S A REAL NAME?
WHAT'S GREEN AND GOES RED AT THE FLICK OF A SWITCH?
SOCK!
HOO HOO!
UH-RIGHT.
SO TELL US, WHAT'S THE MOST IMPRESSIVE CRIME YOU'VE EVER COMMITTED?
I ROBBED A BANK UNDERWATER, ONCE. THE CLUE FOR THAT WAS LEFT ON A GIANT CROSSWORD PUZZLE, ON THE SIDE OF THE CROSS CLEANING COMPANY BUILDING.
THEY TORE IT DOWN, YEARS AGO. I THINK IT'S IN HERE SOMEWHERE.
NONE OF THIS STUFF WORKS ANY MORE. THEY'RE ALL RUSTED UP AND FORGOTTEN.
YOU KNOW WHAT THEY CALL THEM NOW? CAMP. KITSCH. CORNY... DUMB...
...STUPID.
1ST PLAYE
WELL, I LOVED THEM--THEY WERE PART OF MY CHILDHOOD.
BACK THEN, THEY ALL WORKED PERFECTLY. THE GUNS FIRED. THE CAMERAS TOOK PICTURES. THE PENCILS WROTE.
NOBODY COMES DOWN HERE ANYMORE.
...NOBODY BUT ME.

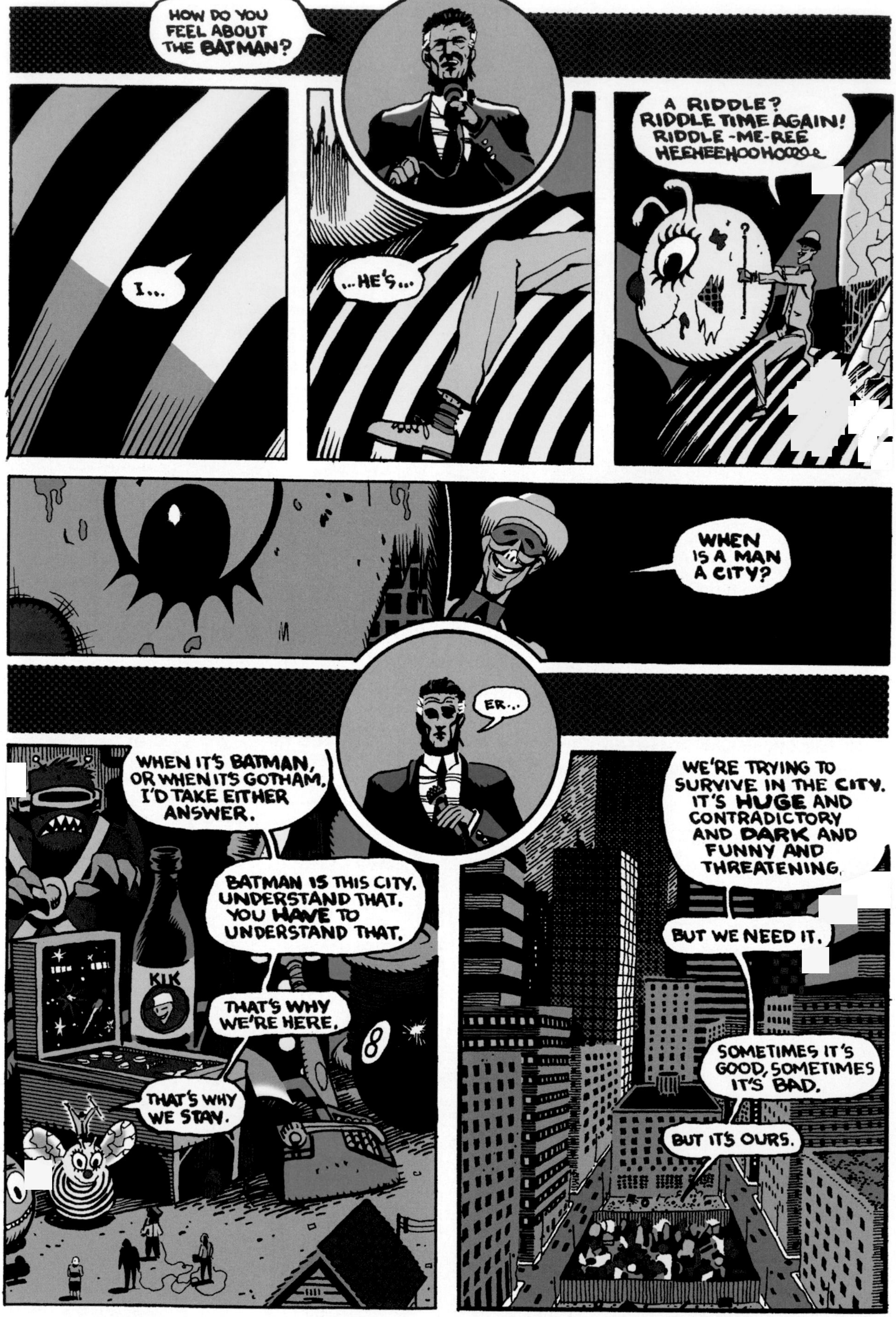

HOW DO YOU FEEL ABOUT THE BATMAN?
I...
...HE'S...
A RIDDLE? RIDDLE TIME AGAIN! RIDDLE-ME-REE HEEHEEHOOHOO
WHEN IS A MAN A CITY?
ER...
WHEN IT'S BATMAN, OR WHEN IT'S GOTHAM. I'D TAKE EITHER ANSWER.
BATMAN IS THIS CITY. UNDERSTAND THAT. YOU HAVE TO UNDERSTAND THAT.
THAT'S WHY WE'RE HERE.
THAT'S WHY WE STAY.
KIK
WE'RE TRYING TO SURVIVE IN THE CITY. IT'S HUGE AND CONTRADICTORY AND DARK AND FUNNY AND THREATENING.
BUT WE NEED IT.
SOMETIMES IT'S GOOD, SOMETIMES IT'S BAD.
BUT IT'S OURS.

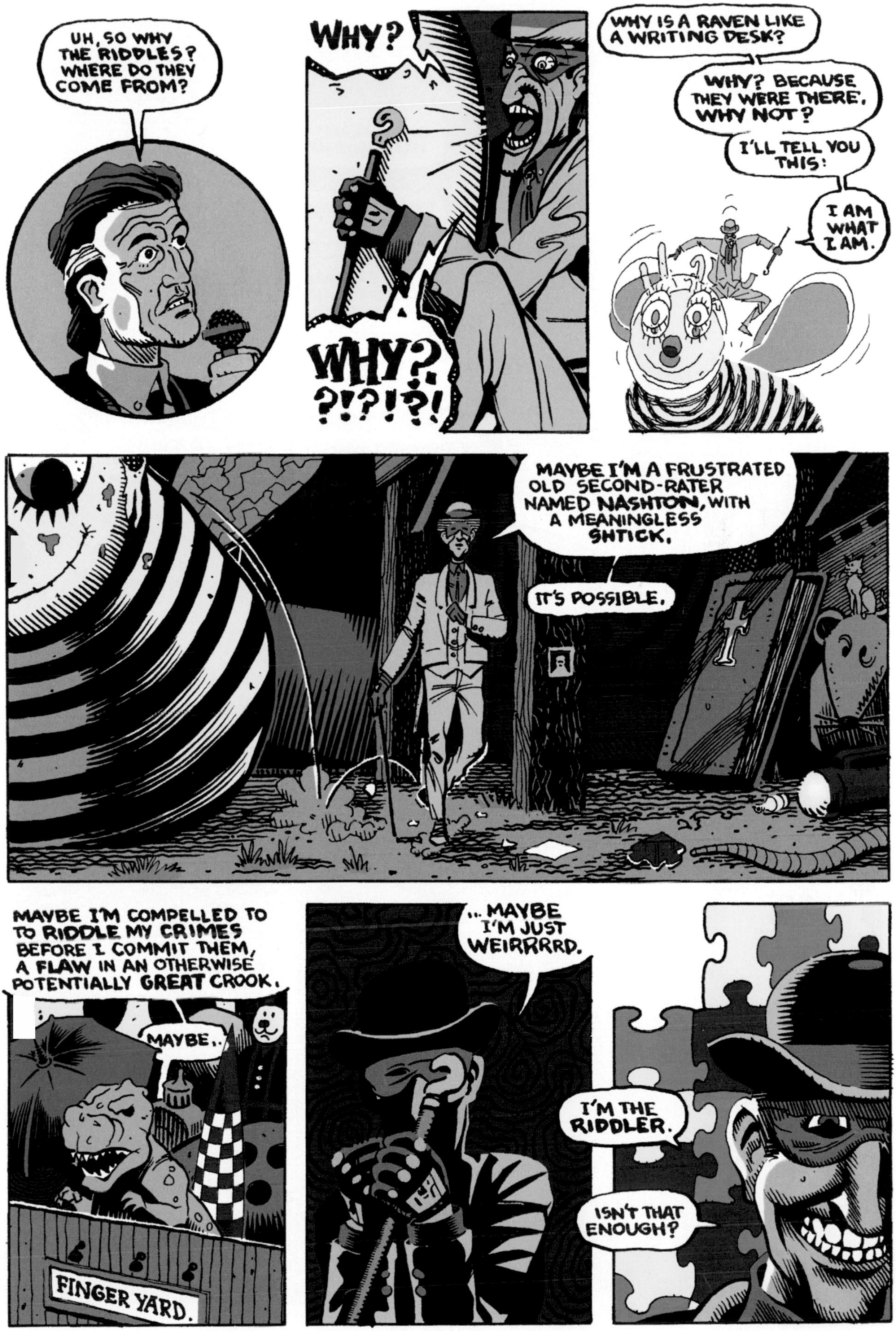
UH, SO WHY THE RIDDLES? WHERE DO THEY COME FROM?
WHY?
WHY?, ?!?!?!
WHY IS A RAVEN LIKE A WRITING DESK?
WHY? BECAUSE THEY WERE THERE, WHY NOT?
I'LL TELL YOU THIS:
I AM WHAT I AM.
MAYBE I'M A FRUSTRATED OLD SECOND-RATER NAMED NASHTON, WITH A MEANINGLESS SHTICK,
IT'S POSSIBLE.
MAYBE I'M COMPELLED TO TO RIDDLE MY CRIMES BEFORE I COMMIT THEM, A FLAW IN AN OTHERWISE POTENTIALLY GREAT CROOK.
MAYBE..
FINGER YARD.
.. MAYBE I'M JUST WEIRRRRD.
I'M THE RIDDLER.
ISN'T THAT ENOUGH?

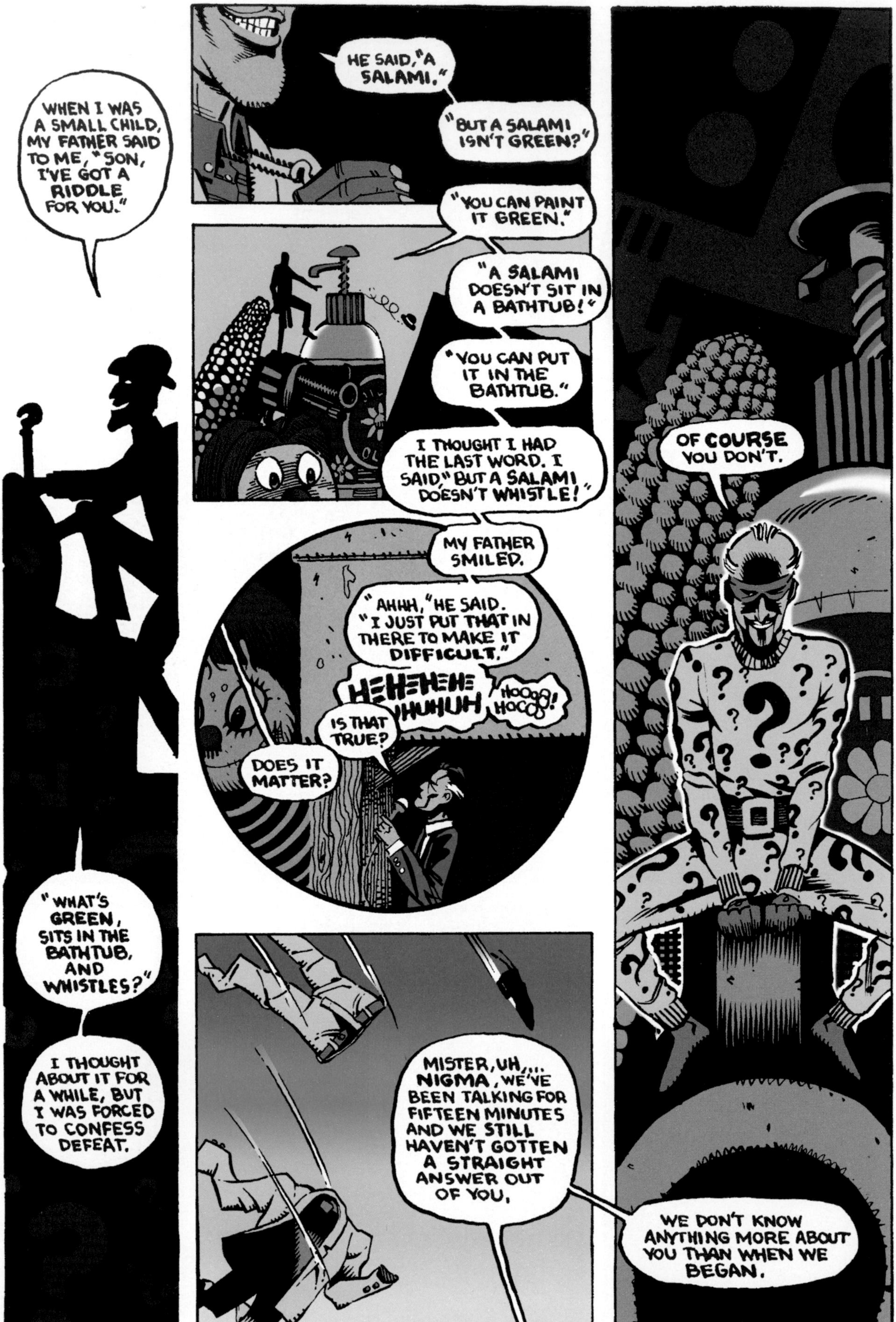
WHEN I WAS A SMALL CHILD, MY FATHER SAID TO ME, "SON, I'VE GOT A RIDDLE FOR YOU."
"WHAT'S GREEN, SITS IN THE BATHTUB, AND WHISTLES?"
I THOUGHT ABOUT IT FOR A WHILE, BUT I WAS FORCED TO CONFESS DEFEAT.
HE SAID, "A SALAMI."
"BUT A SALAMI ISN'T GREEN?"
"YOU CAN PAINT IT GREEN."
"A SALAMI DOESN'T SIT IN A BATHTUB!"
"YOU CAN PUT IT IN THE BATHTUB."
I THOUGHT I HAD THE LAST WORD. I SAID, "BUT A SALAMI DOESN'T WHISTLE!"
MY FATHER SMILED.
"AHHH," HE SAID. "I JUST PUT THAT IN THERE TO MAKE IT DIFFICULT."
HEHEHEHEHE HUHUHUH
HOOOO! HOOOO!
IS THAT TRUE?
DOES IT MATTER?
MISTER, UH,... NIGMA, WE'VE BEEN TALKING FOR FIFTEEN MINUTES AND WE STILL HAVEN'T GOTTEN A STRAIGHT ANSWER OUT OF YOU.
WE DON'T KNOW ANYTHING MORE ABOUT YOU THAN WHEN WE BEGAN.
OF COURSE YOU DON'T.

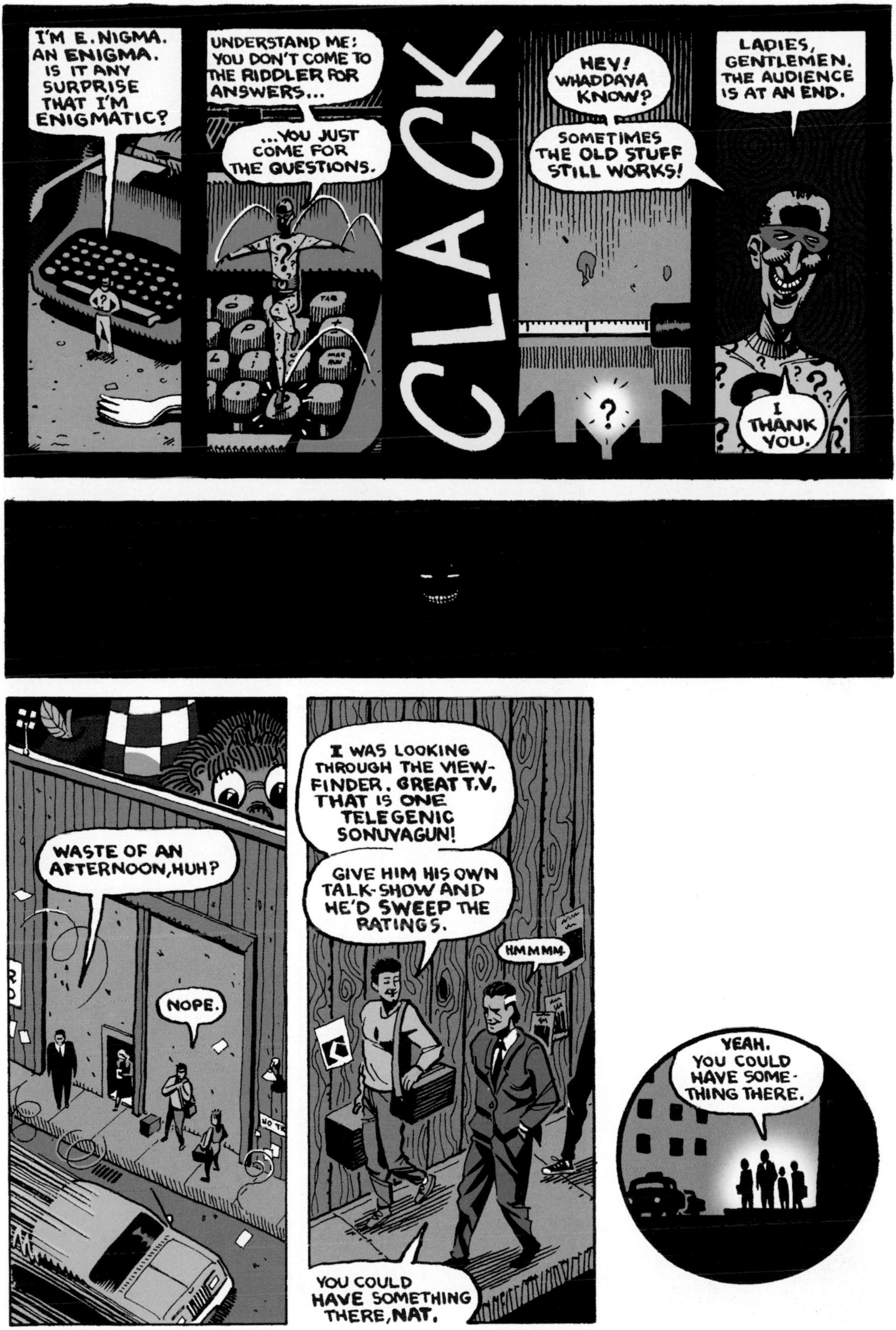
I'M E. NIGMA. AN ENIGMA. IS IT ANY SURPRISE THAT I'M ENIGMATIC?
UNDERSTAND ME: YOU DON'T COME TO THE RIDDLER FOR ANSWERS...
...YOU JUST COME FOR THE QUESTIONS.
CLACK
HEY! WHADDAYA KNOW?
SOMETIMES THE OLD STUFF STILL WORKS!
LADIES, GENTLEMEN. THE AUDIENCE IS AT AN END.
I THANK YOU.
WASTE OF AN AFTERNOON, HUH?
NOPE.
I WAS LOOKING THROUGH THE VIEW-FINDER. GREAT T.V. THAT IS ONE TELEGENIC SONUVAGUN!
GIVE HIM HIS OWN TALK-SHOW AND HE'D SWEEP THE RATINGS.
HMMMM.
YOU COULD HAVE SOMETHING THERE, NAT.
YEAH. YOU COULD HAVE SOME-THING THERE.

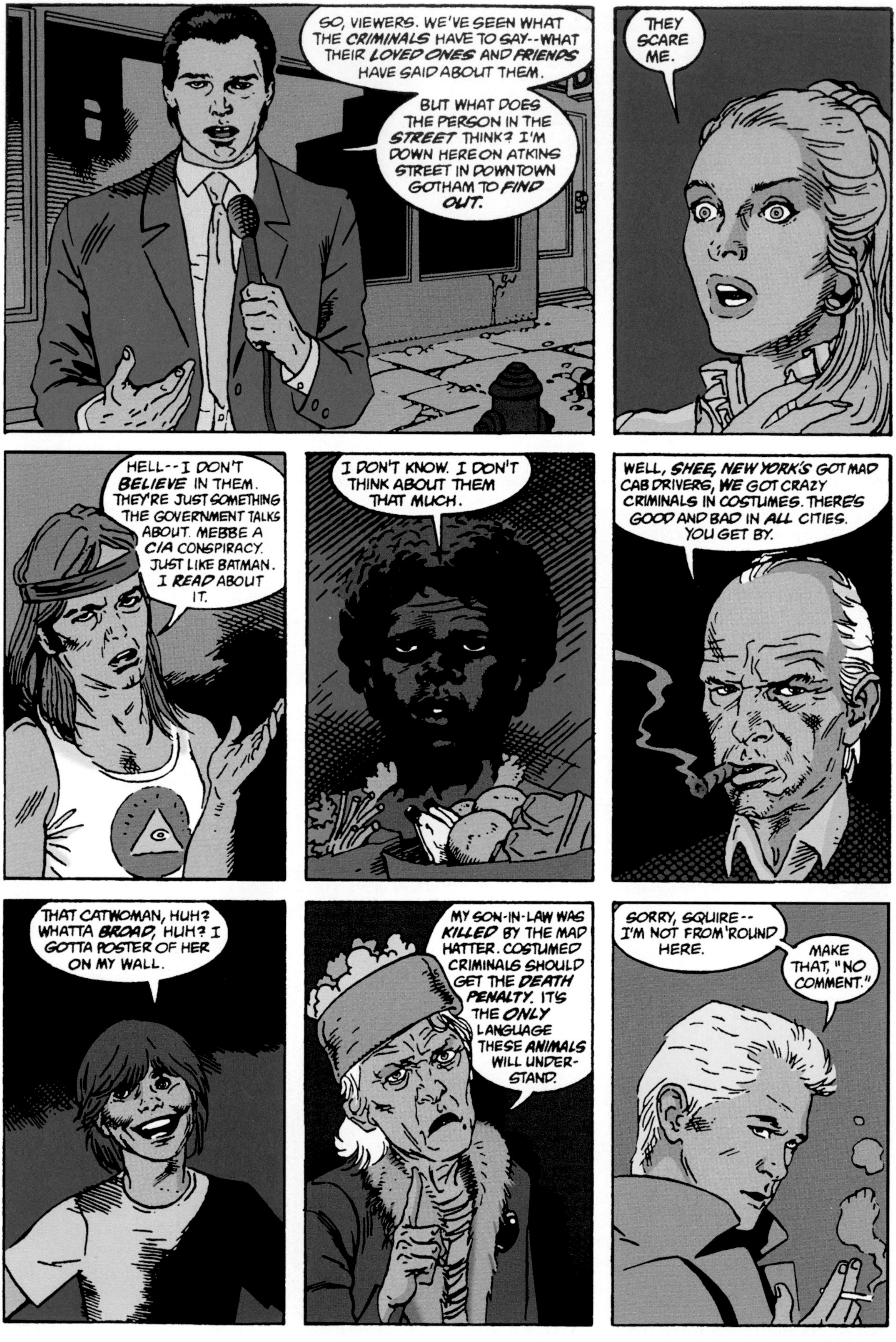
SO, VIEWERS. WE'VE SEEN WHAT THE CRIMINALS HAVE TO SAY--WHAT THEIR LOVED ONES AND FRIENDS HAVE SAID ABOUT THEM.
BUT WHAT DOES THE PERSON IN THE STREET THINK? I'M DOWN HERE ON ATKINS STREET IN DOWNTOWN GOTHAM TO FIND OUT.
THEY SCARE ME.
HELL--I DON'T BELIEVE IN THEM. THEY'RE JUST SOMETHING THE GOVERNMENT TALKS ABOUT. MEBBE A CIA CONSPIRACY. JUST LIKE BATMAN. I READ ABOUT IT.
I DON'T KNOW. I DON'T THINK ABOUT THEM THAT MUCH.
WELL, SHEE, NEW YORK'S GOT MAD CAB DRIVERS, WE GOT CRAZY CRIMINALS IN COSTUMES. THERE'S GOOD AND BAD IN ALL CITIES. YOU GET BY.
THAT CATWOMAN, HUH? WHATTA BROAD, HUH? I GOTTA POSTER OF HER ON MY WALL.
MY SON-IN-LAW WAS KILLED BY THE MAD HATTER. COSTUMED CRIMINALS SHOULD GET THE DEATH PENALTY. IT'S THE ONLY LANGUAGE THESE ANIMALS WILL UNDER-STAND.
SORRY, SQUIRE--I'M NOT FROM 'ROUND HERE.
MAKE THAT, "NO COMMENT."

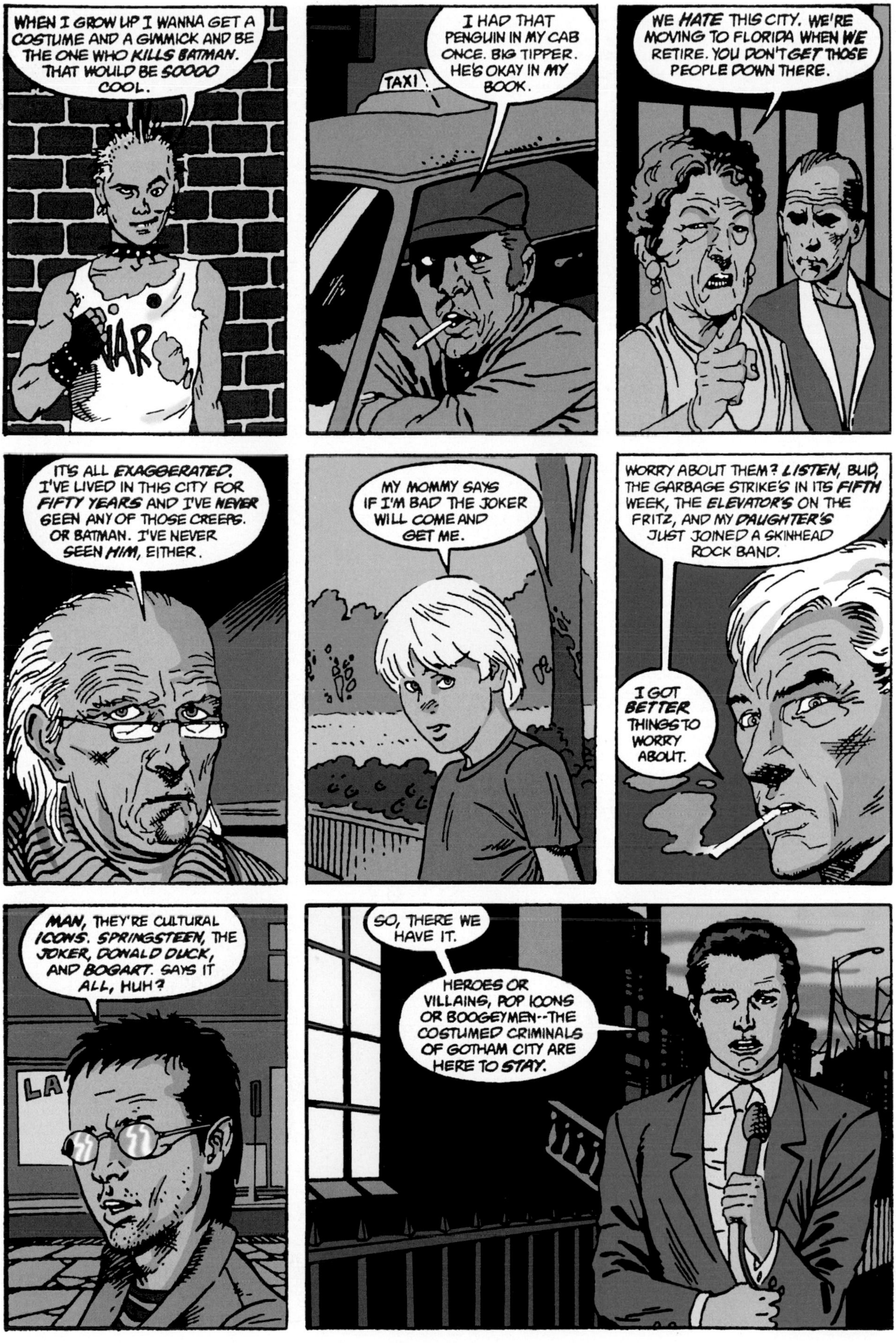
WHEN I GROW UP I WANNA GET A COSTUME AND A GIMMICK AND BE THE ONE WHO KILLS BATMAN. THAT WOULD BE SOOOO COOL.
WAR
TAXI
I HAD THAT PENGUIN IN MY CAB ONCE. BIG TIPPER. HE'S OKAY IN MY BOOK.
WE HATE THIS CITY. WE'RE MOVING TO FLORIDA WHEN WE RETIRE. YOU DON'T GET THOSE PEOPLE DOWN THERE.
IT'S ALL EXAGGERATED. I'VE LIVED IN THIS CITY FOR FIFTY YEARS AND I'VE NEVER SEEN ANY OF THOSE CREEPS. OR BATMAN. I'VE NEVER SEEN HIM, EITHER.
MY MOMMY SAYS IF I'M BAD THE JOKER WILL COME AND GET ME.
WORRY ABOUT THEM? LISTEN, BUD, THE GARBAGE STRIKE'S IN ITS FIFTH WEEK, THE ELEVATOR'S ON THE FRITZ, AND MY DAUGHTER'S JUST JOINED A SKINHEAD ROCK BAND.
I GOT BETTER THINGS TO WORRY ABOUT.
MAN, THEY'RE CULTURAL ICONS. SPRINGSTEEN, THE JOKER, DONALD DUCK, AND BOGART. SAYS IT ALL, HUH?
LA
SO, THERE WE HAVE IT.
HEROES OR VILLAINS, POP ICONS OR BOOGEYMEN--THE COSTUMED CRIMINALS OF GOTHAM CITY ARE HERE TO STAY.

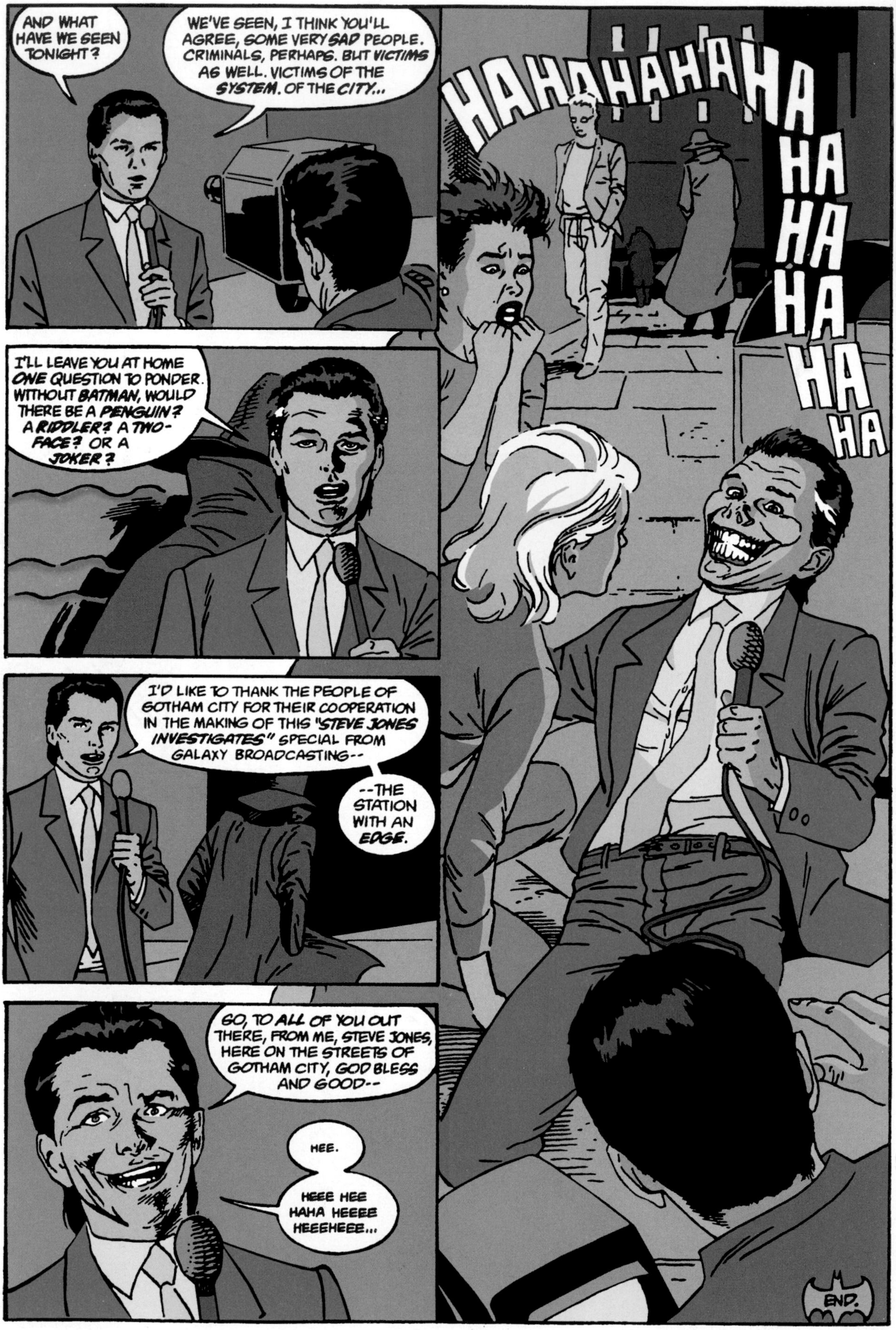
AND WHAT HAVE WE SEEN TONIGHT?
WE'VE SEEN, I THINK YOU'LL AGREE, SOME VERY SAD PEOPLE. CRIMINALS, PERHAPS. BUT VICTIMS AS WELL. VICTIMS OF THE SYSTEM. OF THE CITY...
I'LL LEAVE YOU AT HOME ONE QUESTION TO PONDER. WITHOUT BATMAN, WOULD THERE BE A PENGUIN? A RIDDLER? A TWO-FACE? OR A JOKER?
I'D LIKE TO THANK THE PEOPLE OF GOTHAM CITY FOR THEIR COOPERATION IN THE MAKING OF THIS "STEVE JONES INVESTIGATES" SPECIAL FROM GALAXY BROADCASTING--
--THE STATION WITH AN EDGE.
SO, TO ALL OF YOU OUT THERE, FROM ME, STEVE JONES, HERE ON THE STREETS OF GOTHAM CITY, GOD BLESS AND GOOD--
HEE.
HEEE HEE HAHA HEEEE HEEEHEEE...
HAHAHAHAHAHA HA HA HA HA HA HA
END.